ORAL TRADITION AS HISTORY

JAN VANSINA

# ORAL
# TRADITION
# AS
# HISTORY

THE UNIVERSITY OF WISCONSIN PRESS

The University of Wisconsin Press
114 North Murray Street
Madison, Wisconsin 53715

Printed in the United States of America

Library of Congress Cataloging in Publication Data
Vansina, Jan.
Oral tradition as history.
Bibliography: pp. 229–245
Includes index.
1. Oral tradition. 2. History—Methodology.
3. Oral tradition—Africa. 4. Africa—History—Methodology.
I. Title.
D16.V2784        1985        960        84-40504
ISBN 0-299-10210-6
ISBN 0-299-10214-9 (pbk.)

# CONTENTS

CHAPTER TWO
# PERFORMANCE, TRADITION, AND TEXT  33

CHAPTER THREE

# GETTING THE MESSAGE 68

CHAPTER FOUR

# THE MESSAGE IS A SOCIAL PRODUCT 94

CHAPTER FIVE
# THE MESSAGE EXPRESSES CULTURE 124

CHAPTER SIX

# TRADITION AS INFORMATION REMEMBERED   147

# PREFACE

*Tete ka asom ene Kakyere*
Ancient things remain in the ear
(*Daaku,* p. 45)

This Akan (Ghana) proverb puts it succinctly. The marvel of oral tradition, some will say its curse, is this: messages from the past exist, are real, and yet are not continuously accessible to the senses. Oral traditions make an appearance only when they are told. For fleeting moments they can be heard, but most of the time they dwell only in the minds of people. The utterance is transitory, but the memories are not. No one in oral societies doubts that memories can be faithful repositories which contain the sum total of past human experience and explain the how and why of present day conditions. *Tete are ne nne:* "Ancient things are today" or "History repeats itself." Whether memory changes or not, culture is reproduced by remembrance put into words and deeds. The mind through memory carries culture from generation to generation. How it is possible for a mind to remember and out of nothing to spin complex ideas, messages, and instructions for living, which manifest continuity over time, is one of the greatest wonders one can study, comparable only to human intelligence and thought itself. Because the wonder is so great, it also is very complex. Oral tradition should be central to students of culture, of ideology, of society, of psychology, of art, and, finally, of history. It is with this last aspect that we are concerned in this book.

Among the various kinds of historical sources traditions occupy a special place. They are messages, but unwritten; their preservation entrusted to the memories of successive generations of people. Yet, until a generation ago, little had been done towards the study of what this means in terms of historical methodology. This is all the more astonishing in view of the fact that traditions were constantly used as source material. Not only are such data the obvious sources for the history of oral societies or for information about the past of illiterate groups in literate societies, but they are the fountainhead of many ancient writings as well, be they those of early times in the Mediterranean, India, China, Japan, or those of later times, such as many writings from the European Middle Ages before the turn of the first millennium in western Europe.

"Ancient things are today." Yes, oral traditions are documents *of the present*, because they are told in the present. Yet they also embody a message from the past, so they are expressions *of the past* at the same time. They are the representation of the past in the present. One cannot deny either the past or the present in them. To attribute their whole content to the evanescent present as some sociologists do, is to mutilate tradition; it is reductionistic. To ignore the impact of the present as some historians have done, is equally reductionistic. Traditions must always be understood as reflecting both past and present in a single breath.

Does this situation and the reliance on memory automatically deprive oral tradition of all validity as a source of history? Or may " . . . belief upon unwritten story fondly traced from sire to son"(Wordsworth, "The Excursion," VII:941–43) be justified? The answer cannot be a simple yes or no. Rather, as with other types of historical sources, this is the question which leads to an examination of how the reliability of various particular traditions can be evaluated. It is the question with which this essay deals.

In 1959 I wrote a book to answer this question in the hope of drawing attention to this lacuna in the methodology of history and to provide an introductory guide to the characteristics of oral tradition as history.[1] Since then many articles and some books have been devoted to this and related questions, such as the study of traditions as forms of art. The book needed to be brought up to date. Much experience has been gained meanwhile, many discussions have found their way into print, and my own thought, like memory itself, has not stood still. So this has become a new book. Its goal is unchanged. It still aims, in brief compass, to introduce the reader to the usual set of rules of historical evidence as they apply to oral traditions. These rules of evidence form a body, a logical train of thought. One cannot apply some and neglect the others. They are a single whole. They are the method of history. Our goal is to present them. In the notes I introduce the reader to the discussions pertaining to them.

Given the scope of the project, this book should not be limited to any particular period or place. This should be all the more the case because I hold that all human thought and memory operates in the same way everywhere and at all times. Some will still deny this and in discussing "modes of thought" confuse the object of thinking with the process of thinking. As an inevitable consequence of its goal, this essay should also stress the unity of processes of thought among all humans, and hence avoid limitations of place and time. And yet in practice most of the traditions and studies on which this book is based deal with twentieth-century peoples. This is so because we have here sufficient information to enable historians to evaluate the reliability of many traditions, which is not the case for most traditions that reached us in writing from distant pasts. The reader will no doubt also notice that there is a preponderance of African examples and of examples deriving from my own researches within that body itself. For these last cases further book-length analyses are available and even the raw material of sources as taken down is accessible to the interested reader.[2] No harm is done in using one's own experience or predominantly African cases as long as they are representative of general conditions. In order to show that this is so, illustrations from different parts of the world have been included or referred to in notes. Oral traditions have now been studied in most parts of the world and allow us to confidently state that we are dealing with general conditions. A massive volume along the lines of this essay could show this, but within the compass of a study about method, conciseness is a crucial virtue and points made should be illustrated rather than documented *ad nauseam*.

I begin this examination with a description of the process we call oral tradition. This allows me to better define what is meant by this expression. Then this can be followed up with a discussion of how a tradition becomes a record, a testimony or a text to which the rules of textual criticism should be applied. From there I can turn to elucidation of its social context, and its character as an expression of culture. Tradition is information remembered and as such raises fundamental queries which are addressed next. Once this aspect has been studied, the value of traditions to the historian can be assessed.

This itinerary, however logical it may look, is not the only possible one. Indeed, it differs from the plan of the earlier book. The plan was chosen so as to guide the reader with the least amount of repetition from a consideration of what oral tradition is to a consideration of its value for historical reconstruction.

# ACKNOWLEDGMENTS

Anyone writing about oral tradition as a process rooted in a collectivity becomes aware of the degree to which she or he is immersed in the flow of a tradition of historiography and scholarship in general. Within this wide river, eddies can be found; teachers, colleagues, students, and writers one has never seen. Beyond these, others have passed on knowledge, life experience, and traditions, be they family partners in dialogue about specific traditions or friends. And they are not less wise or relevant than professional scholars are. Then there are the institutions that house research and feed researchers: the museums, institutes, and university departments. Even if one could list all one's debts, how could one disentangle everyone's share? Here and there, cognoscenti will recognize debts and influences in this work, while institutional readers—if they exist—will see what has been done with their support.

In the past, we are told, there is a long duration and there is a very recent past. In the first I must mention at least one person and one institution, although that subsumes another person. The first is Prof. J. Desmet, *quondam mentor*. This distinguished medievalist certainly must have found me an unruly student. Later he saw himself saddled with me plus the topic. He performed wonders, querying my views and their expression with such a zeal that he drove me sometimes to distraction, as I probably did him. No one understands the finer points of historical reasoning better than Desmet, no one was in the end more committed to the goal of this book than he, and of course it was only later that I realized how much energy and time my "professor" had put into this project. The institution is the now defunct *Institut pour la recherche scientifique en Afrique centrale (IRSAC)*, which for nine glorious years allowed a bunch of us to research what we liked. That institute was in effect the doing of the late and magnificent L. Van den Berghe, who will never be forgotten by his footfolk.

In the recent past I must thank the Vilas Trust Fund of the State of Wisconsin, the Graduate School of the University of Wisconsin, and the Alexander Von Humboldt Foundation of the Federal Republic of Germany for the support that gave me time to research and write this essay. And how can I omit Ms. S. Grabler, who put all of this on a word processor and then had to retrieve it from there? In the middle of her own research work, she still found the dedication to show what modern technology can do and why it is good to do it that way!

Jan Vansina
Frankfurt a / Main and
Madison, Wisconsin
May 1984

# ORAL
# TRADITION
# AS
# HISTORY

## CHAPTER ONE

# ORAL TRADITION AS PROCESS

The expression "oral tradition" applies both to a process and to its products. The products are oral messages based on previous oral messages, at least a generation old. The process is the transmission of such messages by word of mouth over time until the disappearance of the message. Hence any given oral tradition is but a rendering at one moment, an element in a process of oral development that began with the original communication. The characteristics of each rendering will differ according to its position in the whole process. We must in a first section discuss the whole process, even before we define oral traditions as sources for history and discuss their major characteristics.

## I. The Generation of Messages

Any situation in which people speak generates messages, some of which may be repeated and hence start a process of transmission. The infinite variety of situations that prompt people to speak to each other and to repeat what others said should not be reduced to classification. Nevertheless, among the messages that are repeated a historian will recognize two major groups: communication that presents "news" and communication which represents an "interpretation" of existing situations. We discuss these in turn.

### (1) News

The essence of news is to give information about something that happened not long ago and is not known to one's audience.

The news must be of some interest to the audience and often has some sensational value. The more sensational the more it will be repeated. The main point is that such communications do *not* concern the past, but rather the present, and imply a future. Such information comes from eyewitnesses, hearsay, or internal experience such as visions, dreams, or hallucinations.

(a) Eyewitness

Every reader of this book has been an eyewitness at one moment or another. Everyone has given an account of events in which he participated or which he saw to others who were not there. Eyewitness accounts are supposedly the fountainhead of all history. Most manuals of historical method therefore have discussed them.[1] They stress that in order to be reliable the witness should have been able to see, able to understand what he saw, and not so involved that his or her *parti pris* would have completely altered what he saw. The first point is obvious, the others are not so obvious. Reports of soldiers in battle are often deficient on both these grounds. They saw only a fraction of what was happening and often through screens of smoke. They did not really understand what was happening as the general confusion and their own positions prevented them from observing at leisure the development of the whole battle.[2] From my own experience in taking down accounts by eyewitnesses of battles during the Italo-Libyan war (1911–32) it is clear that with a single exception, none of about one thousand informants could observe the whole battle. The exception was a man who during the battle of Taghrift (1927) stood on a hill overlooking the battlefield and followed the fate of his camel, which had been requisitioned by the Libyan forces. The battle was small; the battlefield a round depression bordered by hills on all sides. Even so he could not detail to any extent the coming and going of forces during the action, which lasted for several hours.

In the best of circumstances, even the best of witnesses never give a movielike account of what happened, as all accounts of accidents show. Eyewitness accounts are always a personal experience as well and involve not only perception, but also emotions. Witnesses often are also not idle standers-by, but participants in the events. Furthermore, an understanding of what happened cannot occur through mere data of perception. Perceptions must be organized in a coherent whole and the logic of the situation supplies missing pieces of observation. The classical cases of car accidents or purse snatching document this to satiety. A witness reporting a car accident typically first heard a smash, then saw it, then deduced how it happened—how both cars were traveling *before* the accident after which he or she built up a coherent account of the incident. Usually he did not see the two cars before the accident drew attention to them. Most witnesses cannot resolve themselves to build up a story starting with a noise and the result of the accident first. If a witness was traveling in one of the stricken cars, much of what took place happened at a speed greater than his own reaction time allowed him to perceive. Such persons often only remember one or two images of the accident. Yet when called upon to tell what happened, they must become coherent and build up a tale in which the logic of the situation makes up most of the account.

Eyewitness accounts are only partly reliable. Certainly it is true that complex (battle) or unexpected (accidents) events are perhaps rarer than simple, expected events. Yet even here the account remains imperfect. The expectation of the event itself distorts its observation. People tend to report what they expect to see or hear more than what they actually see or hear. To sum up: mediation of perception by memory and emotional state shapes an account. Memory typically selects certain features from the successive perceptions and interprets them according to expectation, previous knowledge, or the logic of "what must have happened," and fills the gaps in perception.

Thus from the very first step, valid for all messages, oral or written, the hypercritical analyst can already deny validity to an eyewitness account. In strictest theory such an analyst would be correct. In practice, as we know from daily experience, he is wrong. For if our observations and their interpretation were so uncertain, we could not function at all. We would not remember nor efficiently act on remembrance for the situations, we find ourselves daily involved in. Still, it is well to remember that the forces which already impinge on eyewitness accounts should always undergo scrutiny before being accepted as such.[3]

(b) Hearsay

Hearsay or rumor is transmitted from ear to mouth. It still deals with news—indeed, with sensational news, since otherwise no rumor would build up. Even if the bare facts of such accounts are true enough, the spectacular parts are always overdone and accounts are cast in a form which directly appeals to other people's empathy with the speaker. "Do you realize what so-and-so has done now?" involves an appeal to the emotions of the listener who is supposed to share basic values in the matter with the speaker.

Many rumors have a basis in fact, especially in a society without writing or mass media, where speech is the medium of information. Yet we all know that many rumors are untrue, and the saying "Where there is smoke, there must be fire," is as often proven false as it is shown to be true. Especially when rumors serve practical purposes, such as to dishearten opponents or to galvanize supporters, they are untrustworthy. In practice most false rumors tend to die out as the expected consequences of the rumors do not occur. They are then replaced by new rumors. Rumors that are not contradicted survive and become part first of the store of oral history, later also of oral tradition. While the above holds for hearsay which should be followed by changes perceptible to the public, false rumors that were not expected to have such effects can linger on and turn into tradition.

Hearsay is the fountainhead of most tradition or most written documents. Eyewitness accounts in both categories of sources are in fact rare. Very often, one can no longer ascertain whether the rumor derives from an eyewitness account or not.[4] In most cases internal evidence itself will have to guide us as it did the Kuba informant who commented about the story of the first man: "How could he know about his own creation, if not by hearsay?"

Rumor is the process by which a collective historical consciousness is built. The collective interpretations resulting from massive rumors lead to commonly accepted interpretations of events, nonevents, or sets of events. Hence a tradition based on rumor tells us more about the mentality at the time of the happening than about the events themselves.

(c) Visions, Dreams, and Hallucinations

Visions, dreams, and hallucinations are quite common perceptions. Some, in certain societies, are news, not only for the person who experiences them, but for whole communities. When
such experiences are told by the person who underwent them,
such stories become hearsay and spread. All information of this
nature is perceived as communication from the supernatural to
the living, and is news. Visions of celestial beings or divine
voices are prime examples of such sources. Often visions by
"innocent" persons such as children lead to the creation of sanctuaries and to pilgrimages.

In oral societies such occurrences were and are frequent.
They pass into tradition either as glosses on the meaning of history, as often happens with prophetic sayings, or they remain
known because they gave rise to novel situations which they legitimize, or explain. A prophecy about the coming of the Europeans in the Rwandese tradition translates historical consciousness.[5] The dream of King Dingiswayo, which ordered him to
bring peace through universal conquest, legitimizes—*ex post
facto*?—the Zulu (Natal) imperialism of his age.[6] The prophecy
of Nongqause in 1856, who promised the return of their ancestors
to the Xhosa (South Africa) and victory against the European
encroachment in the Cape province if they sacrificed their cattle,
is an example of a prophecy remembered for its consequences.
Many Xhosa heeded her and the ensuing famine broke determined Xhosa resistance against European pressure.[7]

Such sources should be recognized and not summarily dismissed as physical impossibilities and hence useless embellish-
ments of some later age. Their very survival in tradition means
something in terms of historical consciousness and of contemporary mentalities and ideologies.

## (2) The Interpretation of Experience

A whole class of original messages does not deal with news at
all, but with the expression of experience. This includes personal reminiscences, etiological commentaries on existing objects
(iconatrophy), linguistic expressions (folk etymology), tradi-

tions (explanatory glosses), and literary expressions of experience such as occur in oral art. All these sources are reflexive, the
product of thought about existing situations as well as about
existing messages. They represent a stage in the elaboration of
historical consciousness and are among the main wellsprings of
what we often call "culture." Such sources testify sometimes to
events and always to situations existing at a given time.

(a) Reminiscence
Reminiscences are perhaps the most typical product of human
memory. Prodded by questions or not, they primarily are the
recollections of past events or situations given by participants
long after the events. Reminiscences are bits of life history.
Everyone holds such reminiscences. They are essential to a notion of personality and identity. They are the image of oneself
one cares to transmit to others. Reminiscences are then not con-
stituted by random collections of memories, but are part of an
organized whole of memories that tend to project a consistent
image of the narrator and, in many cases, a justification of his or
her life.[8]

Here we see the full power of memory at work. Events and
situations are forgotten when irrelevant or inconvenient. Others
are retained and reordered, reshaped or correctly remembered
according to the part they play in the creation of this mental self-
portrait. Parts of such a portrait are too intimate or too contradictory ever to be revealed. Others are private but, depending
on mood, can be told to the very near and dear. Others are for
public consumption. These often deal with a public career.[9]
People in many cultures tend to create two portraits of themselves. One is a mask or a public image built up in terms of roles
and statuses, values and principles—the noble mask of oneself.
The other portrait is much less often limned and reveals traces of
doubt and fear as quite contradictory experiences are remembered. The distinction between the mask and the face varies
from culture to culture according to current notions of individ-
uality.[10] In some cultures, such as Japan or Central Africa, the
distinction is weak. In others, such as the United States today,
the gap becomes a chasm. Even in the cases where the gap is

minimal, there still remain remembrances that can be told to anyone, others to intimates only, and some perhaps to no one.

By being sensitive to notions of personality and to the requirements of privacy in given cultures, the researcher can often acquire a good insight of the gap between the past as it may have been and its rendering. The internal consistency of a life history will allow one to find the principles of selection which link individual reminiscences and hence to evaluate their impact on each reminiscence.

Such sources are the main input of oral history. Therefore a discussion of how they are generated, how to gather them, and how to use them is of paramount importance to oral historians. Here, however, we must content ourselves with this small digression, for we limit ourselves to reminiscences as input for later traditions. The main points to be remembered are that such sources deal with situations as often as they do with events, that they are communicated in dialogue with significant others, that these messages deal with such others, be they family, neighbors, or associates in a common organization or community, that such sources always include hearsay along with eyewitness accounts, and that human memory is such that it rules out certain types of "correct" reminiscence—one cannot correctly remember opinions once held and later changed, unless they led to dramatic action. One cannot remember lists of similar abstract items such as figures. Childhood memories should portray objects or people as larger than actual size, and the meaning attributed to childhood memories should correspond to the understanding of a child of that age in that culture and in that situation. These brief indications along with later remarks about interviewing and about the ways in which memory restructures give an idea as to how such sources for oral historians should be approached.[11]

The famous story of the reminiscences of Rossini about his only meeting with Beethoven may serve as a warning to the unwary. When he first told it, a few years after Beethoven's death, Rossini said that he went to Beethoven's house, had great difficulty in being admitted, and in the end did not speak to the master whose command of Italian (Rossini's language) was insufficient. This last bit we may doubt—at least from this source. Towards the end of Rossini's life the story had become quite a tale. It involved the tortured master, in the throes of creation, receiving Rossini, advising him to continue his great work, and above all praising *Il Barbiere di Siviglia* as the greatest comic work ever written.[12]

(b) Commentaries

All sorts of existing situations prompt explanations as to why they exist. Such explanations arise *ex post facto* and are therefore newly created messages. One set of explanations is thus often given for remarkable features in a landscape or to explain monuments. People often explained small depressions in rocks as imprints of hands or feet of founding heroes, kings, or prophets.[13] In Rome the existence of an ancient statue of a woman seated on what looked like the papal *sedia gestatoria* gave rise to the legend of Pope Johanna, a woman pope.[14] This class of spurious explanations is called iconatrophy. Next to spurious commentaries others may exist which do indeed stem from the time of the site or monument itself. It is therefore necessary to treat all stories tied to archaeological sites with some caution. They cannot, as a class, be rejected out of hand, nor can they be accepted wholesale.

Popular etymologies are another class of commentaries. Often they are spurious, but a few are correct, as can be shown by the regularity of their linguistic derivation. Thus the quarter Kintambo in Kinshasa (Zaire) near the rapids means "fishery" as the people have it. But when they say that the next quarter Kalina preserves the name of a local headman, they err. Despite its apparent Bantu form, the name belongs to the Austro-Hungarian officer Kallina, who drowned there in 1884.[15] By 1957 the name had been encrusted in some local genealogies of claimants for headmanship! As this example shows, popular etymologies are seldom innocent. Popular etymologies do not apply merely to place names but also to personal names and titles, and often give rise to tales.[16] Thus the ethnonym Baule (Ivory Coast) is explained as *Ba-ule* ("they threw") and comes with the tale of how the queen who led the Baule in their exodus from central Akan lands, arrived with her people at the banks of a large river.

Looking for a ford she asked the diviners what to do. They told her to throw her young son into the flood, and that then a ford would be revealed. She did so and was rewarded by seeing animals cross the river. She followed with her people and having arrived on the other bank reminded them of the sacrifice and imposed the ethnonym as a memorial.[17]

Explanatory glosses of obscure passages in traditions of any type—often poetry—form yet another class of commentary. Sometimes their explanation goes back to the events themselves, as in the Rundi case of the saying: "It is cracking at Nkoondo." This refers to a battle in the late nineteenth century in which the rebel Twaarereye was defeated at Nkoondo. One is tempted to accept this as historical fact were it not for other versions in which the names of the parties involved in the battle are different. Thus even if the commentary stems from the period right after the battle, it has still been altered several times since then.[18] In most cases, however, such commentaries are created long after the original tradition had been in existence. They explain archaisms of speech, allusions which are no longer understood, customs which no longer exist, and the like. They testify at least that the tradition which they explain has not been altered.

Speculative commentaries explain the existence of cultural traits by giving them an origin. Etiological tales or the upper reaches of many genealogies belong to this group. Thus several Tetela (Zaire) genealogies show a set of brothers, the ancestors of various Tetela groups along with younger siblings, Oluba and Okuba, as the supposed ancestors of the Luba and Kuba people.[19] H. Baumann has aptly remarked that such tales are excellent sources for providing information about cultural history.[20] Like explanatory glosses they often contain memories of archaic features. They are, moreover, indispensable for the study of the cosmological concepts of a given culture.

(c) Verbal Art

All art is metaphor and form. Verbal arts, such as poetry, song, sayings, proverbs, and tales, conform to this rule. They express the experience of contemporary situations or events, morals to be drawn from such occurrences or situations, or express intense emotions associated with them. From the point of view of the historian the form is important, as some categories such as poetry require a composition by a single author. Quite clearly one person brought a new message into being. Even so, compositions can be significantly altered by the successors of the creators who perform these pieces. Each genre has its own profiles of metaphors and stereotypes. Dirges, for example, use a stock of images specific to them. A new dirge created for a specific funeral remains original in its choice and concatenation of images, and in the presentation of novel images, the new images must be in the same line as the existing imagery.[21] Some scholars maintain that preliterate bards improvise as they go. This happens with praise poetry. But deliberate composition by a poet who delivers his work only when the poem is completely finished also occurs. I have seen a poet on a hill in Rwanda, mulling over his compositions for hours, presumably day after day until he felt they were perfect. There is reason to believe that pre-Islamic poets in Arabia created in a similar fashion.[22]

Improvisation on an existing stock of images and forms is the hallmark of fictional narrative of all sorts. Such tales develop during performance. They never are invented from scratch, but develop as various bits of older tales are combined, sequences altered or improvised, descriptions of characters shifted, and settings placed in other locales.[23] Unlike poetry and its sisters there is no moment at which a tale is composed. Innovation is only incremental from performance to performance. Therefore such tales, which do contain quite a bit of historical information, are difficult to use. One does not know what refers to which period. A tale such as "Puss in Boots" in Europe obviously contains archaic elements—but of what period? Similarly, tricksters' stories elsewhere also contain archaic elements—recognized because they could not apply to life today—but we don't know of which age.

## (3) Oral History

The sources of oral historians are reminiscences, hearsay, or eyewitness accounts about events and situations which are contemporary, that is, which occurred during the lifetime of the informants. This differs from oral traditions in that oral traditions are no longer contemporary. They have passed from mouth to mouth, for a period beyond the lifetime of the informants. The two situations typically are very different with regard to the collection of sources as well as with regard to their analysis; oral historians typically interview participants in recent or very recent events, often of a dramatic nature, when historical consciousness in the communities involved is still in flux. Some of them call this "immediate history."[24] Interviews of this nature are always compared to available written or printed information and, if possible, also information from radio and television as well. The goal is to save sources from oblivion, to come to a first assessment of the events/situations studied, and to promote consciousness among the actors of the happenings themselves.

Most oral historians typically deal with accounts of events. In practice, research design is a major problem to them, as it involves a selection of all potential witnesses. Many tend to bypass in-depth analysis of individual testimony because the masses of accounts cross-check each other. Other historians concentrate on one main personage but still cross-check statements against other oral information.[25]

## II. DYNAMIC PROCESSES OF ORAL TRADITION

As messages are transmitted beyond the generation that gave rise to them they become oral traditions. Among traditions exist different classes according to the further evolution of the message. A first class consists of memorized messages, and within it one distinguishes messages in everyday language (formula, prayer) from messages subject to special language rules (poetry). Memorized traditions behave very differently over time from others. Among the latter, one distinguishes again between formal speech (epic) and everyday language (narrative). Narratives themselves belong to two different classes according to the criterion of factuality. Some are believed to be true or false, others are fiction. Factual traditions or accounts are transmitted differently—with more regard to faithful reproduction of content—from fictional narratives such as tales, proverbs, or sayings. The criterion hinges on the notion of truth, which varies from one culture to another and which must be studied.[26] At this point we are interested in the existence of two different ways to transmit narratives. I cannot say whether this practice is really universal or not, but certainly it is widespread.[27] This does not, however, exclude a case in which a given tradition may now be considered to be true and later to be false.[28] Nor are shifts from factuality to fiction excluded, as is shown in some societies by the existence of historical tales.[29] Lastly, the degree of difference in the treatment of accounts and tales can greatly vary from one society to another. Each case must be investigated on its own merits.

Given the different modes of transmission, I now turn to a brief presentation of the resulting categories of oral tradition.

## (1) Memorized Speech

Once created, a composition to be memorized is supposed to remain unchanged from recitation to recitation, although in fact its actual wording will vary over time. Goody has remarked that there was no standard against which the accuracy of a recitation could be checked and hence small changes in the composition would remain undetected.[30] The closest one could come to a standard was to have recitations checked by others who also had learned the poem, as was the case with the liturgical texts of the Rwandese *Ubwiiru*,[31] and to a certain extent in the case of Arab pre-Islamic poetry.[32] Whether there was a difference in faithfulness of transmission according to the use of everyday language or of poetic form is unclear. In theory the additional linguistic form should help mnemonic retention, but we know in practice that simple formulas and prayers tend to be very well remembered. Such is the case of the Lord's Prayer among Christians and of the *fatiha* among Muslims. But, of course, these are prayed in literate societies, and most direct prayers in oral societies are much more variable.

One does encounter formulas which indicate great age by their archaic features. The Kuba exclamation *nce boolo boolo* has lost its meaning. Through comparative linguistic reconstruc-

tion we know that it means "the crowd is powerful" and is prop-
erly uttered at big mass meetings. A magic formula used by the
Mbuun (Zaire) for chasing away rain also has old characteristics.
It runs as follows:

> I beseech thee: Go to the Kwilu of Pombo of Zombo,
> which receives many tributaries.
> Ngul of Kaam
> The Mbuun of Mbanza Wemba have chased men of the hut
> with the chiefly insignia of the Samba.
> They wear little pads on their heads.
> The mountains lie at their feet.[33]

The names date from a period of migration for some Mbuun, and
the memory of a quarrel with the Samba people, far from present
Mbuun country, is preserved also. In such a spell the wording
may have changed, especially in the last two sentences, and formulaic expressions such as "which receives many tributaries"
may have been substituted for others, but the core of the spell
has remained stable for a very long time, because heavy rain is
wished on adversaries who have not been neighbors of the
Mbuun since centuries ago.

Poetry is of necessity memorized, if it is to be reproduced
exactly. Variations do occur over time when one word or group
of words can be replaced by another which respects the metric
form. Nevertheless, the difference between epic and poetry is
that in the former the exact wording does not matter and improvisation is encouraged, and that the latter is memorized. It is
not surprising then that different renderings of Somali or Rwandese dynastic poetry differ very little from each other.[34]

Sometimes poems are explicit, as in this dirge:

> Ntim Gyakari, the wealthy noble
> Who led his Nation to its doom at Feyiase
> Ntim Gyakari's grandchild hails from
> Feyiase, the field of battle.[35]

But one must still know that Ntim Gyakari was the last king of
Denkyira (Ghana) and lost his kingdom to Asante at the battle
of Feyiase in 1701.

Sometimes the poem can only be understood with the commentary, as in this Oromo (Ethiopia) example:

> O red sky at night (bis)
> The falseness of Goobana Daač̄uu
> The cunning man does not bind people.
> A hero is not boastful.
> What is this blackness of night? (bis)[36]

The poem, composed by Walgaafaa Qumbii of Qaqaldii, was sung in jail after the conquest in 1876 of the poet's homeland by Goobana, general of the Ethiopian emperor Menelik II.

Because poetry and formulas are composed at a given moment and are transmitted by rote, it is possible to reconstruct archetypes—the hypothetical wording of the original composition—exactly as one does for written texts. A comparison of the extant versions shows whether the transmission has in fact been as faithful as claimed and, when variants are minor, how to reconstruct an original. These are the only traditions where such a procedure can be followed. In all other cases archetypes cannot be reconstructed, or, indeed, as for tales and some epics, an original never existed.

Usually the exact date of origin for spells, prayers, and formulas is unknown, and dates for poetry, as the above examples show, must be derived from the commentaries that accompany them. The total time span during which such sources are transmitted thus remains often unknown, and, archaisms apart, there are no indications of greater or lesser age. For these sources are not gradually transformed, but fall out of use. For a while a line or two might be remembered and then they are no longer performed at all. Some poems may be several centuries old,[37] but on the whole they tend to fall out of use after a century or so.

Songs are not a special category of tradition. Most songs, however, fall in this category insofar as they are poems or set speech, that is, they are in everyday language but memorized. The fact that messages are sung helps faithful transmission because the melody acts as a mnemonic device.[38]

## (2) Accounts

When accounts of events have been told for a generation or so the messages then current may still represent the tenor of the original message, but in most cases the resulting story has been fused out of several accounts and has acquired a stabilized form. The plot and sequence of episodes changes only gradually after this. Nevertheless, it will be impossible to discover what the inputs into such traditions have been, even soon after the events. So there is no question of reconstructing any original or even of assuming that there was but one original.

The dynamics of accounts start with historical gossip or personal traditions. The latter subsequently become group traditions and eventually traditions of origin. We present these different types in turn.

### (a) Historical Gossip

All sorts of news and hearsay generated as events occur and communicated through the usual channels of communication in a community do not disappear when the novelty has worn off. A child is born and this is news. But even later people will know that this child exists and the names of its parents. A village once founded on a given spot may be deserted fifty years later, but one may still remember which man was responsible for its foundation and perhaps why it broke up. Thus a great mass of information survives beyond the generation in which it happened and can then be kept for long periods of time, recalled when the person, the marriage, or the village foundation, is in question again, perhaps when his descendants, later marriages, or heirlooms are discussed, or when a village site is passed on the way to another destination. In Busoga, Cohen found that such data include information about the environment, settlements, migrations, marriages, and the meanings of words or phenomena (etiological material and folk etymology). None of these are strictly in the historical consciousness of people, but they are nevertheless transmitted as gossip, when the occasion warrants.[39] A typical example is the story related in 1954 by a caravan guide in

southern Libya. He said that west of the Teda (Libya/Chad) live
people who do not know how to make fire. They are called the
sun-fire-people. They live around a big well into which the sun
sets every night. Then the water gets hot and they can cook their
food. Thus they only eat once a day. Confirmation of this was
given three weeks later by another guide. I cite this bit of gossip
rather than another because it has already been told for the same
general area by both Herodotos and Pliny.[40] This bit of gossip
then is some 2,500 years old, and dispels the notion that gossip
must be ephemeral. In fact, though, most gossip about people
will be forgotten over the shorter periods, namely when their descendants have died out, have moved away, or when the gossip
is of no interest anymore, because it relates to situations or
events too far away. As for places, there are other indications
that extremely old information may be preserved, such as the
tales about the lost cities of Haithabu (West Germany) or Ger-
govia (France).[41]

(b) Personal Tradition
Reminiscences become family traditions, known and told by one
or more people even after the death of the person whose reminiscences they were. A common case is illustrated by the Mbosi
(Congo Brazzaville) example of the person who told me of the
time when his grandfather put his wife in a big round fish weir
and let her fall from the roof of their house to punish her. This
story surfaced in the course of a conversation about relationships between the genders. Chances are that the man's children
may never hear of it. Then again, they might. Under suitable circumstances such anecdotes, quite similar to historical gossip,
crop up, often in a stable form. They are hard to recall on demand, but in a proper setting the cue recalling them is triggered
and they are told. Personal traditions of this sort tend then to be
transmitted in the fashion of jokes or historical gossip, but unlike
gossip they are not considered of great importance. On the other
hand, certain persons were leaders or otherwise deeply affected
their communities, and their adventures will not remain as personal haphazard tradition for long. They are remembered by

many, are recalled more often, and tend to form the basis of anecdotes in group traditions. Insofar as such information does find its way into group traditions, it is quickly lost, surviving only one or two generations after the death of the persons involved.

(c) Group Account

Group accounts are the typical "oral traditions" of many authors. They are the oral memories of groups such as villages, chiefdoms, kingdoms, associations, and various kinship groups. I have called them "groups" because they embody something which expresses the identity of the group in which they are told or substantiates rights over land, resources, women, office, and herds. They are all institutionalized to some extent. They are told officially on formal occasions. They are often the property of a group. When they deal with royal history they stem from state officials, whose duty it is to remember and relate them to constitutional matters (succession, rights of kings and councils, precedence, and obligations and perquisites of offices). As reminiscences or news become institutionalized traditions their content has to be adapted. They have become part of an existing corpus of history relating to the institutions they related to and through this to a corpus relating to the whole society. There are very few examples of cases recorded precisely at this juncture so that we can follow exactly which transformations take place.

An illuminating case involves the Hopi of Arizona. Sometime between 1853 and 1856, ten Hopi were attacked by a party of Navaho as they returned to their home at First Mesa from a visit to the army Fort Defiance. At least four were killed. The Hopi village chief was among the dead. As a result a new clan took over the headmanship of the town. The affray led to retaliation and peace was concluded some time later when a boundary between Hopi and Navaho was agreed on, one passing quite near the place of the ambush.

Two versions of the event were recorded late in 1892. First a generalized one giving the bare facts, followed three weeks later by the reminiscences of one of the survivors, Djasjini, who had been an adult at the time of the events. This second version is

long, has greater detail, but essentially still narrates a sequence
of events. So almost forty years after the events there was still
an eyewitness in the town. In fact, there were two. Hani, who
had been a boy badly wounded in the affray, was still alive, had
become chief of the Singer's Society, and had directed the whole
Wuwutcim ceremony of 1892 at which occasion the first generalized version had been told. He may have been the one who told
it.

A third version now clearly oral tradition was published by
a Hopi in 1936. The tradition from personal narrative to collective narrative is completed. The differences with the previous
versions consisted mainly in the addition of elements that altered
the whole character of the story. A motivation was added to explain why the Hopi went to Fort Defiance. This was set out in
characteristic ways: two men, rivals for a woman, decided to
show their bravery by sacrificing themselves to be killed at the
boundary so that that boundary would be marked forever. The
whole affair was predestined to happen, and in the narrative two
incidents, one with an eagle/buzzard and one with a rabbit, are
added to make this clear. There was not much accident left in
the whole story. The part of the wounded boy, Hani, grew and
he is in fact the hero in 1936. His role was slightly idealized so
that it recalled the little Twin War Gods of mythology.

The material has been fitted into the corpus of tradition,
made important by reference to a significance and imagery also
found in other parts of the whole body of tradition. This probably happened because the incident led to changes in leadership,
became a charter with regard to the boundary, and had affected
a senior chief in the town. It was therefore a remarkable event
and could not be allowed to be forgotten. This case neatly presents both the reasons why the tradition was kept, and the kinds
of transformations messages undergo when they become part of
a body of tradition.[42]

Thus group traditions can be created quite rapidly after the
events and acquire a form which strikingly makes such a tradition part of a complex of traditions. After this, and in due course
of time, such accounts undergo further change. In general they

tend to become shorter and be single anecdotes. As new accounts enter into the storehouse of change further changes occur in individual traditions as well. The whole corpus of group accounts is constantly and slowly reshaped or streamlined. Some items acquire greater value. As the corpus grows, some items become repetitive or seem to have symmetrically opposed meanings or mnemonic streamlining occurs. Collective memory simplifies by fusing analogous personalities or situations into one. Whole groups of traditions, now abraded to anecdotes, are set up and contrasted so that in every account details are sharpened, altered or left out to imprint the mark of their association to other accounts.[43]

This process continues to the point that most accounts are lost or fused into each other beyond recognition. Especially characteristic of this process is the part played by stereotypical elements or clichés.[44] We saw with the Hopi example how clichés enter into the account to explain it, to make it understandable in terms of worldview and the folk theory of society. Once there, clichés may well remain stable over long periods of time or can proliferate further (as with the omens in the Hopi account) until in the end the whole account is boiled down to one typical cliché, which then tends to recur in all similar situations. All migrations in the Upper Nile area are caused by a quarrel between brothers over an item of little value.[45] In Central Africa marriages are often clichés to express relationships between chiefs.[46] In the end group accounts are either lost or move as a cliché or set of clichés into the realm of accounts of origin.

## (d) Traditions of Origin and Genesis

Every community in the world has a representation of the origin of the world, the creation of mankind, and the appearance of its own particular society and community. Such traditions of origin or genesis are what anthropologists term myth.[47] They are accounts that originate out of speculation by local sages about these questions, out of preexisting material of the same nature or borrowed from other communities, and out of heavily fossilized group accounts (that is, accounts reduced to clichés). Traditions of origin are new accounts and they may or may not remain stable over long periods of time.[48]

Often, logical constructs are used, in many cases put in a genealogical form.[49] A first being appears and then gives birth to others who pair and produce more offspring. The paradigm allows the expression of the relations between different groups of peoples, between different taxa of animals, plants, and spirits and their relationships to people in a single creation. Borrowed materials were very useful when some such groupings had to be explained. The Tower of Babel story is one of these. Known over large parts of Africa, the motif was used to explain why different populations had come to be different.[50] Such borrowings need not stem from other traditions of origin but come straight out of tales. The appearance of the first king of Burundi included in some versions the wholesale adoption of the future king dressed as a sheepherder, who overcame and slew the ruling, but false, king.[51] Borrowing to flesh out an account through the addition of further revelations also occurs. The Kuba (Zaire) held that migrations must stem from the common cradle of humanity, which must lie at the furthest downstream point possible. Hence, when they heard from Imbangala traders (Angola) about the ocean, this information was added to the mention of the point of origin with details about tides, beaches, waves, and the immensity of the ocean.[52]

The use of logic is evident in all stories of migration, since mankind originated in one place and now lives in others. Migration stories should be understood as cosmologies, just as creation *in situ*, but here elements that once were part of group accounts can be incorporated. Thus, the very last stages of the Kuba migration accounts reflect the location of the chief's capitals, just north of the present country. In the same way, "logical" genealogies are cosmologies, but in their lower reaches transitions do occur to what once were genealogical accounts about people who had lived. Moreover, whole bodies of group accounts have collapsed into a single cliché or crystallized around the figure of a single culture hero, who stands for long periods of time.[53] Some may just be logical constructs or were perhaps once revered as spirits and later humanized into culture heroes—a process known as euhemerism.[54] Perhaps the Chinese succession of five imperial culture heroes who invented society and culture belong here, especially the mystical yellow emperor.[55] But Shih Huang Ti, the first emperor, who was held responsible for creating the imperial institutions and the unity of China, was no spirit.[56] In all these cases, then, traditions of origin should not be rejected out of hand. But, as best as one can, one should separate logical construct and cosmological representation from what may be historical accounts condensed beyond easy recognition. One can never conclude that certain events occurred, but the study of accounts of genesis and origin can lead to formulation of questions to be pursued by other means.

Accounts of origin, group accounts, and personal accounts all are different manifestations of the same process in different stages.[57] When the whole body of such accounts is taken together there typically appears a three-tiered whole. For recent times there is plenty of information which tapers off as one moves back through time. For earlier periods one finds either a hiatus or just one or a few names, given with some hesitation. There is a gap in the accounts, which I will call the floating gap. For still earlier periods one finds again a wealth of information and one deals here with traditions of origin. The gap is not often very evident to people in the communities involved, but it is usually unmistakable to the researchers. Sometimes, especially in genealogies, the recent past and origins are run together as a succession of a single generation.

Some anthropologists have taken such stages to represent different functions in society. The first is myth and corresponds to a timeless past, the second is a repetitive (cyclical) middle period, and the third deals with linear time. Mythical accounts justify the bases of existing society and correspond to Malinowski's myth as social charter. The middle period justifies the working of present day society and is a static model of it. The recent period is the description of causal change, perceived as a disturbance of legitimate order. R. G. Willis talks of "the correlations between oral-traditional statement, social evolution, and form of historical consciousness."[58] But his representation is too static, and does not explain the dynamics of any tradition in particular. Moreover, the gap becomes a middle period.

The gap is best explained by reference to the capacity of different social structures to reckon time. Beyond a certain time depth, which differs for each type of social structure because time is reckoned by reference to generations or other social institutions, chronology can no longer be kept. Accounts fuse and are thrown back into the period of origin—typically under a culture hero—or are forgotten. The shortest such time depth I know of is that of the Aka of Lobaye (Central African Republic), where it does not exceed one generation of adults.[59] Historical consciousness works on only two registers: time of origin and recent times. Because the limit one reaches in time reckoning moves with the passage of generations, I have called the gap a floating gap. For the Tio (Congo), c. 1880, the limit lay c. 1800, while in 1960 it had moved to c. 1880. If the Tio were still a fully oral society, the arrival of de Brazza in 1880 would now lie in the period of origins. As it is he has become a culture hero, but can still be dated.

(e) Cumulative Accounts

Cumulative accounts are accounts such as lists or genealogies which have to be continually updated. They form a basis for the local chronology by providing epochs, units of duration used to evaluate how far in the past something happened. But this is not why they exist. They are of direct relevance to the social structures today. Genealogies show what the relationships between contemporary groups and between individuals today are and when these change they are manipulated to reflect the new relationships. Hence their transmission has a strikingly different dynamic from that of other accounts and not only because names have to be added at each birth. Lists of rulers exist to prove the continuity and to legitimate the institution of chieftainship, and justify why X occupies that office today and why he has the authority of the office. Such lists can also be manipulated and are subject to confusion because lists do not fare well in memory unless they are backed up by mnemonic devices. Both genealogies and lists are crucial to chronologies and will be discussed fully later.[60]

## (3) Epic

Epic is a class of traditions all on its own. We call epic a narrative couched in poetic language, subject to special linguistic rules of form. Usually epics contain hundreds or thousands of verses and present a complex tale full of wonders and heroism, centered around a main personage. These latter requirements are not essential. What is essential to the historian is that the wording is totally free, provided the form is kept. The generous use of stock phrases and fillings explains how a performer can innovate and still adhere to the required form. Epics in this sense exist primarily in the old world.[61] As innovation by performers is admired, it is not surprising that very different versions of the same epic exist, for example, in the Balkans, or of the Finnish epic.[62] Great variability occurs as different performers string different episodes together or change the order of episodes, and not only because individual passages are expanded, contracted, or altered.

Many epics have a historical dimension: The hero once really lived, as in the cases of Alexander or Marko Kraljevic, or some of the incidents, usually the main plot, correspond to actual events of minor or major importance. There was a war of Troy in which a king Ulysses may have participated. The historian uses them much more as reports about existing situations in a recent past than as a source about these persons or incidents. Some epics can be quite old. Thus the epic of Jaziya, known from Jordan to Algeria, is still told. It refers to the invasion of the Banu Hilal into Tunisia in 1049–53, and was already mentioned by the historian Ibn Khaldun shortly after 1400.[63] Epics may well be much longer lived than poems. They may well disappear, not into oblivion, but as their substance is cannibalized for later epics or passes into tale.

## (4) Tales, Proverbs, and Sayings

Tales are performed in everyday language chosen by the performer, and a certain amount of innovation is highly appreciated. They are considered to be fiction. We have already seen that there is no original and there cannot be an original. Some anecdotes or episodes or motifs can be very old, just as old as the tale about the Fountain of the Sun, which is historical gossip. Every performance is a premiere and appreciated as such by the audience. The public likes to hear known tales in new garb. This is similar to the attitude of the public towards production of an opera, where the performance should be original in setting, style of singing, acting, costume, and other details, but not alter either score or wording. The public for a tale expects partly novel wording and novel expression. Over time tales alter much more than accounts and in a different way. They never have a beginning, a composition, and they never end, but rather disappear into later tales. This means that tales, which are important sources for the historian, contain material of very mixed age and parentage. Anyone hearing or now reading "Puss in Boots" realizes that the social setting is archaic but cannot pin it down to a given place and time, even if the sixteenth–seventeenth centuries and northern Italy seem most attractive. There is too much mixing of materials from different times and places. In nonliterate societies this handicap is so great that one can only use material from tales for situations which no longer exist today and then date them to the *last* possible date, in many cases the later nineteenth century.

Among tales occur historical tales. They differ from accounts in that they are told for entertainment and are subject to the dynamics of fiction. Names and settings can be changed at will. Thus among the accounts about kings in Rwanda, there is a cycle of such tales dealing with King Ruganzu Ndori, which is quite popular and fancy.[64] Many pseudo-epics, that is narratives about historical personages that are not couched in a strict poetic form, belong here and should be handled as tales. Comparison of the popular tales about Ruganzu Ndori and historical accounts about him show obvious influences from other tales on the popular version and exhibit the full effects of artistic license. The main difference with other tales of the type "There once was a king" is that now the king is given the name "Ruganzu." This development occurs not only with kings but also with tricksters and other narrative heroes. Thus one of two Kuba tricksters, Kot a Mbo, was a historical personage, only a few generations back. Some of his adventures may have occurred as pranks, but most have been borrowed from the stock of anecdotes about the other trickster.

Besides tales, proverbs, sayings, and what E. Bernheim called *Geflügelte Worte* ("famous words") also belong in this class of traditions, for neither exact wording nor any special linguistic form is required of them.[65] Moreover, any formulation that sharpens the punchline is readily appreciated. Large scale collections of proverbs and sayings bear the variability in wording out.[66] As to famous words—usually famous last words—they sum up programs or persons and are mostly apocryphal. "The ocean is the border of my ricefield," said King Andriampoinimerina, thus laying down a program for his heir to conquer all of Madagascar.[67] Goethe's last words were "Mehr Licht" (more light), and that exemplified his career. Stanley, dying, heard Big Ben strike the hour and exclaimed at the sound: "So that is time," which summed up his life in Africa.[68] None of these can really be believed, but the occurrence of such tales tells how a later generation summed up a person.

The dynamics of proverbs and sayings are not well known. They seem to evolve like any metaphor in the language, which becomes just an expression, such as "His heart sank into his boots." They could be old or they could be freshly coined. There is nothing in a proverb that makes it old by definition, only wise. The situation is therefore exactly as it is for tales and in fact even more dfficult. For, as aphorisms, such sayings are shorter and more allusive.

## III. Oral Tradition as a Source of History

### (1) Definition

We are now ready to define oral traditions as verbal messages which are reported statements from the past beyond the present generation. The definition specifies that the message must be oral statements spoken, sung, or called out on musical instruments only. This distinguishes such sources not only from

written messages, but also from all other sources except oral
history. The definition also makes clear that all oral sources are
not oral traditions. There must be transmission by word of
mouth over at least a generation. Sources for oral history are
therefore not included. On the other hand, the definition does
not claim that oral traditions must be "about the past" nor that
they are just narratives. They encompass all the classes that we
have described above.

Such a definition does not rally all suffrages. Henige would
add a further restriction, namely that they should be commonly
or universally known in a given culture.[69] Versions that are not
widely known should rightfully be considered as "testimony."
To us this distinction is unnecessary here, and we prefer rather
to use "testimony" in its widest sense as "evidence about something." Henige would stress that traditions represent common
historical consciousness, and while this is a crucial criterion for
any sociological analysis of traditions, it is not usable as a source
for history.

J. C. Miller restricts traditions only to conscious historical
statements: The person who tells them wants to communicate
the past to us.[70] And in practice the same author seems to imply
that such statements must be narrative. He further argues that
the heart of such statements consists of stereotypes or clichés,
which remain very stable over time in his view and are the genuine unchanged formation that the historian must decode. But
his view is far too restrictive. Traditions need not be clichés or
narratives, nor is the conscious intent to testify about the past
necessary. Much can be learned about the past from oral sources
that are not concerned with the past and hence testify despite
themselves. Indeed, that characteristic makes them more reliable
precisely because they are unconscious contributions.

Obviously, our definition is a working definition for the use
of historians. Sociologists, linguists, or scholars of verbal art
propose their own, which in the first case (sociology) might well
stress common knowledge, in the second features that distinguish the language from common dialogue (linguists), and in the
last features of form and content that define art (folklorists).

Such specialists normally will be much less impressed by the importance of oral transmission over time than historians will be. Indeed, in practice they fuse oral history and oral tradition. Understandably, they stress the features most crucial to their analyses just as I have stressed the ones that are crucial to oral tradition as sources for history.

## (2) Oral Tradition as Evidence

(a) From Observation to Permanent Record
The relation between the event or the situation observed and the final recording made of it, either written or on tape, may be described in two ways. Whatever the model used, there must be a link between the record and the observation. If there is none, there is no historical evidence. Hence a tale that has no beginning in time is of itself no evidence, but those portions that were observed as existing situations and then incorporated into the setting or action of the tale do go back to an observation and are evidence.

The first and simplest model supposes that an observer reported his experience orally, casting it in an initial message. A second party heard it and passed it on. From party to party it was passed on until the last performer, acting as informant, told it to the recorder. A chain of transmission exists in which each of the parties is a link. From the definition and from the previous section dealing with oral tradition as a process it is evident that to a historian the truly distinctive characteristic of oral tradition is its transmission by word of mouth over a period longer than the contemporary generation. This means that a tradition should be seen as a series of successive historical documents all lost except for the last one and usually interpreted by every link in the chain of transmission.[71] It is therefore evidence at second, third, or nth remove, but it is still evidence unless it be shown that a message does not finally rest on a first statement made by an observer. It cannot then be evidence for the event or situation in question, even though it still will be evidence for later events, those that gave rise to the "false" message.

Some students of oral tradition realized this crucial fact many centuries ago. In Islam the traditions relating to the sayings of the Prophet have canonical value as *hadith* and these statements have been evaluated since the second century A.H. by an examination of the links in the chain of transmission. The possibility of transmission, the reliability and quality of each intervening witness between the first, the "Companion of the Prophet," and the recorder were all evaluated and *hadith* were accepted or rejected or kept in abeyance on the basis of the results.[72]

The sketched model has drawn criticism. It has been said that it was idealized and often not truly realistic, applying at best only to a minority of traditions.[73] To a certain point this is correct. Cohen, who used historical gossip to great effect, and Rosaldo, who used personal reminiscences, point to the fact that a neat single line of transmission simply does not often exist. Rather, most oral tradition is told by many people to many people. News, such as the birth of a boy, gets about and is transmitted by many people as gossip which in time becomes historical. Even in the generation after this and later, messages do not go from one link in one generation to a link in the next one in an orderly way. People hear performers and all the auditors have heard that message. Some tell it in turn to still others. Some who tell it have heard it several times from different people, and fuse all that they heard together in a single statement. Hence the transmission really is communal and continuous. There are no neat lines of communication reserved for all oral traditions. This information flows along the usual channels of communications, and has consequences that are discussed in chapter six. It is important to realize that we should not stick to a model that handles oral messages as if they were written, with originals and copies, rather than statements of information with all the flexibility of oral expression and their evanescence.

While this is indeed true, it is still crucial to realize how central problems of transmission remain. A link must be maintained between observation and record, if there is to be evidence.[74] What the second model emphasizes is that in practice such a transmission cannot often be traced, and that in many cases the messages recorded are fusions of several earlier messages re-stated. Yet the information was still passed on, in fact by more people and more continually than in the first model and with a better control on the accuracy of information than in the first model. The information coming from more people to more people has greater built-in redundancy than if it were to flow in one channel of communication. Multiple flow does not necessarily imply multiple distortion only, rather perhaps the reverse.

After a tradition has been recorded it does not die out *ipso facto*. On the contrary, for a while traditions continue still to be told and may at a later time once again be recorded. In their turn written records may serve as a fountainhead for oral tradition. Thus a mixed period of transmission comes into existence, and can last for a long period, as in Madagascar. Historians should be aware of this, examine oral traditions for feedback from earlier writings, and trace whether a tradition has been recorded several times, rather than be content with the last recording.

## (b) Evidence of What?

Any message containing historical information tells us about events or sequences of events, describes a situation of the past, or reports a trend. A car accident is an event, a description of etiquette at funerals a century ago is evidence of a situation, and remarks about inflation in bridewealth are evidence of a trend.

Most situations and trends in tradition seem to be summaries of events generalized. Thus the memories one has of etiquette concerning funerals derive from one's participation in one or more funerals plus what was then said to be proper on such occasions (that is, normative data rather than observed data). An observation about change in bridewealth may rest on actual observation (of how many cases?). It usually translates an opinion also held by the community, whether the facts substantiate it or not. Therefore statements about situations or trends need not in fact relate to actual events or observations. Often they derive from generalizations made by contemporaries or later generations. Such data testify then to opinions and values held, to mentalities, and that is their value, not as testimony of fact. It is therefore important to scrutinize traditions for signs that they are in fact expressions of generalizations or norms rather than statements of observations of events or situations. The converse holds true as well.

Such distinctions are important when we consider the various classes of oral traditions discussed. Only accounts directly testify to events, with very rare exceptions in poetry. All classes report on situations and trends. Tales especially, by creating a lifelike setting, give evidence about situations as they were observed as well as about beliefs concerning situations. For this reason, these sources, which are still very much neglected, can be of great value. An excessive concentration on accounts—even historical gossip—can mislead when it comes to reconstructing actual situations because accounts are the historical consciousness of present and past generations. More than once we shall underline the processes of selection that affect all accounts to bring them in line with a commonly held view of the past, concentrating on certain aspects of that past only—for instance, what happened to the elite—and on certain activities—for instance, on migrations or battles.[75] The use of tales and memorized traditions helps a great deal in obtaining less-biased and different sets of data.

Having described oral traditions in this chapter I can now turn to the application of the rules of evidence to them, and to begin with, how a tradition relates to a text that stems from it. As historians we deal with stable texts, permanent messages. But this record is only one manifestation occurring only once in a stream of renderings or performances. Can we accept a text as a valid rendering of a tradition? This and related questions form the subject of the next chapter.

## CHAPTER TWO

# PERFORMANCE, TRADITION, AND TEXT

The task of a historian working with written documents starts when he or she finds or takes up such a document and begins to read it. There is no relation at all between the historian on the one hand and the ready-made document that confronts him or her on the other. Hence the classical rules of evidence are straightforward. What is this document, both physically and as a message? Is it an original, written by the person who composed it? Is it authentic, truly what it claims to be, or is it a forgery? Who wrote it, when, or where? Once the answers to these questions are known an internal analysis of the content can proceed. As long as they are not known, one does not know to what, if any, analysis of content they relate. So the analysis of the document itself comes first.

But to historians dealing with oral tradition the situation is very different. Some of these are indeed faced with a piece of writing that claims to be the record of a tradition. The usual questions must be asked, but will refer only to the record, not to the tradition itself. In most cases, however, the relationship of the historian to the document is totally different. He or she did not find the piece of writing, but rather created it. He or she recorded a living tradition. The questions now are: what is the relationship of the text to a particular performance of the tradition involved and what is the relationship of that performance to the tradition as a whole? Only when it is clear how the text stands to the performance and the latter to the tradition can an analysis of the contents of the message begin. This means that the questions of authenticity, originality, authorship, and place and time of composition must be asked at each of these stages. The crucial link is the performance. Only the performance makes the tradition perceptible and at the same time only a performance is the source of the ensuing text. The peculiarities of the text derive from the relationship it has to one or more performances. Hence I adopt an order which examines first the performance, then its relation to the tradition from which it stems, then the process of its recording, and only then the resulting text.

# I. PERFORMANCE

## (1) Performing

The best-known situation of performance is the telling of tales.[1] A performer sits, often in the evening, surrounded by listeners and spins a tale. It is never just a recitation. The voice is raised or lowered, used as a means of dramatization. Nor does the storyteller just sit there. The tale is acted out with body gestures, even when the storyteller is sitting. Sometimes he or she may stand up, move around, and mime parts of the action narrated. In most cases the public is not just watching. The public is active. It interacts with the teller, and the teller provokes this interaction by asking questions, welcoming exclamations, and turning to a song sung by all at appropriate points of the action. The teller and public are creating the tale together. The teller leads the event, but responds readily to the public and leads his or her public to experience the tale. He or she tries to frighten, delight, worry, and put the listeners on tenterhooks, in turn, and skillfully builds on the passages which move them most, expanding the exciting parts and condensing or transforming the ones where the attention of the audience lags.

No wonder then that, as with actors, some tellers of tales are better and more famous than others. They are more creative, they have a better technique for making a tale come alive through sound and sight and involvement of their public, and like actors they have a repertoire. Some are better at dramatization, others at comic relief. Some personalities dominate and are spellbinders, others are better at involving the public. Some come across

as sages, whose tales will be pondered by many after the performances, others as wizards who take the audience out into a
dreamland, far from reality. Of course, the same tale handled by
different talents and for different audiences becomes something
quite different, even if the plot, settings, personalities, and the
sequence of episodes remain the same.[2] The tale must be well
known to the public if the performance is to be a success, for the
audience must not be overly preoccupied with the task of trying
to follow painstakingly what is being told in order to enjoy the
tale. They must already know the tale so that they can enjoy the
rendering of various episodes, appreciate the innovations, and
anticipate the thrills still to come. So every performance is new,
but every performance presupposes something old: the tale
itself.[3]

   This situation is the paradigmatic one described by folklorists. It is not, however, the only one. There exists quite a range
of situations of performance depending on what is performed.
Praise poetry in the great lakes area of Africa is shouted during
martial dances by a warrior stepping out of the ranks to the
front of the dancing area. The speed of delivery, the height of
the pitch, the martial attitude taken are part of his performance.
Praise poems for kings among the Zulu (South Africa) were delivered in front of the king by the poet during a public gathering
in a different attitude.[4] Historical accounts in Burundi were
short because they were told by a person sitting in a circle sip-
ping beer. Everyone contributed more or less in turn with
proverbs, jokes, small tales, or accounts. There was no time for
a long performance here. To the contrary, historical accounts
(*ibitéekerezo*) in Rwanda could be quite long, as the performer
was the entertainer of a lord and his guests for a whole evening.
He talked quietly, affected a subdued voice, and acted in accord
with a restrained, dignified atmosphere. He painted landscapes,
persons, actions, and emotions all in words rather than in
gesture or intonation. Historical accounts among the Kuba
(Zaire) were given in front of men sitting in council who could
not be easily interrupted. Indeed the king could never be interrupted.[5] This telling was in the nature of a testimony given in
measured tones and careful language. The epic singers of the

Kalevala (Finland) sang their lines, seated on a chair faced by another man on a chair. Both held the opposite ends of the same stick which they swayed to and fro to the rhythm of the epic. In Yugoslavia (Bosnia) epic singers were accompanied by a stringed instrument, the *gusle*.[6] When Nzebi (Gabon) wise men fought wars of wisdom in court, proverbs were thrown at their opponents as if they were their javelins. And we should mention also the masquerades, the tale that has become theater. The Javanese shadow play *wayang* is only one type. Masquerades miming historical accounts occur among the Natchez (United States), Tonga, and Bini (Nigeria).[7]

The actual technique and rules of performance situations vary. They will exert an impact on the fidelity and the stability of the tradition being performed. It therefore behooves anyone who publishes traditional texts to inform readers as to the context of the performances. One cannot assume that only tales and fictional data will be performed in the sense of "acted out" while somehow historical accounts would be recited *recto tono* in measured cadenza and in religious silence. Whether that ever happened with any tradition anywhere seems doubtful.

Readers should also be kept informed of date, place, and author of the performance. Such information can become crucial in interpreting the text. Thus in 1906 L. Frobenius jotted down a tale in which the dwarf antelope was killed by the leopard. It was told by a Lulua slave in Kuba country. Without this information no one could discover that an anomaly in the tale (one of two) was an expression of defiance. The dwarf antelope is the trickster hero in Kuba tales. The slave had the hero killed. In this case, the *who* was important, so important that it is one of the very few tales in the collection for which Frobenius gives an explanation.[8]

## (2) Performers

Of these questions, description of the performer, the author, needs the most elaboration. Performers could be specialists or not. Indeed, some persons were specialized in one particular type of tradition, say, tales, and sometimes in some tales only—their repertory. They would not necessarily count as "specialists" in their society since they did not practice this occupation for a living. This is the case with Mazitatu Zenani, the woman teller of *ntsomi* in Xhosa land who has become famous because of her work with H. Scheub. She was known as a good performer especially to women and children in her neighborhood, but not to most men—they do not listen to *ntsomi*—nor to anyone outside of her district.[9]

With regard to historical accounts, poetry, or epic, however, some specialists are known to everyone in the community. In many West African states there were *griots*, professional and casted praise singers and tellers of accounts.[10] In Polynesia specialists were widespread, such as the Ha'a Ngotā Motū's belonging to the Ha'atufunga clan of Tonga who specialized in the traditions of royal ritual, just like their counterparts in Rwanda, the *abiiru*.[11] Specialists in Tikopia were trained persons authorized to speak.[12] These differ from knowledgeable persons who have learned many traditions without being designated socially as specialists. They enjoy a prestige status as wise persons, such as the Kuba *bulaam* or the Tonga *fefine 'ilo* and *tangata 'ilo*. Anglo-Saxon scôps (Celtic bards or druids) and epic singers in Yugoslavia are specialists in a different sense, rather closer to the status of griots, but without any castelike status and enjoying a very high prestige. All these people, like the Arab *rawi*, were not full time specialists, only part time performers to be hired for festivities, but professional performers nonetheless.

In states, an official was often found whose duty was to perform the state's official history at public ceremonies.[13] Thus the *baba elegun* of Ketu, a Yoruba (Rep Benin) city, had to know the city's history. The office was hereditary in the Oyede family and the information was passed from father to son. The traditions were recited at each enthronement. If the *baba elegun* succeeded on that occasion in reciting the traditions without a mistake, he was offered a reward. If he failed, he was deemed to be punished by supernatural sanction.[14] Such a man was a walking reference library, to be used when state occasion demanded it. And indeed these men were, but one can doubt whether their main functions were to be but walking archivists. The description for Rwanda sketched by Kagame is clearly overdrawn.[15] There were genealogists (*abacurabwenge*), memorialists (*aba-*

*teekerezi*), poets who told the panegyrics of kings (*abasizi*), and
*abiiru* who preserved the secret ritual code of the dynasty. With
the exception of the last group the Rwandan terminology is
not a titulature. It indicates merely what people can do. Thus
those that could recite panegyric poems of kings are *abasizi*. In
contrast, *abiiru* were special people whose main duty was not the
remembering of, but the carrying out of, the rituals of kingship.
Memorizing these rituals was only an accessory part of their
main duties.[16] Connected with this was a sense of ownership.
Not everyone could publicly perform or recite everything one
knew. It is in this sense that the answer of an informant to
Kagame must be understood. The man said that it was not his
fault if he did not know the answer to the question put before
him, since he was not responsible for the preservation of that
particular tradition.[17]

With reference to the Akan states of Ghana, E. Meyerowitz
mentions as specialists: minstrels, masters of ceremony, royal
drummers, royal hornblowers, the king's spokesman, his grave
priest, his stool-carrier-chief, female "soulbearers" of the souls
of the deceased queen mothers, masters of ceremonies to the
state-gods, court functionaries, and the administrator of the capital—each of whom had to remember a particular part of the history of the state and transmit it to his or her successor in office.[18]
Assuredly, every one of these persons was a specialist, but to do
certain things at court and know their historical specialization
merely entailed knowing those portions of past history that
related to the office. In the case of the royal drummers this meant
knowing the state historical compositions in drum language,
which are important sources for its history. In contrast, a female
soulbearer needed only to have some historical background
knowledge about the queen mother whose soul she was concerned with.

While it is easy to overemphasize the degree of historical
specialization in nonliterate states, one should not forget that
specialized knowledge was kept by those specialists at court who
needed it. Thus a royal archivist general was not found in the
Akan states, and the one that E. Torday mentioned for the Kuba,
the *mwaaddy*, was in fact limited to questions of royal succession

for which he had to know the precedents. As a rule, the degree of specialization in traditions corresponds to the general level of specialization in a given society. Every specialist knows what was historically relevant to his function.

In addition to such people, research has turned up many cases where performers were found to be truly encyclopedic informants, ones knowledgeable about all aspects of local history. In many societies there are men of memory, local historians, who collect all the information they can and weave it into a reconstruction of their own. Sometimes their attitudes are more akin to those of an antiquarian, but other times they are more those of a historian building the information up into a grand design. Among the Kuba, Bope Louis was the antiquarian, a connoisseur especially of historical slogans, while Shep Mathias was more concerned with the grand design and meaning of the past. A debate has raged around the reliability of the testimony of such encyclopedic informants.[19] Whatever side one takes in this debate, one thing is clear: collectors should always indicate whether a performance was due to such an especially interested and talented person or not.

## II. PERFORMANCE AND TRADITION

A performance is the normal expression of a whole tradition. The conditions of its reproduction are those of the tradition itself. I discuss them first, with regard to the occasion and frequency of performances, the intent to reproduce a tradition as faithfully as possible or not, and the processes by which a performer remembers the tradition as he or she performs. Beyond this I need to deal with the questions of the variability within a given tradition, of authenticity of authorship and of date.

### (1) Reproduction of Performance

(a) Frequency, Time, and Place
Performances are not produced at random times. [20] The occasions for performances are limited and can be observed in the field. In most cases the rules relating to this have little to do with

a desire to maintain the faithfulness of the message. They are rather inspired by the practical use of traditions. Thus, a formal recitation of a royal list of successors to the throne or a royal genealogy is appropriate at a coronation, and perhaps the genealogy may be recited once a year when the chiefs are assembled at the capital. Many rituals containing historical messages, like the *kava* of Tikopia (and other Polynesian islands), are performed when appropriate. The "Work of the Gods" in Tikopia is performed only twice a year while ordinary *kava* occur much more often.[21] Legal precedents and proverbs are often cited during litigation, clan slogans at funerals or, as among the Kuba, in eulogy to praise star dancers.

In many parts of Africa and elsewhere tales are not to be told during daytime.[22] No good reasons are given for this, and unlike the previous examples we do not see an evident link between use, purpose, or situation and this rule here. Economic factors often are said to be the cause of such a constraint. The rule was not made with economic uses of time in mind, but probably grew out of the observation that people do not tell tales during the day, because they are all busy doing other things and often not at home.

The location of a performance is to be appropriate to its use and purpose. Such a location is often prescribed where it would not seem to matter. Thus tales in Benin City should be told in the *itun* or central place of the house and nowhere else. In the villages, the village square is the proper setting.[23] In Kuba villages, the square is not appropriate; tales should be told in the houses or in their yards, or perhaps just in front of them, but never in the middle of the yard!

Each sort of tradition has its appropriate occasions for performance, and that also determines the frequency of a performance. Among the Dogon (Mali), the Sigui ritual was performed, it is said, only once every sixty years.[24] One wonders who after such a lapse of time would still remember the details and order of the complex rituals and, indeed, in the absence of a calendar how one knew exactly when to perform them.

Frequency of repetition helps to combat forgetfulness. But

frequent repetition does not itself guarantee fidelity of reproduction. Tales told many nights in the month may in fact change
faster than tales which are told more infrequently. Thus, to
know the occasion and the frequency of the performance is not
by itself enough for evaluating the faithfulness of a reproduction.[25]

(b) The Intent of the Performance
The intent of the performance greatly matters. Where, as in the
case of tales, innovation on a stable scheme is at a premium, the
pulse of change beats faster. Where, to the contrary, the performers intend to stick as closely as possible to the message
related and to avoid lapses of memory or distortions, the pace of
change can almost be stopped. In some cases controls over the
faithfulness of the performance were set up and sanctions or
rewards were meted out to the performers. The Kuba used only
a mitigated form of sanctions. In theory no king could succeed
if, during the coronation ceremonies, he could not give a general
description of Kuba history,[26] and the candidate for the female
office of *mbaan* could not be appointed if she could not
enumerate the names of her predecessors in office. Of course
such sanctions were fiction. Who would dare to correct the king
on such an occasion, and would the *mbaan* not be briefed by
those who knew the information—if any? No inspectors were
set up. Control was exercised by the consensus of the public
among the Kuba. Nevertheless, the very explicit requirement,
however fictive, seems to have encouraged successors or *mbaan*
to study the required traditions so as to deliver them fluently.

In Polynesia ritual sanctions were brought to bear in case of
failure to be word-perfect. When bystanders perceived a mistake
the ceremony was abandoned. In New Zealand it was believed
that a single mistake in performance was enough to strike the
performer dead. Similar sanctions were found in Hawaii. This
implied that when a performer was not struck dead his performance had to be correct. Such beliefs however had visible effects. Thus in Hawaii a hymn of 618 lines was recorded which
was identical with a version collected on the neighboring island

of Oahu.[27] Certainly this is remarkable, at least if we are certain
that one of the performers did not have access beforehand to the
written version of the other one. Sometimes controllers were appointed to check important performances. In Rwanda the controllers of *ubwiiru* esoteric liturgical texts were the other performers entitled to recite it. In such cases two difficulties arose.
First, since there was no written text, there was no absolute
standard against which to measure a performance. The only acceptable standard was the remembered performance of the
teacher of the performer. If he said it deviated, then the sanction
could be applied, and it was death. Secondly, it is evident that
such specialists, all belonging to a single or closely related house-
holds, were not ready to point out a failure that would have
such drastic consequences. No failure is remembered.

The reward system would seem to work better. In Rwanda
performers of dynastic poems were exempted from corvée labor
and given small gifts when they recited.[28] This does not relate to
the faithfulness of the reproduction, only to its pleasing character. Still, as there was competition between different poets,
perhaps fear of rivals prompted performers to reproduce the
poems as faithfully as possible. Indeed, we find little variation
between different performances.[29]

The intent of the performance with regard to the faithfulness of the message it contains must be investigated for every
separate circumstance. Whether innovation is appreciated or to
the contrary word for word delivery is required should be investigated for every type of tradition in a given culture. Moreover,
whether or not the intent to be faithful succeeds, and to what
degree, will appear from the variability of the versions collected
at various performances.

(c) Remembering: Cueing and Scanning
The role of memory during a performance is astonishing. Lord
says it well: "If we are fully aware that the singer is composing as
he sings, the most striking element in the performance itself is
the speed with which he proceeds. It is not unusual for a Yugoslav bard to sing at the rate of from ten to twenty syllable lines
a minute."[30] Lord goes on to uncover the technique of compo-

sition which makes composing possible and the use of formulaic material, which allows for breathing space and yet keeps the master constantly in mind.

Studies of memory emphasize that remembering is action, indeed, creation.[31] Its mechanisms are cueing and scanning. Cueing, the main mechanism, consists of attaching a cue to every item that is being memorized. This acts like a label on a library book by which the book can later be retrieved. The cues relate to a single master code, the mnemonic code. Often items are double coded for efficiency of recall: once auditory, which is the main code, and once visually. A subsidiary mechanism for recall is scanning items according to the sequence of accession.[32] This works well when items are related in a time sequence or a local sequence: for example, before the hero comes onto the stage he must be born.

For tales H. Scheub has shown that cueing is crucial.[33] Tales are built around a single core image or a set of images. The cue for each image is a core cliché: a short song, chant, or saying. With this the performer recalls the image and given the recall of a theme she can tell her tale. Skilled performers scan the stock of their other core images (over the core clichés) for details or attributes that will be useful in expanding the image they use. This is not scanning in the mnemonic sense, but it is symbolizing. Symbolizing consists of using the mnemonic code not to recall directly, but to group together unrelated materials with similar attributes.[34] When several core images have to be recalled, stereotyped passages will appear between them to allow for time, exactly as in epic, to produce the next cue and in many cases true mnemonic scanning takes place: the performer recalls items following the first cue over time as she committed them to memory, even though she learned nothing by heart.

In poetry, memorization must be more rigid. Its structural features facilitate this, but it is not entirely clear how recall actually operates here. As to accounts, it is not surprising to learn that when precision in recall is desired, many peoples have turned to mnemotechnic devices. Indeed, writing is the most perfect such device.

(d) Mnemotechnic Devices

Most mnemonic devices were cues destined to recall a memory and could therefore, unlike writing, yield new information. These devices were objects, landscapes, and music.

(i) Objects

Objects as proof of a certain event or as mementos of a past happening are quite common. In the Hopi case mentioned earlier, we see the Hopi produce a feather shrine (*tiponi*) in 1938 as proof of an earlier agreement about the boundary between Navaho and Hopi.[35] *Wampum* were used in the eastern United States in similar ways as proofs of treaties and clues of memory.[36] Similarly a firebrand kept by an Anyi (Ivory Coast) family substantiated their ancient royal status.[37]

Figurative objects or iconography on them could be more than this. The same Anyi had figurative goldweights. In the treasury of a ruler one finds a weight showing a chicken coop. It helps to recall how the Anyi were protected by Boafo Nda, the son of the great warrior-king Ano Aseña.[38] Luba initiates into a certain cult received a *lukasu* or "long hand," an emblem covered with signs which helped them remember the main teaching of their initiation.[39] The Sioux "winter count" consisted of a buffalo skin for a given winter on which the owner painted figures acting as cues for the important events that had taken place during the winter.[40] This brings us close to pictographs and ultimately to writing systems. A set of figurative goldweights kept in a package *dja* was for Niangouran Bouah a proof that the Akan (Ghana, Ivory Coast) had a system akin to writing,[41] and similar claims have been made wherever sets of pictographs have been found, especially standardized pictographs. Easter Island, Benin, and Maya codices are all examples of such developments. The ultimate development here is the use of a piece of writing as a cue to other information. Thus, the memory of a whole correspondence was attached to a letter preserved in Masina (Mali).[42] People knew what the correspondence leading up to the letter had been and what the outcome from the letter had been, and this is not an isolated case.

Repetitive information was remembered by adding knots to

a rope, cutting pegs onto a stick, or adding objects such as twigs or stones to a bundle. This seems to have been common practice all over the world. A beautiful instance is that of an Iroquois (United States) cane with pictographs and fifty pegs. It served as a cue to lists of chiefs, rolls of councils, and chants, and in its discussion alternate mnemonic aids made of kernels of corn, wampum strings, and drawings were produced.[43] Many objects had no importance by themselves, serving only to count, but some, such as Akan thrones, were kept as repositories or altars for the cult of the deceased chiefs and only incidentally served as mnemonic supports.[44] Skulls, jawbones, and umbilical cords were all in one or another case kept as relics of past rulers and served incidentally as mnemonic aids.[45] A curious case is that of the Igala (Nigeria) where carved canes were relics of former rulers, but where their number could not exceed nine. So whenever a new one was added, the oldest one was destroyed.[46]

A case by itself is the *quipu*, which was used in Peru. It consisted of a series of knotted ropes of different colors and lengths which were tied together and attached to the headdress in the form of a fringe or kept in an archive. The colors, knots and length of string were all significant, as was their order. The Inca imperial officials used this process to preserve quantitative, including chronological, data, and apparently qualitative information as well. Father Morua was astonished to discover how wide a variety of things concerning the past these knotted ropes could report: the length of each king's reign, whether he was good or bad, brave or cowardly, in short the *quipu* could be read as a book. He adds that a monk of his order had conducted conclusive experiments with an old Indian. The man understood his *quipu* just as if he were reading a book. After their conversion, Indian penitents at confession often read off their sins from a *quipu* they had constructed for this purpose.[47]

### (ii) Landscape

The landscape, changed by man or not, often was a powerful mnemonic device. A vivid example are the *tee* grounds of the Mae Enga of New Guinea. Such grounds were the stage where leaders competed with each other in the giving of pigs and where they displayed their wealth. Trees were planted on this sort of battlefield to commemorate just how long each line of pigs had been. The grounds acted as a mnemonic device for recalling the history of the institution of *tee*, the history of all the exchanges and hence the whole political history of the area.[48]

Abandoned towns, battlefields, and royal gravesites all act as mnemonic cues. L. Frobenius described royal tombs in Upper Volta as "historical records carved into the landscape,"[49] and this applies to many other cases where royal tombs were kept up or built as mausolea.[50] Indeed, they were "carved as historical records" to the point that a Shilluk (Sudan) monarch apparently built a fake tomb in order to substantiate a traditional history! The most common historical sites that evoke traditions, apart from tombs, are battlefields, capital sites in kingdoms, and estates of the crown (Pfalz) or House estates of ruling lines.[51] Such is the importance of landscape that among the peoples of the Luapula (Zambia) a number of traditions are only recited when passing the site mentioned in them,[52] and I had to use such features as a major element in the spatial distribution of a sample for collecting traditions in Burundi.[53] Ritual sites such as the *kava* sites or *marae* in Polynesia are less used as mnemotechnic sites by themselves, even though they are the scene of much telling of tradition. Such sites are sometimes chosen for a spectacular natural feature to which an etiological story is then attached. The historian should beware of such cases of iconatrophy.

### (iii) Music

Among mnemonic aids other than objects or landscapes one must mention melody and rhythm. It is well known that these provide mnemonic support. Many people recall the words of a song by working from the melody. In Rwanda the dynastic poets first learned a melody and afterwards the words of the poem they wished to remember. One of the poets actually explained that the melody serves as a means to remember the words. In various parts of Africa south of the Sahara and in New Guinea, where the languages are tonal, drum rhythms are used to transmit information. In some West African kingdoms drum slogans and poems recorded historical information.[54] Elsewhere, where drums were used for long distance communication, the drum names and slogans often preserve historical information.[55] Tonal languages can also use the melody of a sentence as a mnemotechnic means. This is evident, for instance, in tonal riddles.[56]

(e) Learning
Most traditions are learned in the same way that other skills are, that is, by imitation. Thus Xhosa (South Africa) children imitate the performance of *ntsomi* tales, performed by their mothers.[57] Learning by attending performances is always crucial. The Iwì Egúngún chants among the Yoruba (Nigeria) could only be acquired in this way.[58] According to J. Goody, this was the main way in which the long Bagre account (Ghana) came to be known to the performers. Goody at first also cited learning by rote, but later he dismissed this type of transmission.[59] There is no doubt that attendance at performances was always crucial and in some cases may have been the only means of transmission. In order to become a competent jurist only those who assiduously sat in on court cases would acquire the required expertise. By attending performances one learns to recognize cues and formulas and how to use them in a creative way, but often this was not deemed to be sufficient. When a high fidelity of reproduction was required, memorizing was enjoined. The Arab poet's *rawi* (official performer) learned the poem by rote as the poet was composing it.

Many examples exist where instruction was given by recognized teachers, often in appropriate places, whether the traditions were learned by rote or not. R. Firth learned many Tikopia traditions during breaks in *kava* rites, and he noticed that when traditions were told to him by competent persons, they often were accompanied by one or more persons who were also learning the tradition or acting as a control to ensure that nothing would be omitted.[60] Formal schooling existed in Rwanda, Hawaii, the Marquesas Islands, New Zealand, among the Inca, and perhaps certain Akan groups.[61] Such cases seem to occur among people with a considerable degree of centralized state apparatus. On the Marquesas Islands a father desiring to give his children special instruction built a house, hired the services of a bard, and gathered a group of about thirty men and women. All went to live in the schoolhouse and during the period of instruction the pupils were taboo. Instruction lasted for a month, followed by a two-week recess, after which the next period of instruction began. If the pupils did not learn well, the bard closed the school. Everything that had to do with the school was taboo because of the sacred nature of what was taught.[62] This case reminds anthropologists of teaching in noncentralized societies, either during boys' initiations or when initiating new members into an association. These are found all over the world. Instruction was by conversation, teaching of songs and riddles, through the use of icons, by acting out what was to be learned, or through other means. Systematic memorizing was not often required, tests of knowledge acquired did not exist, yet instruction clearly imparted a great deal of information to the pupils, including traditional accounts.

## (2) Variability within a Tradition

Although much can be learned from a study of performance, still the historian needs to know more about the tradition it expresses. One must know first how representative the message of a given performance in relation to the whole tradition is. Hence different performances of the same tradition must be compared to assess the variability of their message.

(a) Poems and Their Kin
One extreme case is Rwandan. It involves the dynastic poem *ukwibyara*. As recited by different performers in different performances, the poem remains substantially the same. Variants are claimed to be few and often minimal.[63] Yet the length of the five full versions varies from 396 to 441 verses, while a sixth version is a fragment of 277 verses. The variants, verse by verse, are

usually quite small. Thus verse 3 has *Buhanzi* except for one version *buhanza* which makes no sense in the context and must be an error. The same performer has verse 4 *Nyamuhanza* instead of *Nyamuhanzi* and although this variant does make sense, it is likely to be an innovation patterned after the change in verse 3. Such variations strongly suggest the poem was learned by rote. Variations of this type occur every few lines if one counts them in any of the six performances, including those whose differences may be negligible. Thus verse 62 *abagusigiranye* ("those who transmitted to you") vs. one variant by one person *abagusigira* ("those who left you"). Another class of variation, omission, is more serious. Thus the so-called fragment omits verses 18–52, but others omit one or two verses here and there as well. More serious still is the situation in verses 220 and following and 280–94, where one performer inverted the verses. They deal with two kings, both called Mibambwe, both in the first and in the second passage. The performer confused them.

There is no doubt here as to the actual message and the wording of the tradition. Nor is it doubtful that the original was composed at one time by a single person. The comparison of variants not only makes clear which passages have remained stable, but in many cases where one variant must be an error of another one. The individuals and groups which vary do so with some order; that is, one can reconstruct a genealogy of the poem's variation and discern from it the order in which they learned one from the other and ultimately from the composer, as the relationships of all six performers to each other is well known.

This example is a paradigm of a message, learned by rote, and constrained by special language rules applying to poetry. There is an archetype and it can be reconstructed. But the example is also an extreme case of faithful transmission.

Much more common is the case of the Kuba clan slogans, where we deal with set speech without special linguistic form. If we take the largest Kuba clan, Ndoong, we are confronted with recorded performances. Using a small sample of those is enough to illustrate our argument. A number of instances have:

A. *Makum a Labaam amiin mel aNdoong*

Various other sections give:

B. identical to A + *Mbul aNdoong yashyaam bwiiky*
C. identical to A + *Ibul yashyaam bwiiky*
   C differs in one element only from B.
D. identical to A + *Ibul inyaamk imitetl*
   D is closest to C but the difference is bigger than be-
   tween C and B.

*Mbul* means "rain," *Mbul aNdoong* "the rain of Ndoong." The
second sentence in B and C means "The rain (of Ndoong) sur-
passes others in quantity." This leads us to check with the slogan
for rain:

E. *Yooncdy inyaacdy mateem ikaangl byeenc yaan adik
   dimaan. Makum aLabaam amiin mel aNdoong. Kweemy
   acik Mimbyeem bwil abwil.*

Clearly, the second sentence corresponds to the simple Ndoong
slogan. Further analysis shows that the first sentence is derived
from the slogan for the Bieng people and the third one is the
slogan for the clan Kweemy. Links between these elements are
provided by the close ties of Kweemy and Ndoong clans with the
chieftaincy of the Bieng people.

Obviously, one can continue further with the comparison
and further document, first, that the stable element in the
Ndoong clan slogan is the element *Makum aLabaam amiin mel
a Ndoong* (Makum, child of Labaam, among the names of
Ndoong) and, second, that other elements given as short sentences relate to other groups or concepts. Working from one
through the other, one finds oneself in a network of slogans,
apparently without end.

It is possible to compare versions, group them, and put
them in order so that a *stemma codicum* or "genealogy of writings" appears. One must then recognize that many slogans have
"interpolations" from other slogans, such as E would have from
slogans of the Kweemy clan and the Bieng people. True, in the
case of the clan Ndoong, the mass of versions makes this proce-

dure quite cumbersome. When mutual influences are so numerous, a *stemma codicum* of the full corpus would in practice refer to hundreds of other slogans—not to speak of the difficulty of actually proving in which order mutual influences are to be put.

Further thought makes it clear that to work by analogy with procedures for comparing written versions, as the *stemma codium* approach implies, falsifies reality. Here versions are not due to errors in copying, but to minor (examples B, C, and D) rephrasing of the same idea or to major differences in discourse (E). E actually links rain to the Bieng chiefdom, the Ndoong clan, and the Kweemy clan. This is a different discourse from A. B and C are a different discourse also: the second sentence links Ndoong to rain. And D, while close to B and C in intent, actually says something different about rain. The versions in fact either present a novel discourse or the same discourse but with replacement of words, like *ibul* vs. *mbul* (C+D/B), or a portion of E that we compare to the onset of the slogan of the Bieng:

E. *byeenc yaan adik dimaan*: "his litter high"
F. *bakidy adik dimaan*: "his friends high"

No scribe would make that last kind of error.

The first type of version cannot be seen as a question of "error," but is one of choice of discourse. The second one can involve the notion of error. One can show that *ibul* should be *mbul* and that *bakidy* makes much less sense than *byeenc*. For the second type of error one could elaborate a genealogy of versions, but for the first type one cannot. Comparative analysis of versions yields in this case very short set speech patterns, which have been learned by heart. Such patterns are very stable in many cases, encompass the message of tradition, and are the parts that were once composed by a single individual. Kuba slogans then are a discourse made out of successive formulas.

(b) Epic
Formulas are also the stable elements in epic, along with the special linguistic form in which the message is couched. A con-

cept of "the original" makes no sense here.[64] Strictly speaking, where there is no original there can be no variant, argues Lord, even though epic pieces are related to each other. To reconstruct an ideal form would merely be to establish a list of elements common to the messages of the examined performances, which always are but a percentage of actual performances over, say, a generation. Yet such comparisons establish at least what the total field of discourse is in a given epic, in terms of plot, setting, personages, themes, and obligatory episodes and formulas. For epic works with formulas as well. In comparison they stand out as common to different versions, as in the song of Alijaga Stočević performed in 1935 and then again in 1950 by Halil Bajgorić.[65]

| 1935 | 1950 |
|---|---|
| Razbolje se Stočević Alija | Razbole se Stočević Alija |
| Usred Stoca grada kamenoga | Usred Stoca grada bijeloga |
| Pa boluje za punu godinu | absent |
| Vazda misle age Stolačani, | absent |
| Da j'Alija svijet mijenijo | absent |
| Pa boluje za dvije godine, | Te boluje za dvij'godine dana |
| Pa boluje i trecú godinu. | absent |

| | |
|---|---|
| Stočević Alija fell ill | Stočević Alija fell ill |
| midst Stolac, stony city | midst Stolac, white city |
| He was ill for a full year | |
| Even the aghas of Stolac think | |
| that Alija has changed worlds. | |
| He was ill for two years, | And he was ill for two years |
| And he was ill also a third year | of days |

In the continuation it is sometimes the version of 1935 which is more detailed, sometimes the version of 1950. The variation is due to differences in discourse, but there are common lines, with minor variation—as in the case of Kuba clan slogans.

Epic is a narrative with major and minor plots. These can all vary. In the Yugoslav case Lord was struck by the conservativeness, the stability of the tradition. The basic story is preserved. Changes are either in ornamentation or in detail of description, in greater or lesser contraction, in "interpolation" from other epic material and even in substitution of one theme for another. Such variation is also found in other epics, for instance in the Central African *Mwindo*.[66]

To the historian this poses the same problems as the Kuba clan slogans, only more so. He now must be careful to determine what belongs to the corpus of epic traditions in general (the so-called interpolations) and what belongs to the traditions of one particular epic, determined by a stable story line, its plot. There may have been a first composition, but in this case much more than in the case of clan slogans, the variation that we find in contemporary performances is due to many performers over time, and we cannot even be certain that all of the formulaic lines belonged to the first performance.

(c) Narrative
These conclusions are just as true when we compare different tales, with the added difficulty that even plots shade from one tale into another so that it is almost artificial to separate one tale from another. Also, we have seen in chapter one that there never need have been a single moment when a single person created a new tale.[67] Here the historian is faced with a source whose versatility severely limits any conclusions from any performance with regard to the past. On the other hand, one performance is as good a source as the other. Only references to archaic situations which no longer exist can be used in such tales and then only for the most recent past when they existed.

Historical accounts, however, differ from tales or epics in this respect. Variability is often much less pronounced. There is substantial commonality in plot, setting, personages, and even succession of episodes, although the types of variability noted for the epic do obtain to a certain degree. Thus, expansion or contraction of descriptions, omission or addition of detail, are common. Two versions of a historical story told by Gakaniisha (Rwanda) in 1952 and 1957 differ less than the versions of the epic of Alijaga Stočević cited above.[68] Such cases allow us to conclude that the stability of the message inherent here is as great or greater than what is found in epics and set speech that is not learned by rote. Still, we cannot think of an archetype, and we cannot claim for certain that the parts common to all versions existed in a supposed original.

The timespan of a tradition is important in this regard. If it is small, then we can come close to the message told by contemporaries after eyewitness accounts have been conflated with rumor. More often we come close to the message as it stabilized in the generation after that. Examples are too cumbersome to detail here. The reader is therefore referred to the case of Macoonco where the versions allow us to grasp the differences between two accounts that crystallized shortly after the events they relate.[69]

When the timespan is greater, we must know how the process of tradition alters messages and with this in mind attempt to interpret the present-day messages. What in them is likely to stem from a first generation of accounts and what is due to transformations brought about in due course of time?

## (3) Authenticity, Antiquity, and Authorship

Questions of authenticity, authorship, locality, and dating are at the heart of the external critique concerning written documents, because they allow us to establish the context for a critique of their content. With oral tradition these questions receive very different answers. All we have are performances. As we have seen, original compositions do not exist in several genres of oral tradition. It follows that the question of authenticity is posed very differently. We can only ask whether a given performance that claimed to be part of a tradition is indeed part of a tradition or not. The poems of Ossian were claimed to be the record of an old tradition in Scotland. Yet MacPherson invented them. They were not based on any performance at all.[70] The *Walam olum* of the Delaware or Lenape Indians (United States) was said to be a very complex ensemble of traditions backed by pictographs as mnemonic aids. They were for many years treated as the most significant body of American Indian traditions from the eastern United States.[71] Constantine S. Raffinesque, who first worked with these materials, said that he had bundles of sticks and glyphs from a Dr. Ward in Indiana in 1820 and then in 1822 received the songs annexed to these—that is, the tradition itself—from an unknown source. Raffinesque moved to Philadelphia in 1825 and translated the tradition and published it in 1833. The tradition is likely to be a forgery. Did Raffinesque himself fake the objects and invent the tradition? Or was this an effort by Delaware Indians involved in a revival movement?[72] We don't know, but we know enough to discount the *Walam olum* completely as a tradition.

Authorship of a tradition does not exist for most genres. Each performer of genres which are not memorized word by word is an author. We know only those whose performances were recorded. We can only comment on the age, gender, and status of performers who usually render a given tradition and know whether they are professionals or not.[73] This does not mean that these attributes have always been those of performers in the past, nor that—in cases such as accounts—where there has been an original composition the original composer of the tradition shared any of these characteristics with contemporary performers.

Nevertheless, it is important to note who the author of the recorded version was. If he was a professional, did his performance belong to a genre reserved to professionals? Was he entitled to perform or not?[74] Was he a "person of memory" or not? That is, was he or she interested in the past history of that community to the point of having learned many traditions and having produced his or her own vision of the past? Such persons exist and have been called encyclopedic informants or men of memory.[75] Obviously, in all these cases the status and circumstances of the author will influence the contents of the message performed.

It is useful to inquire from whom the authors learned their traditions, even if, in most cases, nothing very definite emerges. It is useful because one does find out that many learned their traditions primarily from other people, still living, to whom one can turn for other versions. Thus, among the Kuba, Mikwepy Anaclet gave me a very few names of kings. Later he added more.

These he had just learned from his uncle Mbop Louis, to whom I could turn for a much fuller version. Moreover, Mbop Louis turned out to be a man of memory who was very knowledgeable about many traditions. In cases of memorized compositions one can also sometimes learn who the original composer was, as in the instance cited above of *Ukwibyara*, composed by Nyaka-yonga around the middle of the nineteenth century. Such information stems from another oral tradition, which explains also why Nyakayonga composed certain passages as he did.[76] The genealogy of his descendants was known in the 1940s and 1950s when A. Kagame recorded it all, and it was possible to correlate this with the different versions recorded by him. Such cases of parallel written sources are rare indeed.

The only place and date that can be given about a tradition is that of the recording of a performance. Beyond this we usually do not know when a tradition was composed, whether at the time of the events or situations discussed or later. The variants of the slogan for the clan Ndoong which we cited can be dated to 1953 as far as the performances go, but we do not know when this slogan originated. It may be as old as the clan, or it may be much younger. Events themselves can often be situated in a relative time scheme, expressed in units of measurement that are local. The problems of chronology involved are difficult even here. We discuss them in chapter six along with all other chronological matters, but we may underline here that weakness in chronology is one of the greatest limitations of all oral traditions.

## III. Recording Traditions

When the researcher has to evaluate conclusions based on oral traditions or studies oral traditions recorded long ago, he or she does not deal with performances, but with records of performances, usually in written form. Two questions then arise: To what degree does a written or taped record correspond to the performance? How typical is that performance, given that records are not often made during normal "live" performances, but during a recording session, which can be a very different situation? Furthermore, printed records can be full transcripts, mere summaries, or even just mentions either of items known in tradition or in the guise of: "Oral tradition says." I distinguish between incidental mentions or the incidental record of traditions and full records based on systematic research.

## (1) Incidental and Accidental Mentions

Incidental records of traditions tended to occur in older writings. Purely accidental conservation happened from time to time in the European Middle Ages when a scribe was testing his pen and wrote down a poem or song as a sample of writing.[77] This must be clearly distinguished from incidental mention. Thus we find a mention of Roland, the hero of the *Song of Roland*, a medieval tradition, in Einhard's *Life of Charlemagne* written in about 830, fifty years after the events in 778 with which the *Song of Roland* deals. The best known surviving manuscript dates from between 1125 and 1150. Einhard tells us here of an ambush which is also mentioned in the *Royal Annals to 829.* Other official histories do not mention Roland nor is he mentioned in most manuscripts of Einhard's *Life*. Perhaps the name was inserted long after the composition of that text, because the ambush was felt to be the same story as that of Roland. In this case there would be nothing accidental in the casual mention of this name. Other evidence shows that by the eleventh century the song was known and the Einhard manuscripts that do mention him may well date from that century. One manuscript from that century has an editor's comment to the effect that Einhard "leaves a gap in relation to these facts about the Emperor, which the vulgar tongue celebrated in songs."[78]

Intentional mentions of oral traditions summarized in passing were once very common. Authors typically would state "According to oral tradition . . ." or something to that effect, and then give a summary.[79] Even if the author has not conflated speculation and traditional data from one or more traditions—the standard situation—the distance between what must have been a performance and its record remains enormous and correspondingly great caution must be exercised in using such data. They can hardly become major pieces in a historical argument.

## (2) Systematic Research

Some accounts of traditions, even in older days, were based on a systematic search and on many performances. Njoya's history of the Bamum kingdom, of which he was king, is one example of this.[80] Another is the case of the Ko-jiki, the oldest record (dating from c. 712 A.D.) of Japanese political traditions. The Emperor Mommu ordered a systematic search for the traditions of the great families, pruned them, and built an official tradition out of them which was learned orally by Hieda-no-Are. The next ruler, Empress Gemmyô, later ordered a Chinese scholar to record this version from Hieda-no-Are.[81] The Japanese case is remarkable because it explicitly details how a selection of data was made, approved officially after "untruths" had been eliminated, and then constructed as one account conflated out of many others. This no doubt happened also in Cameroun and wherever authorities ordered the creation of official histories out of tradition.

Scholars in our century, studying oral tradition and then publishing their results, usually work systematically as well. They should publish or make otherwise available all versions they have recorded and relevant other materials, including all their fieldnotes.[82] They rarely do. Authors should provide a clear account of how they proceeded and list what comes from different informants in the synthesis. This happens more often. It allows readers to have an idea of what research design (if any) was used, which motives performers had to collaborate, and eventually who controlled the acquisition of data.

The concrete case of research on the Italo-Libyan war (1911–32) by the Institute of Libyan Studies in Tripoli shows why all this information is necessary. The goal was to interview all the surviving veterans of this war in the whole country. They had to be found and the most reliable way to do this in the end was by inquiry in every village of the country. The public cooperated, among other reasons because to be recognized as a veteran meant to be entitled to various veteran benefits programs. This did induce some who had not fought to pose as veterans. It also made difficult the search for Libyan veterans who fought for the Italian side. In some places, accounts could only be taped in alternate villages because of enmity between adjacent settlements. All the recording was done by trained Libyans using a standard guide to information required. There were therefore few language problems. Yet there were some when it came to Tuareg or Tubu informants who spoke their own languages, rather than Arabic. Trained inquirers usually worked very well in their own home districts, but on occasion difficulties arose. The most remarkable case was that of a young man in charge of the collection of traditions about a famous figure in his district. An analysis of how he had found his informants showed that he was in fact teleguided by a few leaders in the area. Informants referred him to other informants but always within the same circles. Thus he wound up hearing only one side of a raging argument about this famous figure, until the systematic nature of these references became clear and corrective action was taken.

Such problems of sampling, research design, language difficulties, and social position of the inquirer occur during all research and should be addressed when traditions are published or used in publications. Unfortunately, this occurs all too rarely and makes critical use of oral traditions difficult for anyone other than the person who constructed the collection. Nevertheless, any historian who plans to use evidence derived from published traditions should attempt to fully elucidate the research situation.

## (3) The Recording Situation

Performances for recording are often different from the usual circumstances under which a tradition is performed. In the best of cases the person who records participates in a normal performance and manages to capture the message either on tape or on paper, without disrupting the normal flow of events. Even in

such favorable circumstances, however, the product only partially reflects the proceedings. The visual elements and the reaction of the audience are lost, unless videotape is used. When a
gesture of approval, denial, despair, or joy is used, rather than a
description of such behavior, even the tape gives no clue. Videotape would correct this to some extent, but even videotape
works only from a single angle. Moreover, most performances
on record eventually are published as written texts. Here one
loses not only the image but even the sound. While this is
universally deplored, no adequate solution has been found to
the problem.[83] The problem is most acute when dealing with
narrative, especially tales. It is least acute with memorized
messages, especially with poetry. Even here, there is an unde-
niable and substantial loss.

The second difficulty deals with the difference between performance and recording session. Very often indeed a recording
session is an interview situation which is more or less structured
by the interviewer. In the best of cases the performer puts on a
special session for the benefit of the recording. The Kuba king
recited official Kuba traditions in 1953 in front of his court, even
though normally he does this only at his coronation.[84] No questions were asked, the text was taped, and there may have been
only minimal difference between this and what might be expected during a "genuine" performance.

In the normal course of events though, and especially to
elucidate historical accounts, or even tales, interviews are set up.
This introduces two types of alterations. First, the performer
handles the interviewer as an audience and dialogues with him.
He structures his content so as to make points relevant to this
situation. Thus when L. Haring was collecting accounts in Kisii
(Kenya) in June 1971 his informants emphasized their positive
feelings towards Europeans and tried to use the interviewer as an
arbitrator who would agree with them about the superiority of
the Kisii over their neighbors.[85] The same accounts would
hardly have been told in this manner in front of another audience. Even performances in front of a "normal" audience at a
"normal" time differ in emphasis according to the present situation of the day and its points of interest.

Information about such recording situations should be made available. Again, this rarely happens. A researcher is often unaware of such matters unless he or she has conducted a large number of interviews and been present at performances in other settings. Nevertheless, anyone using such records must be acutely aware of the impact of circumstances on both form and content of the record.

Interview techniques have often been discussed and we therefore limit ourselves to a few principles.[86] Any interview has two authors: the performer and the researcher. The input of the latter should be minimal, even though it can never be absent since he is at least part of the audience. His input is maximal when he asks questions. Indeed, if the questions are leading questions such as, "Is it not true that . . .," the performer's input tends to zero. [87] Ideally, the informant alone should talk, but in practice this is only possible in cases where the content of a well-known performance, such as a tale or a poem, is wanted. Even there, the researcher needs to obtain further information about allusions in the performance or to clarify obscure or controversial points. In other cases, the interview must at least be structured by the researcher, who decides what should be talked about and attempts to keep the informant to the topics being discussed. This should be done unobtrusively and informants should not be interrupted, even when they do seem to wander off the topic. After all, unexpected links with the topics discussed may turn up and most unasked for information comes from such diversions.

An interview is always a somewhat tense situation, especially at first. The interviewer cannot use a questionnaire but must be certain that all relevant topics will be discussed. The interviewee wonders what the interviewer wants, how to please, and perhaps what advantages can be gained from the situation. Hence it is advisable, if at all possible, to repeat interviews so that the parties get to know each other better and develop confidence in each other. The extent to which this can be done is of course limited by material factors of time available and means, but also by the natural talent of the researcher for getting along with people.

Group interviews, while not desirable in principle, are often unavoidable and in certain circumstances become desirable. During such interviews informants rarely say all they know, but only what they all can agree on. The information is minimal. But group testimony may also be customary and a guarantee of truth. The recital of traditions relating to Kuba groups should be public. The officials hold a secret conclave or *kuum* before the meeting, appoint a spokesman, and rehearse what will be said. Statements acquire the character of official accounts. It is always possible for a researcher to talk to each of the participants individually after such a meeting and to obtain further views and elaborations on the matters being discussed. Whenever this is possible a group interview should be followed up in this manner. Where group interviews are not customary they should not be introduced just for the sake of convenience, however much one informant repeats statements already made by others.

Interviews should be held as confidential information. One should not tell B that A had a different account about such and such a matter and ask, what does B have to say to that? Such behavior easily leads to tension and ill will in a community. Nevertheless, sometimes confrontations and disputes between informants do occur. In such cases a courtroom atmosphere is created. Confrontations end with compromising, by standing firm, or by one side adopting the other's point of view. An example of a compromise is the case of Bokila (Kuba). The chief of the Bokila people had stated that they were the first inhabitants in the area, but another group in the district made the same claim. They all agreed finally that the latter were first, but that before they arrived, the Bokila had already set up a trading station in ivory within the district, so they were also first occupants. As the example blatantly shows, such compromises have very little if any value, since they are invented on the spot. In the other situations very little usually transpires that had not been known before. Even in the case of a retraction and the adoption of the position of the adversary, the historian is left with the question of whether that party first lied and later told the truth or the reverse. Confronting parties rarely pays.

Researchers should also realize that what one does and asks

is often of great interest to the whole community or society in which they work. People will talk about them, form opinions, develop rumors about them, and sometimes even discuss what to say if asked this or that. Even if interviews are kept private, which is not possible in many cultures anyway, the interviewee is of course eagerly asked what this meeting was all about. Just as the researcher reports to other scholars, the interviewee reports to his friends. Thus the pursuit of historical research involves all social relationships of the interviewer in the community at once. In time he or she will be adopted or be kept at arm's length. This explains in part why informants suddenly begin to volunteer information only after many months have passed. The other reason for this common situation is that by this time the interviewer is finally acculturated and knows what to inquire about.

To sum up: Interviews are social processes of mutual accommodation during which transfers of information occur. If no social relationship can be established—as with the administration of questionnaires—the information given will be minimal, often inaccurate, and usually perceived as extorted under duress —not a situation conducive to relations of trust and frank exchange.

## IV. Testimony and Text

When a performance has been recorded, the information acquired becomes permanent and becomes testimony, whether the information is widely known or not. It is not always clear whether testimony should be defined as a single statement or as the statement of a single party, whether it be one or several persons. This is the subject of the first section after which I will turn to the text.

## (1) Verbal Testimony

Verbal testimony is the sum of statements made by any one party, concerning a single topic, as long as all the statements relate to the same referent. A referent is that of which an account is given. The topic can be a single series of events, or a given situation as seen by the one who testifies: the witness. The topics of the analyst may not be those of the witness. For example, it is rare to find a single testimony concerned wholly with women's rights in oral tradition. The analyst can, however, conceive of this as a topic and use bits in different statements by a witness as different testimonies.

In this definition the witness is crucial. Because oral testimony is fluid, can be repeated, or later qualified, it will not do to consider every single utterance of a witness as separate testimony. It consists of all statements made by the informant about the same topic under the same conditions. The same conditions mean that the informant has had no further new information in between the times that he testifies. An example makes this clear. A Bushong (the ruling Kuba people) first recited to me a list of kings containing only three names. Then he added to his fund of knowledge by obtaining information from his uncle. Clearly, there are two testimonies here: the list of three names and the later lists, the difference being a difference in conditions of knowledge.

From the formal point of view it is clear that any traditions that occur in memorized speech include every word as testimony. Traditions where the wording is left to the performer include only the ideas expressed and therefore the testimony also includes only such ideas. One cannot conclude anything about the past from the wording itself.

That the nature of verbal testimony really does depend upon the informant is shown by additions to the referent which he contributes without necessarily going over the whole evidence again, and by the fact that what is omitted in the given statements of a referent will not figure in the testimony, even if we know that these are omissions (that is, they exist in the testimony of others about the same tradition). Perhaps the informant does not know them, perhaps he suppresses these points because he wishes to preserve some interest, perhaps he merely forgot or assumes that one knows them already. Similarly, an informant may well lie for whatever reasons. Then his testimony contains the lie. Thus a testimony is a tradition as interpreted through the personality of an informant and is colored by this personality. It is impossible to have "a tradition" as evidence. It has to be a tradition actualized through a person, and every person actualizes it differently.

Ideally, a testimony could be thought of as referring to a single tradition, but in practice nothing is less certain. The informant may have heard several traditions which he conflates, making a single testimony of them. The encyclopedic informant who summaries many traditions, who generalizes and interprets them, is but the most extreme case and one which, as evidence, should therefore be of lesser value, however important such a person may be as a historian.[88] Apart from comparisons with other testimonies, there is no ready means to find out whether a testimony derives from one tradition only or from several. So the link between a testimony and a tradition is indirect. It is not one-to-one at all.

It is best to treat the statements of different witnesses as different, even when they have the same referent and seem to derive their information from the same tradition, for the reasons given above. We know of tradition only through the prism of personality. Similarly, the witness in group testimony is the whole group and we must take their joint statements together as one testimony, but separate these from all other statements made by members individually. Here they are the same personalities, but as a collectivity the coloration of their testimony is different.

It happens that the same persons with regard to the same series of events will tell two different, even contradictory, stories. This could be found in Rwanda in 1958–60 when informants explained how the two different castes, Tutsi and Hutu, came into being. In the one story, Kanyarwanda had several sons, including Gatutsi and Gahutu, who were ancestors of the Tutsi and Hutu and therefore brothers. According to the other, Kigwa, the first Tutsi, fell from the sky on an earth inhabited by Hutu. Informants knowing both stories never combined them; they always chose one as true and the other as false. Never mind here that these stories were then the legitimation for either side in a civil war that was brewing and which explains this situation.[89] These two statements about the same topic cannot be considered as a single testimony and were not by informants, because there are two referents. The case cited may be extreme, but it is hardly unique. In disputes, both parties know full well which historical arguments their adversaries will use. The "similarity of referent" makes certain that there is some relationship at least between tradition and testimony, wherever this becomes clear in statements.

## (2) Text

The concept "text" implies a stable something that exists independently of all those who interpret it. It is a written item. The text is what testifies to something, but is not testimony. The problem with this is that because testimony can be given orally several times, there can be several written versions of the same referent. Do we then have several texts? No. We should only have a single text, in x versions. When we deal with speech there is not much of a problem. Small differences in wording between the versions usually occur. If the witness can still be reached, he will tell us what is correct and what is not, or eventually that both readings are correct. In all other cases the situation is one where one must estimate whether or not the different versions really are close enough to correspond only to a single referent. In many cases they are. We can take the case of Gakaniisha (Rwanda) as an example. He told the same account twice, once in 1954 and again in 1957. The first account is printed, the second exists in archival form.[90] There is but one text here, as he does not seem to have acquired any new information in the second rendering. The second is shorter than the first, merely because it assumes that the researcher knew the story, since he had told it before. Any attempt to fuse both versions into a single text or to reconstruct a so-called original text is a serious mistake. However odd it may seem, there is but one text, one version of which was printed, while the other one was not.

When it comes to publication, difficulties arise. The Gakaniisha case shows this. The first version was published at a time when the editors did not know about the second one. This happens with manuscripts as well. A text edition may well be published before all extant copies have been found. However, even if one had both accounts at one's disposal one would have to print both of them in one form or another since there would not just be minor changes between one account and the other: the wording is free. For memorized speech the matter is simpler. Wording is fixed and hence belongs to the text. Differences should be indicated in notes. In the case of epics the practice is to print all versions separately.

At this point I have completed the discussion of performance, tradition, and text. I can now turn to an examination of the content of the recorded messages. The question is: What does the message mean? My task in the next chapter will be to discuss what must be examined to provide a satisfactory answer.

## CHAPTER THREE

# GETTING THE MESSAGE

Once testimony is on record it can be carefully studied, more carefully in fact than anyone in the oral community could ever have done, for the record remains stable. One can return to it, whenever necessary. The scholar cannot begin with a study of the message contained in the record. His first task is to understand it properly. This requires a study of form and structure first, because they influence the expression of the content. Then comes an analysis of the meaning on two levels: the literal meaning and the intended meaning. The intended meaning is often quite obvious to members of the community that produced the tradition, but not so evident to any outsider. Then one can turn to the aim of the message (what one wanted to communicate). In practice all these operations require that the whole corpus, or at least a large corpus of recorded tradition, be examined. Otherwise it is not possible to find form or structure, nor to determine what the characteristics are of any given testimony in relation to all others.

## I. Form and Content

No message is totally without form. If it were, communication would not occur. The rules of language are a first formal requirement. Linguistic form sometimes goes further. Special rules for rendering a message in poetic or even narrative form do occur. As such rules restrict the choice of vocabulary in expressing a message, they must be known if the content is to be appreciated in full. Beyond this, each message has an internal structure, an arrangement of its exposition aiming at making communication more effective. Finally, all messages fall into genres, a combination of form and content that yields literary categories well recognized and practiced in the society under study, so that no utterance whatsoever falls outside a literary genre, and in return the expectations of the public with regard to genre affect any message.

In linguistics problems of form are strictly to be separated from problems of content, form being a matter of regularity and repetition in utterance, which generates enough redundancy for a message to be understood. But even linguists have to relate content to form after a certain point, otherwise they could not follow through an examination of genres or of internal structure. These matters are usually left to students of verbal art or folklore, for the relationship between form and meaning is what makes art. Therefore the historian will find a large body of literature on this subject in those fields which is relevant to his concerns at this juncture, even if the emphasis in those fields is often very different from his own.[1]

## (1) Linguistic Form

The major distinction here is between "formal" and "informal" texts, meaning that in the first group rules over and above the ordinary rules of grammar must be followed, restricting the free choice of expression to a certain extent. The more special rules exist, the more the expression of what one wants to say is being restricted. At the same time the form acquires a higher degree of emotional appeal.

Some time ago, M. Jousse, in an article that aroused a great deal of interest, maintained that the whole of oral literature was subject to formal laws, mainly syntactical, which made it clearly distinguishable from written literature. Whatever the oral message, wherever it came from, it was bound to obey such formal laws. His thesis, mainly based on biblical texts, is by no means convincing. It turns out that the only marked difference between oral and written utterances is that repetition occurs more frequently in oral communication.[2] This is not surprising. Oral material is told over time and needs more redundancy to convey its message. A written document is an artifact quite divorced from time. One can turn back from later sentences to earlier sentences if need be.

Formal texts do occur in oral art, but so far they have been insufficiently studied. Rules of versification can be based on number of words, number of syllables, number of short syllables (*mores*), length of syllables, pitch (tone), stress, and alliteration.[3] Internal or external rhymes, tonal rhymes, and other features can also be part of the formal rules. A Somali example of the genre *gabay* makes the impact of such rules clear: *I/la ah. ba a.dab/ko o di yo.san/da hay.-da nab ba/do i di i ye* (God has put out their fire and has dampened [the valor of] their heroes.").

Each unit is a more. Five mores form a foot, four feet a verse. The feet are indicated by /. There is a short vowel at more five (*dab*) and a caesura (indicated as - ) after more two of foot three. The distribution of long syllables in each foot allows the classification of feet in eight types. The very first syllable (here "I") is an "anacrouse." It does not count. Moreover, there are rules of alliteration here based on "d." Whereas Somali poets are not aware of the metric requirements which they nevertheless follow, they are cognizant of the alliteration.[4] The example makes the limitations on the choice of words clear. It also shows that members of the community themselves do not always know the rules which they are in fact following. This should not surprise us. We all unconsciously follow a great number of grammatical rules in every one of our utterances. This means that one cannot merely rely on what informants say about the matter. A linguistic analysis is indispensable to discovering regularities in verse. Thus tonal rhyme or parallelism will simply never be found by an unsuspecting European. Only linguistic analysis will do it.[5]

In addition to the above, assonance and morphological repetitions—using the same root but different categories of words—are quite common and can be combined or not with verse structure. See, for instance, the use of the radical *-hiig-* ("to hunt") in: *Baantumye kubaz umuhiigw abahiigi b'Imuhiiganyana* ("They sent me to inquire about the hunt, the hunters of the calf-hunt.").[6]

Obviously, sometimes the structure is so demanding that nonsense words must be introduced for its sake. Such fillers are common, especially in an epic where the lines have to be made up as one goes. In the Serbian *U Prilipu gradu prijelome*, for instance—"In Prilip, that white city . . ."—the filler is "that white city." The singer does not particularly want to stress its whiteness, but it rounds off the meter. Hence we will find the same filler with all sorts of names of cities when the meter requires it. This is what Lord has called a formula.[7] The repetitions of the formula in the epic make its character clear. They also make clear to the analyst that the filler must not be considered when seeking the meaning of the whole.

It takes very great familiarity with a language to see what the choices in vocabulary were for someone who wanted to express a given idea in various forms and hence to find out why one item was chosen over another—which of course adds to the meaning of the whole. Even researchers who do not have such competence can, at least, discover which expressions are so conditioned by the formal requirements that they should not be included in the meaning.

Formal study also helps to understand how stable the wording of a given poem or poetic song may be. One would expect the Rundi song *Remeera ryaaNini, intaaho yabaami* (Remeera near Nini, the place of entry of the kings) to be repeated without any change in wording, given its meaning and its form (almost identical structure in each hemistich). Indeed, I never found another version. But if we consider Serbocroat poetry a great deal of variation will be expected, as formulas can so readily be exchanged. Comparison of versions helps to check on effects of formal structure and hence is useful to disentangle intended from apparent meaning.

## (2) Internal Structure

Any utterance has an internal arrangement. If it goes beyond a single sentence it goes beyond the rules of syntax, but there still is an arrangement there, especially with what seems to be the freest of all expressions: narrative. It is easy to show an internal structure (what V. Propp called a morphology) in narrative, by making use of the concepts of plot, episode, motif, setting, and theme.[8] I first demonstrate this with an account from the Kurumba (Mali/Upper Volta), before further discussing the concepts.[9]

### The Origin of the Chieftaincy of the Ganame*

(a)  1.  There was once a hunter who lived in the bush. The daughter of the *a-yo* (chief) went to the bush. She saw the hunter in the bush. The hunter saw the woman. The woman asked, "Are you here?" He answered, "Yes, I am here." She asked him: "What have you eaten?"– "I have eaten meat. I go in the bush to hunt."– "You will eat." The woman returned to the village. She had prepared food there.

2.  She returned to the hunter, to give him the food. The man told the woman that he owned a horn. In this horn there was fat. She should not touch the fat. She should not eat it. The woman wanted to eat from the fat. The women ate it. She developed a big belly. In the belly came a child.

3.  The family saw this. They said, "The girl expects." She delivered. She had a son. They asked: "Where did you find this child?" She said that she had found the child in the bush with the help of a hunter. The hunter had impregnated her. The family said that this was not true. The child stayed with its mother's family. The mother's name was *Natimbe*. Her family said, "This child has no father."

(b)  4.  Because the child had no father, it did stupid things and was beaten for it. Because of this the child wept and ran into the bush.

5.  It went to search for its father, the hunter. It told the father that the villagers beat it and said that he had no father. The father told (him): "Don't weep. You will receive something." The father made a small drum. He gave a box. He gave him (the son) arrows. He told the child, "When they go for fun in the pond and hit you, leave the pond slowly. Take

---

* The title is the first line of the text.

the small drum which I gave you. Look eastwards and drum. Look westwards and drum. Look in front of you and drum. Look to the side and drum. Take your bow and arrows. Shoot towards the pond. Look carefully at the children in the pond. They will become blind. Then take nothing from what they would offer. Say only that they should give the chief's hat (and emblem) in payment."

6. The child did exactly as the father had told him. The children become blind. They want to pay him. He refuses. The villagers ask the child: "What do you want then?" He gestured towards the hat of the chief. The people say: "What should we do to obtain the hat to give it to you?" The child says: "I don't want any other payment." The people reply that they cannot give him the hat, as good Fortune would abandon them. The boy takes the hat. He puts it on his head. The inhabitants of the village want to take it from him. The boy flees weeping. They do everything possible to recover the hat, but without avail.

(c) 7. The boy runs into the bush to meet his father. He tells him that he had brought the hat.

8. Father and son run to Omo. They stay there. The boy marries. They all return in great numbers.*

An episode is a sequence in the action which can be regarded as a functional unit in the narrative, each episode providing for a new development in the plot. If the narrative were a game of chess, the plot would be the entire series of moves and each episode would be a single move. I have numbered the episodes in the example given. They run as follows:

1. A chief's daughter meets a hunter.
2. She conceives by him.
3. The child is deemed to be fatherless.

---

* As chiefs of Yoro and other villages founded there.

4. The ill-treated child finds its father.
5. The father gives him means for revenge (some internal repetition).
6. The child avenges himself and takes the chieftainship (some repetition).
7. He rejoins his father.
8. They go to Omo to return as chiefly line later on.

The plot is the ordered unfolding of the narrative. In this example we have:

(a) Exordium:    1. Presentation of the situation.
                 2, 3. Conception and birth of the boy.
(b) Main action: 4,5, and 6. Ill treatment of the boy, help from the father, defeat of the villagers.
                 Internal repetition in 5 and 6.
(c) Conclusion:  Hero and his father flee to Omo, but return to take power.

For the purpose of analyzing this account I have made use of the following concepts: episode, plot, and setting. These concepts are essential to discover the internal structure of any kind of narrative. The notions of core image, motif, and theme will also be useful (see below).

The notional statements of a narrative can be used to make a graph of the internal structure of the narrative. One places episodes along one axis in the order in which they were told (plot) and shows the degree of tension conveyed by each episode on the other axis. The chief artistic requirement of all narratives is that they should hold the interest of the listener and keep him waiting with bated breath for the denouement. Hence the construction of a narrative pivots on the attempt to attain this end. The ability to hold the listener's attention can be gauged for each episode, as it mainly depends on the extent to which the listener can foresee what will happen next. An episode ends with a given situation, which can develop in a number of different ways leading to a number of possible new situations. In the next episode the performer has made a choice between these possible new situations and again places his listener in front of another series of possibilities. It can readily be seen that the kind of episode least able to hold interest is one that leads to one out-come only. The listener realizes this and knows in advance what is about to happen. The unexpected is ruled out and there is a complete lack of excitement. Next in order of low degree of tension comes the episode that leaves the door open for a large or even infinite number of possible outcomes. The listener can-not foresee anything and, although interested, is not roused to excitement at all. The tension increases as the number of possible outcomes is reduced from an infinite number to two. At that point the listener foresees them and is very anxious to know which of them will occur. Or he may see that one outcome only is bound to occur, yet feels that it does not fit in with the plot and is left wondering if there may be some other solution. This is a favorite situation in tales of heroes who should be invulnerable but find themselves in a desperate situation. The listener knows this, but cannot see what the solution will be of the paradox in-vulnerable yet desperate. In theory, then, tension is measure-able. In practice only a very rough estimate can be made, as in the graph which follows:

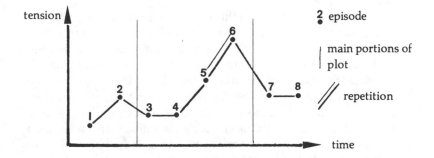

The reader will note that this account is not built to reach a climax just before the end. The end is prolonged and there are, in the main, two narratives rather than one, each with its climax. Repetitions just before the second climax enhance the tension. They are common in oral narrative to build tension. A well-integrated artistic tale would avoid this, shorten the exordium, and have a short decisive denouement, such as "The boy kept the hat and was chief." The reason that the structure here is not perfect is, first, that this is supposed to be an account and not a tale and, second, because tension arises not only out of curiosity but out of emotions suggested by the structure of the imagery as well.

In this account there are two core images:[10] pregnancy through eating and martial display next to the pond. Such ponds are the core of each village, as water is rare in the region. The second image shows magic war on the village. Image repetitions or extensions occur in both halves. In the first, the hunter and the woman eat, when the woman eats the fat. In the second, the drum and arrows are mentioned twice, as is the need for the hat (the overlordship of the village), and the drumming image itself has an internal further repetition. In many analogous cases there would be a song here to be repeated by the listeners. The whole plot, how a special boy (special because of his conception) took over the rulership of Yoro, is expressed in these two core images. The emotional structure of the account derives from that. It is, on balance, more important than the formal structure based on outcomes because most listeners of any performance know the story and concentrate on the images, their development, and their portrayal.

In the present example this is evident from a second version, which has the same succession of episodes, developing the final ones to make links with other villages ruled by the Ganame. But its handling of the core images is different. In different places it develops the aspect of the hunter who looks like a spirit of the bush. It is weaker at the beginning of the first image, as it does not stress food, but chooses to develop an imagery of the horn itself, which was used as a vulva by the hunter, and here lies a link to a well-known shrine for this ancestral hunter in the village of Yoro. It develops the second core image much less. Compared to the first version, it develops the purely action part as to why and how people did things, but waters down the main image: the magical war on the villagers. Still, the hunter in this version is credited with four eyes, which heightens the contrast to the children who will be struck blind.

The present version also allows us to show how core images are expanded. In the first part, eating precedes the eating that conceives; in the second, the drumming, shooting, and bargaining sequence is merely repeated. These are in fact the two major ways to expand core images.

In tales the artistry consists of working with a single core image throughout by repeating it in identical or variable settings as the action develops and transforms its meaning, so as to lead the listener to plumb the depth of meaning held in the image. A similar goal is sought in using several core images which make up a set. The ideal set has image reflections from one image to the other—in our example, between the manner of conception and the manner of defeating the villagers. There is no such link in our example of an account, and this is an artistic weakness.[11] The skill with which images are woven into one another is an even better index of the artistry of a performer than his skill in building up episodes to a climax in terms of outcome. Performers will not hesitate, in tales, to adapt whatever part is required to achieve their intended effects. In accounts the freedom to do this is quite limited, however. In our example the meaning of conception is developed through all the rest. It is what the boy does—gain the chiefdom—and the image of the war near the pond is the same. The version not cited here, despite its artistic weaknesses, contained the inspired comment that the hunter possessed two eyes in front and two in the back, and mentioned this only when the boy ran for help to his father. This is an omen of his magical power but it is a powerful reverse image of the blinding that is to come. Magic of the seeing causes the blindness of the profane.

Besides the functional elements, the episodes, and the imagery, there are other aspects of a narrative which must be taken into account. These are the setting, including the time and the place in which the narrative unfolds, and the characters, named or not, who appear in it. Here the bare mention of the mother's name is sufficient for the audience, who derive all other names from it. The theme is the title or the general subject of the plot, here the first sentence of the account, the origin of the chieftaincy of the Ganame. Theme and plot are not identical in that there are some cases in which the same theme may give rise to different plots, although in this case we know of no alternative plots.

V. Propp and P. Gossiaux have rightly remarked that settings and personages can change from one version to another, by the same or different performers.[12] The reason for such changes has to do with basic image building. A hairy, uncouth king "Ntare" lost in a forest and found by villagers may be better than just "a king" meeting villagers in the fields. This has resonances of "nature" meets "culture."

If this dynamic were universal, we could not trust any narrative to be historical. Fortunately, it is not. It all depends on the genre. Such changes are explicitly forbidden in narratives of events believed to really have happened at some time in the past. After all, this is what distinguishes a tale from an account.

As a general rule of thumb one can say that the more artistic any narrative is, the less it probably reflects a succession of events or an accurate rendering of a historical situation. This rule is not absolute. Any such conclusion should be tested against a generous collection of various versions. In the case of a historical account, one cannot for instance conclude automatically from a brilliant denouement that this could never have happened. The typical situation of the rebel who was executed while the person bearing his pardon was in sight may have happened after all. If all renderings of a fairly recent tradition have this outcome, it would be unwise to think that they all are indebted to some artistic genius in the recent past. Of course, if such a denouement occurs in all versions, but the tradition is an old one, there has been more time for the denouement to spread and its believability declines. As to tales, a great amount of artistry may sometimes capture the essence of a situation better than a mere description, but will do so in present-day terms of reference of the culture involved. The analysis of internal structure along with the availability of other versions allows the analyst to have some idea about the particular dynamic of the item studied. In the case of narratives it will make clear whether the plot and sequence of episodes is stable enough to separate the tradition of this narrative out from other narratives or not. If in a tale, for instance, the personages and settings change so that they become similar to those of other tales and the sequence of episodes changes to the point that one goes over into a different plot altogether, there is no clear tradition of this narrative by itself. The versions rather point to a common, much larger tradition, or to borrowing from other narrative traditions.

On the other hand, if setting, plot, episodes, and personages do not change in the various known versions, these versions clearly constitute one tradition, different from others. In this case all these structural elements "belong" to the tradition and have at least some age. This is often the situation with accounts. This situation will then be a major element in assessing their reliability. By itself it does not establish reliability, but in conjunction with data about the time depth of a tradition, it may do so when the time depth is shallow.

## (3) Genres

An analysis of formal and informal structures does not exhaust the analysis of form and content. It is necessary to go further and to determine to which genre the message belongs. Genre is a concept that includes notions of form and specifications of content. A message is expressed in a given genre when it is put in a given form and internal structure, *and* when its subject matter corresponds to the rules prescribed. Genres are recognized in every culture and are named.

Thus, for instance, Rwanda has a genre called *ibisigo* or "dynastic poetry." *Ibisigo* are subject to rules of form, including specifications of special language, and also to rules of content. At one level certain types of metaphor are required. At a more general level content is specified. All *ibisigo* consist of an introduction (*interuro*), a main body, and a peroration (*umusaayuuko*) which consists of an address by the poet to the king for whom the poem is composed. With regard to the main body three subgenres exist. The first, *impakanizi*, consists of strophes separated by a refrain. Each strophe must extol the reign of a king in the order of their reigns.[13] The *ibyanzu* subgenre is similar, but deals only with a few kings, while the *ikobyo* subgenre is not strophic and only sings the praises of the king to whom the poem is dedicated.

In a given culture the concept of genre is shown by the existence of a name for it in the local language. Thus the Kuba have a genre called *shoosh*. It consists of a short utterance in set speech, but without special criteria of form. Its contents are described as "definitions" of the item to which they refer. We might call them slogans. *Shoosh* are made for individuals, groups, and offices, but also for animals, plants, or objects, indeed, for any item which one wants to "define." Outsiders would never have classified all these slogans together by their contents, which range from picturesque description of places to the listing of clan food taboos to descriptions of administrative offices. Moreover, the outsider would be confused by the form, which is very similar, if not identical, between *shoosh* and *ncyeem* (song), all the more so because *shoosh* can be sung. The form is also identical with that of *mikwoon*, which we might loosely translate as "proverbs." The researcher must then be guided by the local name for the genre and the specification of its requirements. He must follow this guideline, even if to the outsider the works seem to belong to quite different genres.[14] For instance, in Burundi, *umugani* refers both to tales and to proverbs. Yet when one studies what look like tales or proverbs it becomes apparent that in fact they both belong in the same category. This does not mean however that one can never go beyond the recognized genres and discover by criteria of form and content that there are in fact well-defined subgenres of which the local people are unaware. This may be rare, but it happens. P. Smith showed that the Rwandan *umugani* or "popular tale" consisted of three subgenres. One of them stood out by a very visible criterion of form. It had to contain a song. The others did not. This point of departure allowed him to establish three subcategories ("apology," "legend," and "fable"), which are shown to be valid by the study of a large corpus of data.[15]

In most cases one can and does establish a list of names referring to genres with the relevant criteria of form and content for each and encompassing all expressions in that language.[16] This sets off each genre from all the others and throws its characteristics into relief. Perhaps one can go further and elicit a folk taxonomy of all the genres. G. Gossen has published just such a taxonomy created by the Maya of Chamula (Mexico).[17] Thus, "true ancient narrative" is a subgenre of "ancient words," which, along with the branch "recent words," forms "pure words" or "oral tradition." This supergenre is one of three including "conversational language" and "language for people whose hearts are heated." These together form the highest class: *k'op* "words" or "language." Gossen obtained this taxonomy from six informants who also provided most of the texts of his study. To elicit it he used questions of the type "How many kinds of _____ would there be?" along with less-directed information. So, it is quite possible that the informants developed this taxonomy over the year that they worked with Gossen. This might not be an older "genuine" part of Chamula culture. Nevertheless, the interest of such a taxonomy resides in the fact that it tells us how members of the culture relate the genres to each other and thereby better specify the characteristics of each. In this sense it will be useful to try such an approach elsewhere as well.

Genres are thus concepts that are culture bound. It is these literary categories that the authors of handbooks of historical method had in mind, when they suggest that historians must take literary categories into account, when analyzing the specifications to which messages must conform.[18] The reason for this counsel is obvious. The requirements of genre mold the expression of the message. By knowing the genre well the historian will realize what is conventional in the expression and what is not, that is, on what he or she should put weight and what should be considered general embroidery. When an item does not belong in a certain genre, but nevertheless occurs there, the message acquires unusual significance. If in a praise poem a king is *not* praised with the usual stereotypes or even indeed criticized, such passages have more value than the usual praises in the rest of the poem.

Specialists in verbal art have attempted to construct literary categories that would be valid for whole continents or even universal. This is of course felt as a necessity by scholars in comparative studies. If only formal criteria were to be used, such a universal schema could be valid. But in fact content has to be used.[19] A fairly recent attempt for Africa was made by R. Finnegan. She divided messages into "poetry," "prose," and "special forms" (such as drum language and theater). Poetry came in seven subgroups, of which "praise poetry" is one, and prose in four ("tale," "riddle," "proverb," and "oratory").[20] At first such an attempt may seem reasonable, but it soon breaks down. Thus, "praise poem" includes both Kuba *shoosh* and Rwandan *ibisigo*, along with at least two other Rwandan genres. One might think that very elaborate subdivisions could save the situation, but this is not so. Her "tale" and "proverb" will not do for Burundi, where both form one genre.

It is not possible to achieve a universal cross-cultural classification even if it becomes convoluted to excess.[21] Moreover, it is not useful to the historian, because he is interested in the constraints, models and directions that mold a message in a given culture and these are given in that culture's specification of genre. The historian needs no more. It is not possible to achieve this universal goal because its criteria will be bound to a single culture anyway. It belongs to a single worldview in which the phenomenon of messages is classified. By definition every culture differs precisely in its worldview and in its basic taxonomies. In the case of *genres*, their classifications are all different. A universal schema will of necessity wrench local taxonomic units apart and lump others together. If we use West European classifications, for instance, what are we to do with the Shuswap Indian (Canada) story of *The Ant and the Grasshopper*, which explains why the grasshopper jumps or eats grass, although it is derived from the tale of de la Fontaine?[22] De la Fontaine's is a "moral fable" while the Indian story is "etiological." Hence, the same material will fall into two different classes, which does not help the student of comparative literature either.

Of all the specifications required for a given genre, the one that interests the historian most is whether a given genre is supposed to be "true" (that is, cannot be altered at will) or not. Thus

*skazki* in Russian are tales that can vary at will but *bylyny* are a
genre that is supposed to tell what really has happened in ancient
times. Thus V. Propp's analysis of morphology is valid for
*skazki* but not for *bylyny*. Its findings should not be unduly generalized to all genres everywhere.[23] Rather, in each case the historian should ascertain, first, whether or not "true" or "untrue"
are distinguished as categories and, second, whether they are
used in the definition of genres. In Rwanda the genre *ibitéekerezo*, a narrative, differs from the narrative *umugani* in that
the one is supposed to be ancient "fact" and the other is
"fiction." We shall see later however that the notion of "truth"
itself is culture bound and cannot be assumed to correspond to
the "historical truth" familiar to an academic scholar. This problem belongs to another level of analysis.

## II. MEANING

It is so banal to state that one must first establish the meaning of
a message before one uses it, that I blush to write it. But this
matter is often not as simple as it looks. First the scholar works
with a text, not a performance. He has in fact a mutilated message before his eyes. Much of the redundancy of the message
was expressed in tone of voice and body language, and is lost.
Much of the impact of the audience on the performer is lost. Even
with tapes rather than transcriptions problems remain. So,
scholars work with impoverished data in many cases.

Then there is the problem of apparent and intended meaning, which is a problem of culture. Suppose that the historian
knows the language well and has no difficulty in understanding
the apparent meaning. He cannot assume that this was the message as intended. Circumlocutions and word taboos occur, resonances are not perceived, parallels that leap to the mind of every
one reared in that culture are lost. All sorts of cultural clues as to
the meaning of the message remain unperceived. Moreover, in
most cultures intended and apparent meanings are not the same,
although some cultivate the art of double talk to a much greater
extent than others. I must therefore discuss apparent and intended meanings separately. Even the intended meaning will not

yet give us the full impact of the message. I will have to refer to chapter five to deal with those facets that go beyond even the intended meaning.

## (1) Apparent Meaning

When one comes to study traditions in an oral society it often happens, even today, that no descriptions of the language exist or, that if there are any, they cannot be relied upon. It is even more common to find that beyond an outline grammar and vocabulary no serious dictionary exists. In that case a foreign researcher must study the language before he even begins to gather traditions. The historian must then have had a fairly thorough linguistic training or must restrict himself to work among peoples whose language has been studied by a competent linguist. Even if he does learn the language, however, he cannot be expected after a year, or even two, to have mastered its intricacies to the point, say, of noticing choices of expression open to a performer. He takes what is given and cannot see what he could have been given.

This is a strong argument to let local scholars gather the traditions of their communities, but even they may feel hampered by the absence of linguistic materials. Thus a professional historian of the Niger Delta, working among his own people, the Ijo, found it in the end advisable to publish his data in collaboration with a linguist who had studied that language and its dialects for many years. It was not that the scholar could not understand Ijo, but that he wanted to reduce it to writing in the most accurate way possible.[24]

What to say then of many practitioners who have to rely on interpreters or on traditions told in a foreign language by the performers themselves? Every case must be judged individually. How much does the collector know? Enough to follow the interpreter speaking his own language (good passive command, not quite adequate active command of the language)? Or does he know less? Is the interpreter interested, knowledgeable, reliable? Was there one or were there more? If the performances were taped, who translated the original tapes and when? One must have answers to these questions before one can accept any translation of testimony. As to the performers, it is obvious that their style will be hampered by any foreign language. They do not think the tradition in this way. If they often use the language, the situation will be better than if they use it only rarely and are barely fluent in it.

Whoever uses texts in translation must be aware of such problems, just as he must be aware of translation problems in general.[25] Unfortunately, when texts are available in manuscript or in print it is rare to find the indications which allow one to evaluate the reliability of the collection.

The exact meaning of words used in a testimony is never a simple matter when dealing with unfamiliar cultures. The meaning of any word only becomes intelligible when the context in which it has been uttered is taken into account.[26] For most words this poses no difficulty. But some words are key words; they cannot be understood unless one is thoroughly acquainted with the society and culture from which they stem. The words *tabu* (Polynesian) and *totem* (Indian) are two cases where the items have been adopted into European languages for lack of equivalents. Another example is the case of Kongo *nkisi*, "an object, a shrine, a spirit sacredness, a force . . ." which cannot be exactly translated.[27] It is so central to Kongo worldview and thought that one needs a book to describe it, as indeed a whole book was written to describe the idea conveyed by *buloji* ("witchcraft") in the Luba language of Kasai.[28] Such concepts are not limited to the religious. Key words include complex technical terms relating to any sphere of social and cultural life. *Hasina* in Malagasy relates to the whole ideology of kingship.[29]

The problem with these terms in any text is their powerful resonance in the minds of the performers and their public. Every mention recalls a portion of the semantic field to which they apply and gives a particular emotional coloration to them, just as do the Portuguese *saudade* ("longing") or the German *Heimat* ("home"). There exists no literal translation of such terms, precisely because of such emotional overtones. It takes a true knowledge of a whole culture or society to be able to find or rather to feel exactly what the meaning will be in such and such a case.

Some terms in a testimony may be archaic. When the Kuba shout *nce boolo!* they do not know what it means. This does have a meaning in the Mongo language, but the Kuba do not know it. Therefore, the Kuba meaning of these terms is different. An examination of the situation in which the public shouts them tells us that it is a standard part of a shouted exchange with little more meaning than to say to the speaker "we follow you!" Then there are truly foreign terms, such as a foreign language used in ritual, just as Greek intruded into the Roman Catholic mass in Latin. *Kyrie eleison* was not understandable to people who knew Latin. Of course, the Latin mass itself was not understandable to most worshipers. This also occurs elsewhere. The Fang of Gabon developed a new cult in which they borrowed songs, formulas, and performances from the Tsogo of southern Gabon.[30] Then there are the secret languages. The guardians of the esoteric rituals and traditions of Rwanda, the *abiiru*, knew such a language. Further investigation shows that it consisted of words whose meaning had been altered, borrowings from foreign languages, archaic items, circumlocutions, and a number of words for which neither origin nor meaning could be discovered.[31]

It is often impossible to discover the meaning of many words of this kind and a testimony therefore remains partially unintelligible even at the apparent level.

## (2) Intended Meaning

Apparent and intended meaning are often different. Perhaps the best known examples of these cases come from Java where the *pantun* poetry was based on the principle that an innocuous and coherent apparent meaning, concealed an intended meaning— often with sexual overtones.[32] Japanese *haiku* are another well-known example of thorough disassociation between the two levels of meaning. These are obtained by the systematic use of metaphors such as dragonfly = child. To arrive at the intended meaning it is necessary to cope with problems of metaphor, stereotypes, and complex stereotypes or clichés.

## (a) Metaphor and Metonym

Metaphors are very common in any language, but especially prominent in poetry. So are allusions. In Dutch "to put a heart under the belt" means to encourage. The image refers to a man wearing a baldrick from which hangs a sword. Modern Dutchmen no longer understand the image and turn it into "to put a belt under the heart," meaning to bolster courage. "To take French leave" in English and "filer à l'anglaise" in French both mean to abscond. A good knowledge of the language one works with allows one to easily move from apparent to intended meaning. In poetry this may be much more difficult and there is not always unanimity about the intended meaning, which is precisely what makes it poetry.

The following Oromo (Ethiopia) poem leads us through the assonance of *duuri* and *xuuri* to the intended meaning.[33]

| | |
|---|---|
| Silaa arbi bineensa | An elephant would be a wild beast |
| Duuri qabaaf malee | If it did not have duuri |
| Silaa walgayiin Dhidheesa | The meeting place was at the Dhidheesa |
| Xuuri qabaaf malee | If it did not have Xuuri. |

*Duuri* is the hair which grows in the ear. This is a sign common to both people and elephants. *Xuuri* means pollution. For the intended meaning the crucial lines are three and four. This song is said to have been sung by Jote, an Oromo leader, explaining why he was not campaigning against his eastern neighbor. The reason was that this neighbor was his brother-in-law. It was *xuuri* to fight one's brother-in-law. The first two lines are a parallel of the last, the elephant being like a brother-in-law. The form (*silaa*, *duuri/xuuri* and rhyme *bineensa*, *Dhidheesa*) indicates that the last two verses dictated the formal pattern of the whole and initiated the parallel.

In many genres there are rules to be learned. In the dynastic poetry of Rwanda three situations are common: the use of synonyms, homophones, and metonyms. A poet may speak of "the rower" when referring to a personal name or a title meaning literally "to make a river cross" (synonym). He calls a king of Burundi "the hunter of zebras," which is a metaphor for a lion; the lion is Ntare in Rwanda, but in Burundi Ntare designates a king. Hence, that king is meant. The poet who speaks of "the country of the legs," refers implicitly to the lesser tibia and implies that the Rwandan term for this should refer to the name of a country—that the context tells us. The country can only be Burundi because its name is almost similar to the word meaning "lesser tibia."[34]

Such statements are often unintelligible to foreign listeners who do not know the language thoroughly and will not make the necessary rapprochements. Native speakers who know the genre have little difficulty with most of them. Only when metaphors are added to the substitution of the types mentioned will they also need help to catch the intended meaning. There is one intended meaning and only one.

This is still the case with allusions, although here no amount of reasoning will uncover that meaning unless one is given the explanation. In the dynastic poems of Rwanda the names of the kings are usually not mentioned, the names of their capitals being used instead, just as in the British Parliament one speaks of the member from X—a place name instead of a name. One simply must know the connection to understand. No direct mention is made of historic events, but merely of the name of the place where they took place. "This is his Waterloo" is such an example. In Rwandan poetry to mention Kiganda is to allude to the death of King Ndahiro. Around the Mediterranean many allusions are made to the dates of famous events: the first of September, the fourteenth of July, and so on. Indeed, the "Ides of March" refers to the murder of Julius Caesar. It follows from these examples that the occurrence of such allusions in a tradition gives the connection. This will have neither the same characteristics nor the same historical value as the tradition it explains and the historian must clearly distinguish between the two.

(b) Stereotype
Stereotypes are so common in language that we do not even realize that we are using them. All idiomatic expressions are stereo-

types. So are short formulas used in conversation (such as "I know," "I say," "really") which often only add redundancy to a message. Stereotypes of images are also frequent. One need only think in European languages of the metaphorical use of the word "heart" for "emotion, generosity, courage, . . ." It is even harder to grasp stereotypes where the image is not altogether clear. Thus, the symbolism of the numbers 3, 7, and 9 as perfection in various ways continually occurs in European languages, but one needs to be attuned to them. In some messages, "three" means "three"; in others it merely means "perfection." This occurs in many languages. In West Africa "four" is perfection; among the Kuba it is "nine"; among the Maya it is "four." In Yoruba (Nigeria) "one hundred forty four" means infinity.

Beyond these there are the stock phrases or word fillers in poetry which have no intended meaning at all. In the epic *Beowulf* the line "the twisting prow sailed on the road of the whales" (apparent meaning) or "the boat sailed on the high seas" (intended meaning) may in reality not mean anything in the context, as it does not add anything to the text. It is only a *kenning*,[35] just as the epithets of Homer are mere formulas. His "wine-dark sea" was never intended to tell us what the color of the sea was.

Sometimes stereotypes do give an intended meaning. In the following Luba Kasai examples the image of "black people are strangers" is a stereotype but in each case the poem really wants to stress that people are not black:

(a) Bena Ntumba, the chosen ones
    No grass grows on their bodies
    Not one of them is black; if you see a black
    He is a stranger on a visit.
(b) Ciyago of Lita Ngoyi
    Who gives birth to pale children
    No blacks; if you see a black
    He is a stranger, who has come to look after the child.
    He who sent him was Kabongo.[36]

One step beyond this we come to the complex cliché, usually a whole episode or more which is intended to be accepted as it is told. Such complete narratives occur in European oral traditions as well as in written texts and have been named *Wandersagen* ("traveling legends") because the same episode or tale is found in the literature of many communities.[37]

In Africa and in other oral societies such complex stereotypes are also very common. They are now often called clichés. A simple example shows what we are dealing with:

A chief invites his subordinates or his rival to sit down on a mat in front of him. The mat covers a pit in which sharpened stakes have been planted upright or some other means to kill has been provided. The subordinate or rival approaches the spot dancing and either falls in the pit and is killed, or probes the ground ahead with his spear and avoids the trap.

This is told in Central Africa from the Yaka of the Kwango, in Angola to the west, as far east as the people of Luapula across the border of Zaire in Zambia, and northward as far as the Kuba in the heart of Zaire.[38] The story is a stereotype because it is found so many times in different bodies of traditions, but its apparent meaning each time is supposed to be its intended meaning. We are to accept that it happened to the Yaka, the Kaniok, the Luba, the Kuba, the people of Kazembe, and others.

The existence of clichés makes it clear that to establish the intended meaning of a message is not to interpret it. If we stopped with our analysis here, we would accept literally the intended meaning of messages. Clearly, we cannot do that. And why not? Because the members of each culture hold some representations in common, these clichés among them. They are, in a sense, part of their worldview. Interpreting traditions will mean also to understand and account for such worldviews. That operation is the subject of chapter five.

For the moment we are content to establish two groups of stereotypes. First we show items to be stereotypes by showing that they are repetitive in a corpus. They belong to a class in which the apparent meaning intends little or nothing: the stereotype is merely instrumental, a morphological element. Or they belong to a class where the apparent meaning is indeed intended. This can be true for single images, such as "black people are strangers," or it can be true of a whole cliché—a complex narrative. The intended meaning is by definition the explicit meaning. Later we will deal with the next and last step: implicit meaning, that is, a meaning willed beyond the explicit message.

## III. THE AIMS OF THE MESSAGE

Having established the intended meaning of a message we should now turn to the relationship that exists between a message and the intended testimony (the main aim of the message). Intended meaning simply refers to the quality of understanding the meaning of a message in the same way that others in the culture understand it, or as closely as is possible to come to that ideal. Intended testimony or goal refers to what the performer wanted to communicate to his listeners. These two are not the same.[39] All producers of messages have aims in communicating them, but their aim is not necessarily to communicate historical knowledge to us. When a Kuba tells about the trickster Tooml Lakwey he merely wants to amuse his audience. When we learn that in those days slaves could trade on their own account and could trade in blocks of redwood and thus accumulate enough capital to buy themselves free, this is information that was incidental to the story. It was not intended to be transmitted. This was common knowledge to all in the nineteenth century and it simply has been carried over in the tale since then. Nevertheless, it was conveyed, and it is all the more precious for being unintentional.[40] No conscious distortion of the truth is to be feared from such a message.

It is of great importance to determine which messages are specifically designed to tell us about the past and which are not. This is the difference between tales and accounts among narratives, as we saw in chapter one, where we also saw that the process of transmission over time of these two classes greatly varies. Besides accounts, other categories such as epics or some poems may also be intended to transmit history. Even these testimonies are not exclusively designed to record the past, however. A message with this aim would only intend to convey information about events of the past in order to enrich our knowledge of the past. This never occurs in any society, except perhaps among professional historians. All messages have some intent which has to do with the present, otherwise they would not be told in the present and the tradition would die out. So all messages have another aim besides their possible historical aim. When a list of royal ancestors is recited the main thrust is to prove that the present king is the rightful incumbent of the throne and that kingship is the rightful and normal political order in that society. Despite appearances, the historical aim here is secondary and the natural circumstances under which performances occur prove it. They are solemn, public, and occur on occasions when the monarchy is put in the spotlight. Such performances are normal at coronations, investitures of major subordinate chiefs, burials, and often at annual celebrations where the political and ritual significance of kingship is acted out.

Would there be cases where the historical aim is primary and present-day concerns secondary? I no longer believe so. There are apparent cases, such as the recitation by king or council among the Kuba of the list of places where their forebears halted. They have no social importance today. Such places are too far away to be the objects of claims over land, and they do not affect the legitimacy of the institutions that present them. Their main aim seems only historical. And yet it is not. They stress group consciousness (*Wirbewusstsein*) and, more important, they relate the group to the overall worldview of the community. The places do matter on the mental map of the world and they will be ordered to fit such a map, just as medieval Christians mapped the world so that its center looked like a cross.[41]

What we then mean by historical intentional message is that the performer intends to use history as an argument, as proof, as legitimacy. His intention is historical when he wants to tell history, to teach, or to argue. When these intentions are absent, as for instance in much poetry or in telling tales, whatever information about the past occurs is accidental, unintentional. Here, too, the normal circumstances and usages of performance inform us. Tales are told in the evening, often around a fire as a show to please and distract. Songs are often sung for dances. Prayers are recited at shrines to thank, to placate, or to renew spiritual ties. History plays no role in all of this, but whatever snippets of historical information are gleaned are precious because they are unintentional.

In practice many historians of oral societies have confined themselves to concentrate on the collection of intentional historical material. This is understandable, as they thus amass the greatest amount of the most coherent data in a shorter time. They have done this to the point that many limit their explicit or implicit definition of oral tradition to such materials, usually narratives. This is regrettable, since the unintentional materials are often the most trustworthy. In practice, of course, one stumbles on them. A systematic collection of such data would call for the enormous task of gathering all the verbal art of a given culture. Hence many of these unintentional materials will only be found by those who study the oral arts of a given community over long time periods and usually by members of the community themselves. Nevertheless, historians should keep a sharp eye on all collections of such material that are assembled or published.

Having established the intended meaning and the aims of a message, the student is now ready to turn to a critique of that message. He wants to know what can be believed in it and what cannot. An analysis of this matter will occur at two levels. The first and easiest is to discern which social factors of the present or of the past could lead or have led to an alteration of the historical content. At this level such alterations are often conscious. At a deeper level we must examine the ways in which the common cultural heritage of that society has affected and shaped its traditions and, among others, the message we are studying. These are often unconscious forces which pose special difficulties in establishing what they are and how they have affected the material studied. The next two chapters are concerned with these questions.

## CHAPTER FOUR

# THE MESSAGE IS A SOCIAL PRODUCT

Communication presupposes society and all messages are social products. Hence messages of oral tradition have a "social surface."[1] They are significant to members of the communities in which they are told. Otherwise they would not be communicated at all. Would the social pressure not alter the contents of a message? No doubt this occurs, and, as all messages from tradition are uttered in the present, when they are recorded they are strongly influenced by the social present. Therefore one must assess the extent of such influences, the means by which they can be recognized, and the ways in which the interpretation of any message will have to take such influences into account. Some sociologists go further and hold that the total content of oral tradition is only a social product of the present. Oral tradition is created in the present for society, and when the impact of the present is assessed there remains no message at all from the past.[2] This is exaggerated. Where would social imagination find the stuff to invent from? How does one explain cultural continuities?

The sociological stance underscores the obligation of the scholar to investigate how the message relates to its social seat. I therefore start by describing in which social circumstances messages from tradition are produced. Then I discuss their social uses for the benefit of performers as well as for groups, going from the single message and the specific social impact to the corpus and the more diffuse social impact. Finally, I establish the fact that the whole body of tradition is congruent with the structure of a given society and discuss this phenomenon.

## I. THE SOCIAL USES OF MESSAGES

## (1) The Institutional Framework

(a) Performance and Institution

Performances do not occur haphazardly. They appear at appropriate moments during institutionalized social action and their genre as well as their content is related to the occasion. Precedents are cited during court cases, clan slogans and dirges at funerals. Formulas to drive away rain occur at appropriate moments,[3] discussions about a clan's history may find a place at negotiations for a marriage, and so on. Obviously, the collector should indicate what the normal occasion is for the performance of this or that genre, indeed for any type of message that is recorded.

This has not always been done and thus one has often misjudged traditions. The Kuba for instance, like many other people, do not at any moment give a fully detailed performance of their dynastic history. Rather, they tell anecdotes about this or that king in very widely differing circumstances and only give a formal framework of succession at the coronation of kings. Some local wise men (*bulaam*) told me a coherent account of the kingdom's history, but that was neither the usual form nor the usual performance. As a consequence, I long misjudged the supposed coherence of the royal "annals."[4] In many societies genealogies are never performed as a whole. Everyone knows a little bit, gathered in various small scale situations, usually in domestic situations. Among the Luo (Uganda/Kenya) the construction of a large scale genealogy is a matter of agreement among the elders and not a matter for exact recollection, again at least to a degree, and the historian must find out to which degree.[5] A similar situation seems to be true also for the Ewe of Togo.[6]

All performances are not so narrowly tied to institutions. Even if we admit that tale telling in the evenings is an institution in itself, just as dancing to the tune of songs is at full moon, and thereby reach the limits of what is usefully called an institution—one whose goal is to entertain and to teach—other traditions are much more haphazard in that they appear at various moments, during all sorts of conversations. Thus, passing by a historical site with a child can be the occasion for telling him about it. A question such as "where does x come from" triggers a commentary, news about someone's doings prompts an anecdote about the person's village or clan. That is not to say that messages given under these circumstances determine the kind of datum given. For example, the foolish action of a neighboring woman will tend to recall an anecdote of how foolish they were in her village of origin. As Cohen has shown for Busoga (Uganda), haphazard information through the daily channels of communication contains a vast amount of lore about the recent past of perhaps two generations ago.[7] Much older tradition, now formalized, once went through such channels. One especially important situation of haphazard transmission is speculative discussion about points of worldview or obscure points in well-known traditions. Their importance derives from the fact that such speculations often become tradition in their own right as comment fuses with original message or "It could have been" becomes "It was."

There were also the occasions for formal teaching, where traditional messages were not told in their usual setting, but taught in initiation schools at ritual sites or during formal learning processes. Here it is not enough to know when the information came to light, but under what usual circumstances it would appear. Some messages are performed only in initiations, whereas others, such as songs, proverbs, and perhaps traditions of origins, are only taught here. Informal teaching goes on all the time in the household where older women chat with the girls that help them, men teach boys, and everyone instructs smaller children. It is in this framework that techniques and everything that pertains to them are transmitted, not merely by example alone, but also by word of mouth. "Do this" and "Don't do that" are often illustrated with telling bits from messages that normally are performed in other institutional settings of their own. This too the historian must know because content will be conditioned by the original institutional setting.

(b) Social Control of Information
It should not surprise us that in many societies not everyone is entitled either to hear or to perform certain messages from the

past. In the first case we have to do with esoteric knowledge, in the second with copyright. Often the latter point is associated with the official or private character of a tradition.

Esoteric knowledge is a common occurrence among many peoples. The knowledge of herbalists or smiths, for instance, is often not available to everyone. It is not surprising that some traditions are also esoteric. One would expect it in strongly stratified centralized societies such as the Inca empire. There the secret general history was taught in schools by specialists housed and fed at the expense of the state. Access to the schools was accessible only to the elites. Historical poems were given in public performances, but the state controlled their contents. After the death of each Inca, high state officials and the specialists of the secret general history met and decided what the official history was to be, choosing the themes that could be popularized. The keepers of the *quipus*, who preserved all quantitative data, including chronological data, also had access to information that was closed to nonspecialists. Access may not have been forbidden, but in practice the knowledge was esoteric because it had to be taught and not everyone was permitted to take instruction.

It is said that in the Inca kingdom all forms of intentional historical messages were state controlled, some data were diffused for propaganda purposes, others kept secret but nevertheless preserved, while yet others were eliminated from the traditions as harmful precedents. No wonder that Rowe considers that all recorded traditions about the Inca can be traced back to the official traditions of the capital. I think the selection was designed to justify the regime as it then existed and to bolster it.[8]

The Inca may be an extreme example. Yet secret traditions were common elsewhere, too. In the Akan states, ruling dynasties are said to be indigenous, but some have secret versions about their origin showing them to be immigrants.[9] A different case is that of the *ncyeem ingesh*, Bushong songs sung for the ruling Kuba king. They were taught by a female specialist, the *shoong*, to the wives of the king. They are divided into two groups: the "public songs" which all may hear, and the "spirit songs" which may never be performed for an outside public and which only the wives of the king may know. If others know, they keep quiet about it.

Copyright deals only with performance. Traditions may thus be known but not repeated at will. Songs in many parts of New Guinea can be bought like rituals. On the Trobriand Islands, for instance, the song in which the heroic deeds of Tomakam are sung is well known, but only one definite group could perform it.[10] The notion of property was strong enough in many cases for ownership of performance rights to be the subject of sales. Ownership of narratives is well attested by the literature.[11] It is the usual situation for historical accounts concerned with various groups of descent, villages, age grades, or chiefdoms. While everyone may know, only members may tell these and then often only before an appropriate forum. The goal here is not merely to maintain and control the accuracy of transmission, as was often alleged in such situations, but to keep control over the dissemination of the information as well.

### (c) Official and Private Traditions

All traditions can be divided into official and private traditions. Most official traditions are accounts dealing with the history of the corporate group that keeps them. They were performed publicly, on occasions that had great meaning for that group and in the presence of the leaders of the group. The official character was evident to all. They told the "truth" as guaranteed by the group. Hence facts which do not help to maintain the institution or the group transmitting these accounts were often omitted or falsified. Bushong (Kuba) official tradition claims that the ruling dynasty is the first the country ever had, although this is certainly not the case.[12] In the Akan states, although the official history claims that ruling dynasties are indigenous, the members of the royal clans know well enough that this is not so.[13] Private traditions only defend private interests and conformity with more general official tradition is not required. Information conveyed by private tradition about groups other than the group that transmits this tradition can be relied on. For example, the members of a Kuba clan, the Kweemy, say that they are descended of a female dignitary of the Bieng chiefdom. That is for them official and might have been distorted. When they go on to state that the Bieng chiefs were an earlier dynasty for all of the

Kuba, a dynasty eliminated by the ruling Bushong dynasty, there is no doubt that this version is to be preferred over the official Bushong version, which maintains that its dynasty was the first and only one that Kuba ever knew. At the very least, the account by the Kweemy group shows the lack of agreement on this matter.

This example also tells us that "official" and "private" are relative notions. The history of Kweemy by Kweemy members is official. What they say about the history of Bieng or Bushong chiefdoms and about the history of the Kuba kingdom is private. In this sense most historical accounts are official and private at once. Cases of a certain complexity can occur. The kingdom of Burundi had no official historical accounts. The most official data were a short song or two sung during rites of the installation of kings and even here the interpretation was free. So the historical accounts that are given us for the foundation of the kingdom and the rule of the first king, Ntare, are private. But not all and not really. For many of them are tied to annual rites of renewal in the kingdom and were charters for the privileges of particular local groups involved in these rituals, so that each of these groups had its "official" tradition. Here then, they were official at a lower level, but private at the more general level, exactly as in the case of the Kweemy clan. The difference is that there were no general official traditions at all.

One must not, however, discredit all official traditions just because they are official. There is no automatic distortion on every point, and there are advantages to official traditions, especially in more complex systems. These deal with larger areas and deeper time depths than private traditions and thus provide a framework for regional history which private traditions may lack. Kuba official history deals with the whole kingdom and several centuries, whereas most traditions linked to clan sections deal with two generations and a very limited segment of the area. Similarly, village traditions among the Kuba are concerned with a very limited spatial framework and a time depth that is usually less than a century deep. It should also not be forgotten that some private traditions are influenced by official traditions and are distorted as a consequence. In the Akan states transmission of traditions which contradicted the official version of history was expressly forbidden.[14] Fear is a factor to be taken into account when one finds that private traditions conform in every detail with the official accounts. Official historical accounts were often also more controlled and their transmission occurred with greater care, whereas private accounts were more subject to the creativity of individual performers. One could even claim that distortions in official traditions are easier to spot because they occurred under the pressure of very obvious forces, whereas the distortions in private traditions are much less obvious, more idiosyncratic and less tied to specific social imperatives. Yet one should not exaggerate. Perhaps the biggest drawback of official histories in larger, more complex social systems is that they represent only the point of view of elites. When Kuba kings say, "we came from," they mean their ancestors and those of their senior councilors. Even in small scale societies this bias exists. Here the history of villages may in fact be the story of the "big men" in them and the history of so-called clans and lineages was often a construct translating the interests of leaders and alliances of leaders. A major source for the history of the Mae Enga (Highlands, New Guinea) are the accounts about *Tee* exchanges, that is, a sort of potlatch between "big men" (*kamongo*) recording the varying strengths of their communities over time.[15] However, they deal only with the most successful among the Mae Enga. A private source is not of any less interest than an official version *a priori*, nor the reverse. Each type of source has its own value to the historian, the best ones being those which are not intentionally historical, and therefore neither official nor private. To evaluate the impact of society on any given tradition it is imperative to go beyond the official/ private dichotomy, despite its importance, and to study in each case how traditions have been used.

## (2) Messages as Tools

(a) Functions

Every traditional message has a particular purpose and fulfills a particular function, otherwise it would not survive. The significance of its content in relation to community or society at large is what I call a function. But we cannot observe functions. They are elements of social analysis, interpretations of social situations produced by the mind of the analyst. We can deduce these only by seeing how messages are or were in fact used or whom the message benefited. A royal genealogy signifies that monarchy was the form of government here for a long time, that a certain family was entitled to occupy the position of monarch, that it enjoyed certain privileges and obligations, and that the present king is the rightful holder of the office. The genealogy legitimizes the form of government, access to competition for kingship, and the rules of succession as well as the legitimacy of the incumbent. All of these are "functions" because the tradition is to the good of the monarchy, the ruling family, and the present ruler in general. If we can show that the genealogy is recited during succession periods—at accession, for instance—we have a positive sign of use reinforcing our analysis. If we found the genealogy to be used as argument in council or court, the evidence would be even stronger.

It is not enough to postulate functions when one claims influences of society on messages from the past. Functions become compellingly real only when use of the message shows them to be of benefit to X or Y. Expressed or obvious purpose is equally helpful. In this case the examination of different versions of contradictory historical accounts makes a situation clear. Thus, when the inhabitants of the Kuba village of Mboong Bushepy say that the iron mine at Nshaanc spring used to belong to them, as is shown by the tradition that the collector of tribute in iron ore came to their village and not to any of the neighboring ones, the traditional message about the collector is used to legitimize their claim. Indeed, its very purpose in being remembered is that claim. The neighboring village held a contradictory account involving the same tribute collector. Both versions then clearly indicated what the point of their message was.

It is impossible to draw up a list of either all possible purposes or all possible uses that may be connected with a given tradition. They are legion and all traditions, like proverbs, often serve multiple purposes and uses. In order to discover purpose as opposed to use, one should not rely on explicit statements in the message. Anyway, those occur quite rarely. One must be thoroughly acquainted with the community involved. If the historian collects the data himself, he will have to be enough of a sociologist or social anthropologist to analyze the society and community involved, or will have to team up with a sociologist or social anthropologist. If the historian works with data gathered by others, he should systematically search for sociological studies of the place and period involved, and if necessary complement them by personal research in those matters. For example, anyone wishing to use the extensive collection of Malagasy traditions gathered by Father Callet must be conversant with Malagasy social history of the period of collection and before, so as to be able to place the accounts given by Callet in their proper social perspective.[16]

## (b) Tradition as Weapon

The use of messages as tools is perhaps most dramatic in conflict situations. One fights with tradition. Among the Nzebi (Gabon/Congo) the *mboomo* is a palaver consisting of a fight between two masters of knowledge who question the whole social order, the relationship between the clans. Such masters or *mutsundi* are very rare in the country. When they take up a case, they prepare through magic and learning for the duel. The debates turn around clan history and it is the use of decisive formulas that makes points. Thus, if one says, "Mitsimba [the founder of the clan] acquired a following by the harp," one means that the Mitsimba clan is of slave origin. Historical knowledge here operationally creates clan relationships and hence social structure with its ideology. The *mutsundi* are the incarnation of power and among the Nzebi knowledge is the only permanent basis of power.[17]

Elsewhere, historical arguments are common in court cases, where precedent can matter, especially to back up claims over office, land, property, or offspring. The historian has in such cases no difficulty in sorting out conflicting claims and in assessing potential distortion. But it may be impossible at times to find out which account can be trusted. I was once unwittingly involved in such a situation. Among the Bulaang, a Kuba subgroup, several factions started fighting about a genealogy to prove that they were legitimate successors to the chiefly office and that their opponents were upstarts. Having recorded all

positions it was still not possible for me to know who had falsified what.[18] All parties had been at this for two generations or
more and no one really knew anymore what was false and what
was not—it all had begun such a long time ago. In the end none
of the controversial data could safely be used at all.

Traditions were also used in attempts to keep or establish
control over others in the same community. Among the Kongo
in this century, the manipulation of genealogies by the elders in
a settlement allowed them to allot or to deny land rights to
others in their settlement by claiming that they were descended
from collateral kin—allied groups but not owners of the land—
or even descendants of slaves.[19] As such genealogies were not
common knowledge available to all, those who were acknowl-
edged by all as experts were thereby given in fact control over
the whole community. This is but one instance of a very common use of genealogies all over the world. They justify existing
stratifications by denying them (we are all brothers) while at the
same time providing detailed guidance to inequality by distinctions between "elder" and "younger" branches. They also record
alliances by tying allied groups into common genealogies.[20]

(c) Ideological Uses
Less specific but no less important is the general use of traditions
as a justification for existing conditions. An early Ottoman
legend tells how Ertoghrul, migrating across Asia Minor with
four hundred horsemen, stumbled upon a battle in progress and
chose the side of the apparent loser, thus turning the scales and
helping them to victory. These were Seljuk of Sultan Ala-ad-
Din, who as a reward gave Ertoghrul a landed fief, later to be
enlarged by further support of Ertoghrul in a battle against the
Byzantines. In the end the Sultan bestowed the insignia of sover-
eignty in the guise of a banner and a drum on Ertoghrul's son,
the eponym of the Ottoman dynasty.[21] In reality the first Ottoman principality was but one of ten *ghazi* principalities, without
a special connection to the previous Seljuk rulers. The "legend"
established a legitimate succession to the old dynasty, justifying
its rule ever since.

The story of Saint Sidi Mhâmmad is less obvious. It tells us

how he was a herdsman for Sidi Slima. He would take out cattle
and meditate on a hill, during which time miracles took place, the
most noteworthy being the arrival of partridges who lighted on
his body to pick away lice. Sidi Slima being informed of this
realized that Sidi Mhâmmad was a greater saint than he was.
Whereupon Sidi Mhâmmad was given the hill on which he medi-
tated. He lived there as a saint and was buried there. His main
shrine stands there. This is one of the many stories current in the
highlands of northwestern Tunisia in which relationships between saints are taken up. Their sanctuaries are still extant and
the tradition also deals with their precedence. In this case it turns
out that the tradition legitimizes the superiority of the ʿArfawa
over the Ulâd ben Sâyyid who had given them hospitality when
they immigrated into the area c. 1800. Sidi Mhâmmad was the
ʿArfawa saint and Sidi Slima the saint of their hosts.[22] The
function of this story is exactly the same as that so often given in
genealogical terms. It justifies a hierarchical relationship between two groups. Its value could only be established through
the analysis of other traditions, but the connection between the
social groups and the shrines made the claim of the ʿArfawa already evident. That and the use of the account would have been
enough to throw suspicion of distortion on it.

    King lists were very often falsified and for a variety of
reasons.[23] D. Westermann gives examples for Africa of rulers
who were eliminated because they had been a shame to their
country.[24] In Rwanda the rule of Rwaaka was never included in
the official list after the succession of his brother who overcame
him. He was thereafter considered but a "regent."[25] The
Imbangala (Angola) king list is far too short because only for-
mally installed kings could be listed and very few of the rulers
had been so installed. Indeed, the same requirement made it
practically impossible to obtain a list of rulers for Loango
(Congo) and also seems to have affected the memory about even
recent Tio (Congo) rulers.[26] The mechanism involved recalls
such famous parallels in literate societies as the destruction of
royal cartouches in Pharaonic Egypt or the Roman *damnatio
memoriae*. In all these cases the goal was generally to assert an
unbroken succession of exemplary rulers.

Such justifications are quite different from another use of tradition which was often but not always unconscious. Historical tradition established group consciousness (*Wirbewusstsein*). The typical feature in the historical accounts of the Ngoni of Malawi is the recurrent stress on characteristics of any sort —from costume to rules of descent—which made them different from their neighbors. Tradition was to uphold Ngoni "nationhood" at a time when in practice the Ngoni were in great danger of being totally assimilated by their neighbors. This was not merely so that by claiming differences they could also justify the existence of a separate administrative structure, but to assert their own identity to themselves.[27] Such cases are numerous; the most extreme one I know of being the instance of the Lumbee of North Carolina. They claim to be Indians who intermarried with the earliest white settlers of a colony that separated from the Roanoke and was later lost. They used this story first, to identify themselves and, then, to claim a separate status—neither white nor black—and that from at least the 1880s. By their claim they were the first in the land and indeed the first settlers as well. Lumbee do not, however, differ in any way at all from other "white" people in the area. They have no visible Indian heritage whatsoever. Only their claim of origin distinguished them from others and established them as a group, yet they managed to be recognized as Indians in a state where otherwise only black and white races were recognized and separated.[28] They were Indians merely because they believed themselves to be, and their account of origin convinced the ruling whites as well. Historical consciousness of this sort is served in all societies by traditions of origin. The feeling may be rather muted in normal circumstances, but when the account of origin is the only remaining evidence for it or when groups feel threatened by complete absorption the stress in the accounts does stand out to the extent it does among Ngoni or Lumbee.

(d) Idealization
In every society each role or status is modeled after an ideal to which holders must conform. The ideal is common to a whole community and often is preserved in its oral traditions. His-

tory performs an exemplary function and traditions tend over a number of performances to reflect ideal types, a process that is revealed very quickly in tales or in other artistic genres, much more slowly perhaps in historical accounts. Still, apart from very recent accounts such as reminiscences, they too are patterned in "ideals" from which lessons of history are drawn. Thus, fifty years after his death a Kuba king was already held up as the ideal tyrant. "But God finally killed him" was the conclusion of one account I heard. Often heroes or villains are mentioned to young children as examples or warnings. Bundi villagers (New Guinea) will compliment one who acts in warrior tradition by saying "That's Norbriwana, all right," Norbriwana being one of the great warriors whose names have become legendary.[29]

Distortions brought about by idealization were very common and sometimes striking. Some characters became the prototypes for magicians, warriors, wisemen, and lawyers. Anecdotes that originally belonged to other persons who were not so idealized were reattributed to the prototypical character. Culture heroes or founding heroes are but the most extreme among such prototypes.[30] Here it is no longer just the case that one king (as among the Kuba) is the magician and the other the warrior, so that feats of arms are attributed to the second and miracles to the first,[31] or that all rebels in Burundi rebel against a King Mwezi (one of several with that title) and all conquests are made by a King Ntare.[32] Culture heroes are credited with the creation of whole social systems or cultures. For example, among the Iroquois, Dekanawidah was responsible for their special way of life, including the formation of the Iroquois Confederacy, their state.[33] None of this reorganizing and idealizing happens consciously, but it happens nevertheless. The art of the performer, and, as we shall see later, the dynamics of memory itself favor this kind of a development. The results are that overall the corpus of traditions in any given society provides an ideal model of how the society should function even though this never seems to have been the purpose for maintaining the traditions over time. Indeed, history in the telling like history in the writing often is the teacher of life (*magistra vitae*).

(e) Whose Past Is History?

Social structure influences traditions in yet another way. In many African or Polynesian kingdoms it was held that the only true general history was dynastic history. Kingship was the expression of the whole country and the past of the royal house was that of the nation. This is explicitly stated by the people of the kingdom of Kazembe (Zambia).[34] It should not be surprising then to find that the historical tradition of descent or local groups, apart from their stories of origin and foundation, all featured kings along with a forebear of the group in question. Thus, the whole historical perspective was shaped by the existing political structure.

This situation obviously flows from the dynamics of social stratification. Any connection with royalty reflects on the status of descent or local groups, especially if the anecdote recalls a service rendered to the dynasty, or even more when descent from a king is claimed. Such anecdotes went beyond these obviously flattering memories. Even villages created by Kuba kings to house opponents or Kuba clan sections punished by kings by being forced to take up residence in a servile village remember and tell. The court and the dynasty were the cynosure for all in society and the social significance of everything was measured against the court as standard of reference. In smaller scale societies such phenomena exist but are not as obvious. Here the leaders of the village or the "big man" becomes the referent and extinguishes any historical memory beyond family reminiscence.

The historian must always be on the lookout for unconscious distortions, as well as for the obvious alterations which might have been introduced for fun, profit, or esteem. Suspicions should be aroused as soon as characters conform to ideal types. In any given corpus the best way to discover if they do is to compare tales, poems, and historical accounts. In cases of idealization one concludes that whereas one cannot vouch for the messages one cannot rebut them either. Given human nature, the chances are that the message is not to be trusted. When, however, traits or anecdotes run counter to fashion, they should be seen as reliable. These data resisted the trend to idealization.

For instance, when official dynastic accounts tell about kings killed by the enemy or that the sacred emblem of state fell into enemy hands (Rwanda), we accept them, because they run counter to the whole hagiology of state. Should a "magician" king be credited with a victory rather than a "conqueror" king, this too is worthy of notice. Thus those elements that run counter to the use, purpose, or trend of the message will be considered valuable, although still not as valuable as unintentional historical messages.

Other data, and this is the great majority, must be used with circumspection. A victory reported may be a falsification, but it may be true. A culture hero may be an imagined figure, but he or she may be a real person.[35] Often we cannot vouch for the truth of the information given. In such cases one should discuss the evidence and neither accept nor dismiss the data too readily. Lastly, we should never forget that traditions adhere to the "great man" school of history. They thereby fundamentally distort the nature of historical processes but in a way diametrically opposed to all evidence that stems from direct traces of the past in which human personalities play no role whatsoever. In this way they serve as a reminder that all change cannot merely be attributed to faceless forces, but is the result of people's dreams and actions, even if the particular people presented are idealized.

## (3) Performers

Traditions are performed and performers have their own interests. They may want to please, to earn money, to gain prestige, etc. As it is, however, and if only because performances also involve an audience, the interests of performers are almost entirely conditioned by the interests of the community of which they are members. The notions of status, role, career, goal, social arena, and group of reference all make clear that a person is placed in relation to others within a community. If a teller wants to gain prestige, it means that there is prestige in performing in that society, that some more prestige can be won by achievement, and that it is to be won by doing certain things.

One soon realizes that whatever private social interests a person has are socially conditioned and that an analysis of social uses and purposes also will take those of the performers into account. Obviously, we can no longer study the interests of performers who lived long ago, except under exceptional circumstances. A dynastic poem in Rwanda was said (in a separate tradition) to have been composed by a certain Ngogane on the occasion of a murder committed by a member of his family. The murderer fled to the home of Bigeyo, a friend of the family. Bigeyo set intrigues afoot at the court to blacken Ngogane's family and turned the murderer over to the family of his victim. Ngogane, worried for the whole family, composed his poem and as was usual dedicated it to the king. In it he stigmatized the hypocrisy of Bigeyo and warned the king against such duplicity.[36] The separate tradition was remembered because it was in fact an essential commentary on the poem, so that here, as in a few other cases, we know something about the first composer (if there was one) because the composition tells us so. But the case is very rare and we still do not know, except in general terms, why all the other performers of the poem performed it. So we will not make any distinction between the performers of a tradition at any time in the past and merely discuss briefly what can be observed from recent performances.

(a) The Usual Performing Situation
In ordinary circumstances the performers are not put under any extra stress compared to the situations of their daily lives. They play a normal role, are perceived in their status, and pursue activities towards a "normal" career goal. Their status can be high, low, or ambiguous and may or may not be tied in with their actual role as performers. Griots in West Africa are performers by profession. Their status prescribes it and they live from it. If the performance is good, they will be more in demand. But their status is ambiguous. All expert performers, all griots, are viewed as dangerous to others, as parasites, but also as the instruments by which prestige and fame are allotted.[37] In any particular performance a particular griot may pursue a particular goal, which may be to win the favors of a new patron, to defend the family

of his traditional patrons against attacks by others, or perhaps to receive a specific favor from his patron. Obviously the performance will be influenced by it, but these influences go in the general direction of the social uses and purposes of the genre of tradition in that society. So while we never can know all the motives that move a person, the effects can still be perceived, because the performer is, say, but one in a set of many Manding griots. Ngogane had his special motive, but it did not affect the way he praised the king, merely the danger against which he warned him. Even without the additional tradition it is easy to see that this poet held some grudge against Bigeyo.

It is not very difficult to assess distortion stemming from the motives of most performers, but the prevailing social situation must be known. Among the Tonga (Polynesia) traditions are best known by chiefs. Anyone who knows items from the past unknown to most others gains prestige and is an expert, a *tangata 'ilo* (men) or *fefine 'ilo* (women). People take pride in being known as experts and hence guard their knowledge jealously; it is difficult to get them to talk.[38] Among the Kuba such a person is a *bulaam*, a "wise person," but he has to demonstrate this status and does this by telling traditions. Here such persons tell sometimes more then they know. They tend to add a little and to pass on speculation for received knowledge. Social structure here was unambiguous. This meant that some informants would not communicate all they knew for fear of outshining their superiors. And so it was that a performer once begged me to come and record all he knew, after he had refused to tell me much until then. He had learned that another expert had poured his traditions out and now he had to defend his reputation as *bulaam*.

## (b) A Novel Recording Situation

When a tradition is to be recorded on tape or paper, an unusual situation is created, as a performance becomes a testimony. The performer now acts in a different arena, one linking his community or encapsulated society with a wider world, and often with the national state. The performer becomes informant. The informants must take into account what the reactions of their fellow countrymen will be, and they know that the latter will be critical of how they behave. Informants wonder to what uses the testimony will be put. Finding himself in a novel situation and in the role of "informant," the person is never quite certain what to do. It is a situation fraught with tension. The informant must also take into account what the reactions of the person recording the testimony are likely to be. The latter can perceive, or may attempt to perceive, what motivation an informant may have for altering his or her testimony. In such a situation distortions are to be expected when compared to a normal performance.

Individual motives no longer are contained by the usual expectations. In a broader arena new items crop up that are related to that arena. Payment in currency, ingratiating oneself with authorities well beyond the "customary" authorities, a belief in the superior knowledge of the interviewer—all are linked to a much wider arena. The influences of schools should be considered. By the 1950s the Lulua of Zaire were telling that they originated in a place called Nsangu Lubangu, although that was not what their traditions had been saying hitherto. The old men who knew the older traditions believed that they had been mistaken, since the Nsangu Lubangu account was taught in a school and schoolmasters must be right.[39] Hence when an informant perceives from a question asked by a supposedly learned interviewer that the latter believes the answer to be such and such, he or she may simply concur, not just in a desire to please, but also out of a new-found conviction.

The behavior of the informant depends largely on the impression he or she has formed of the researcher. Is the researcher a well-known local person and can one handle him or her within the local rather than the wider arena? Is the researcher foreign? Has he or she been in the area for long? What is the status of the researcher? What motives is he or she credited with? Is the person to be trusted? What does the informant stand to gain by testifying? Is the informant testifying under some form of intimidation or even duress? The fieldworker must know the answer to all these questions in order to tell what might lead the informant to falsify the testimony. A fieldworker must therefore know how the local people label him. In the 1950s the Kuba were acquainted with European state officials, missionaries, business people, and railway personnel. The state officials held power and were therefore always a danger. It was expected that they would want to know all traditions of a political nature and that each political group would make every effort to present these in such a way as to convince the officials that their group was especially important and possessed a maximum number of rights. The missionaries wanted to convert the local inhabitants and to introduce Christian customs into the country. They too were expected to be interested in traditions, but they were not to be told items that went against the tenor of their teaching for fear that they would criticize the informant, who would lose prestige. They might even provoke trouble, as they did, for instance, by striving for an interdiction of boys' initiation ceremonies. Businessmen or railway people were not expected to be interested in traditions. If they took an interest, it worried people because the motives of such interviewers were not clear. As a professional fieldworker I was in a class of my own because my activities made it impossible to place me in any existing category. Indeed, for a while this very observation was used to suspect me of witchcraft. It took quite a while before it was accepted that I was collecting traditions because I was interested in the past history of the country and because that was my job, although it was hard to imagine why anyone should invent such a job. Still, history was important for the Kuba and they had a model for this sort of person: their own *bulaam*. Later in Burundi there was no such local model so I ended up by being regarded as a harmless, friendly lunatic from whom one could hope for some unexpected windfall. The Tio, later still, knew about researchers. In the beginning I was to them one whose purpose was to take notes, write a book, and become rich, or one who was paid to take notes and would throw them all through the window of the plane as soon as I left.[40]

It takes quite a bit of time for a foreign fieldworker to be accepted and to develop relations of mutual esteem with a community and its informants. The tension inherent in the situation of recording can lessen or even disappear in time, both by repeated interviews or social mixing between the parties and by the general reputation the researcher acquires after many months of stay. So it is especially important for researchers to be very careful in their first weeks of interviewing. Interviewers should be friendly, interested, all ears, but nevertheless not show any reaction to the testimony, so that informants will not begin to distort their data according to the preferences or dislikes of the interviewers. They must reward informants in customary local ways or in currency, as is common in the wider world, but at rates that do not vary with the content of the testimony and that are usual in the area. They should not establish themselves in any way as "patrons" of their informants, who often hope for this so that they can get help in legal, political, or even medical matters. In principle the fieldworker should stay completely out of local quarrels, be friendly with everyone, informant or not, and be equally helpful to everyone. In practice this is not so easy, and interviewers should at the very least be aware of the impact of social relations on testimony and account for this.

In the case of a local fieldworker, the situation is different but equally complex. Should such a person be labeled as of faction A and clan I? Could local factions use him or her to present their cases to national bureaucracies? Which favors could they expect, if any? Or are such local persons really to be handled as foreigners because of their ambiguous status, between the local and the wider world? Local researchers should thus be equally aware of the image that people develop of them, and equally beware of falsification.

For the scholar who works from accounts already written down, an evaluation of distortions stemming from the recording situation is obviously harder, especially if the interviewer left no indication about this. The scholar must then work with what can be generally known about the situation. For instance, a record was made by a senior chief of the kingdom of Benin interested in the history of that state and supported by the king. Informants performed almost on command at the capital, and the chief's known interests in the preservation of the state's ideology, in the matter of proving its antiquity, and the extent of its dominions, were known to many informants. The record in fact does not allow one to distinguish easily between what the informant contributed and what the chief made of it, but the drift of general bias is clear.[41]

## II. TRADITION MIRRORS SOCIETY

Even if critical attention is paid to each testimony in particular, it is often not realized to what extent traditions are congruent with the society to which they belong. We therefore begin this discussion by establishing this fact of congruence.

### (1) The Congruence of Traditions and Society

A comparison between the oral traditions of Burundi and Rwanda shows the congruence between tradition and social structure in a way that is all the more compelling because the two former kingdoms and neighbors have so much in common, including much of their culture, while their languages are extremely closely related.[42] Let us merely compare the genres in Burundi to those current in Rwanda:

| BURUNDI | RWANDA |
|---|---|
| *imigani:* all narratives | *imigani:* all tales |
| all proverbs | all proverbs |
| | *ibitéekerezo:* all accounts except |
| | *amakuru:* personal recollection |
| *indirimbo:* all songs (specific | *indirimbo:* court songs |
| court songs are unknown) | *imbyino:* folk songs |
| *amazina:* poetry (mostly martial) | *amazina y'inka:* martial poetry |
| | involving cattle |
| | *ibisigo:* dynastic poetry (unknown in Burundi) |
| *ivyivugo:* synonym for *amazina* | *ivyivugo:* warrior poetry |
| | *ubwiiru:* dynastic ritual code (unknown in Burundi) |
| | *ubucurabwenge:* royal genealogy (unknown in Burundi) |

The roots of the three names for main genres in Burundi recur in Rwanda (*-gani, -rimbo, -zina*), but genre differentiation is clearly much greater in Rwanda than in Burundi. Why? It is easy to show that the additional Rwanda genres are linked to political institutions which do not exist in the same form in Burundi. The Rundi political system did not favor historical memory. The royal family, the *abaganwa* of which the king was but a *primus inter pares*, ruled collectively. Most men of the family held full authority over lands and sought to enlarge their estates to the detriment of neighboring *abaganwa*. Beyond this competition all *abaganwa* were united in two or three blocks between whom a balance of power obtained. When one of the *abaganwa* died, his lands were up for grabs. The sons of the deceased only succeeded to some or most of them if they achieved some power of their own before their father's death. Some parts of the kingdom were ruled by chiefs without any connection to the royal family at all, but who had local following. Each chief in his lands appointed subchiefs. When he died the next chief dismissed all the existing subchiefs and appointed his own men. In addition, the boundaries of the provinces were constantly shifting; the fluidity of the whole political system is striking. There was nothing to favor the rise of detailed oral traditions: no provincial history because provinces were unstable, no histories of important families because besides that of the royal family there were none, and no centralized government, hence no official historians. If they had existed at court, they would have upheld the power of the king and the *abaganwa* would not have welcomed it. It was in everyone's interest to forget the past, whether it was the *abaganwa* who had taken the land, the subchief who had been dismissed, or the king himself who relied now upon one faction, now upon another. The former senior regent of the country told me that history was of no interest at court so there were practically no historical accounts. The political system shows why.

The contrast with Rwanda was great. The king was in command. He governed through great aristocratic families, not necessarily descended from former kings, to whom he allotted lands with relatively fixed boundaries. Such lands were semihereditary. Government was carried out by a territorial bureaucracy assisted by a standing army encamped on the marches of the

kingdom. Government was further indirectly supported by a
patron/client network especially connected with the owership of
cattle. In Burundi patron/client contracts also existed, but they
were of shorter duration and played no big part in government.
With central enduring government and its institutions came a
need for legitimacy and an interest in history. Hence the historical narratives, court songs, dynastic poetry, warrior poetry,
and even martial poetry involving cattle, the dynastic code, and
the royal genealogies. Hence even the fact that historical narratives were liked by all the people. One set that were strictly
historical narrative were performed at the court or at one of the
manors, while the other set (popular historical narrative), which
were much influenced by tales, were performed for the general
public.

The difference in socio-political systems between Rwanda
and Burundi explains the difference in genres, in attitude towards the past, and, where they occur, differences in repertory
and in actual content. For the content of narrative tradition
especially closely corresponds to social practice and cultural
values, which however similar in general outline they may be,
are in fact not identical between Rwanda and Burundi.

## (2) How Is Such Congruence Attained?

(a) The Limits of Society and the Limits of Tradition
The specific institutional seat for each type of performance and
the attendant impact on traditional messages are a first explanation for the congruence between society and tradition. This congruence produces major effects that cannot all be neutralized by
a judicious application of historical critique. For social organization sets spatial and temporal limits to what is told in performances. The spatial limits are obvious. In large-scale societies
the most general history remembered deals with the whole territory of the state, often a large area, and sometimes beyond, but
the most general history of a small-scale society deals only with
the domain of a village, a descent group. These are often tiny, at
least in settled societies. Hunting band history, however, can
sometimes deal with a huge area as in the case of the Dog-rib of

northwestern Canada. The bands here counted fewer than two hundred people, but their activities stretched over hundreds of kilometers.[43]

The historian dealing with small territorial units faces the problem of understanding what the trends are which affected a larger area and many communities. He must combine the history of many small units, but this is never easy to do. Synchronisms between the histories of each unit must be found and, given the general weakness of oral tradition with regard to any chronology further back than a few generations, this often becomes quite speculative. All the historians who deal with central Kenya, northern Uganda, or most of southern Sudan have to deal with this problem, and the resulting historical reconstructions still suffer somewhat from this situation.[44]

Similarly, albeit less obviously, social organization sets time depths to tradition, not only because traditions deal with institutions which only have a certain time depth, but also because of the possibility of expressing time depths. The measurement and expression of time was based in part, for longer periods, on structural recurrence. Where the social structure required the use of long genealogies, as among the Fang of Gabon and Cameroun where one remembered sometimes up to thirty generations in depth, events of several centuries back could still be given a place in time.[45] In most states the structural time depth goes back to their foundation. Yet we can use one kingdom as an illustration for the telescoping of the past into a very shallow time depth because one could not express greater depths of time. The Tio of Congo recognize only two generations backwards from an adult Ego. The third generation backwards is spoken of as if it were the first (father's) generation back and the fourth as if it were the second (grandfather's). So, even though the Tio formed a kingdom they had no way to place anybody in a time further back from the second generation backwards. Some results are surprising. I was told in 1963 that a certain migration occurred at the time of the grandfather of the chief whose title is Ngobila. Stanley, eighty years earlier, was told the same story, which was dated to the grandfather of Ngobila. In the seventeenth century a written source already mentions the same tradition with the same time depth![46] An analogy exists here with the situation obtaining in the Lunda empire of Central Africa. Structural time depth there is four generations at most, and one does find a historical depth of four generations before the first recording in writing of these traditions. Beyond that one goes straight to origins, to mythical founders.[47]

Anything earlier than the structural time depth and anything outside the structural space is ignored or, in the case of the time depth, telescoped to remain within the frame. Time and space become congruent with society.

What is true for the whole corpus in relation to a society also holds for each tradition relative to its social seat. Ordinary family tradition lasts the time a family lasts, village history lasts the time a village lasts (as a social unit) and does not exceed its spatial domain. Although artistic traditions such as poems, epics, tales, and songs can be spread over huge areas, their contents rarely deal with events; when they do, this is usually only by allusion, and the events relate only to the place where the tradition was composed (poetry) and where it is performed (tales).

(b) Significance
Traditions about events are only kept because the events were thought to be important or significant. A selection process is already underway, starting in fact with eyewitnesses or contemporary reports. As time passes and the criteria of importance or significance change, the selection process continues. It is therefore strange to find that after years of debate R. Lowie's main objection against the use of tradition as history was that such traditions often dealt with insignificant items, while events of great importance were not remembered.[48] He cited the case of the Assiniboine Indians of the Canadian Plains as an example. The Assiniboine adopted the horse in the eighteenth century and it changed their whole way of life as a result. Yet the introduction of the horse is not recorded in their traditions. According to those, horses existed since the time of creation. Lowie, however, did not realize that the appearance of the first horse may not

have ranked as an important event, because the people then could not know how it was about to change their lives. Some three generations later when the horse had become central to the Assiniboine, it could no longer be imagined that such an important acquisition had ever been absent, just as one could no longer imagine that life had ever been fundamentally different from what it was then. So significant had the horse become that it "always had been there" and hence belongs to Creation myths. The Nez Perce (United States), however, do have a tradition about the introduction of the horse, but it gives no indication of the importance of the event for their later development. To the Nez Perce, horses were less important than to the Assiniboine, and, because their significance was less great, the perpetuation of a tradition about their introduction in the historical past was acceptable. The Assiniboine situation resulted because they overestimated the importance of what happened, not because they had no sense of that importance.

The importance accorded to events is a matter of general consensus in a community. It is tied to the social impact of such an event. As groups and institutions change over time, the notions of "significance" and of "interest" also vary and may eventually lead to loss of information. Such losses may also occur because the memory of the event never became part of a tradition in the first place as it did, at that time, not seem to affect society very much. The Kuba remember the first European to come to their country, but not the second one. It was no longer a novelty. Yet the first was only a merchant, while the second was taking over the country on behalf of the Congo Independent State, a fact the Kuba did not know. As a result of such processes of selection, the intentional historical content of traditions becomes closely congruent to social concerns of the past and of the present.

(c) Repertory
While it is almost impossible to establish a full repertory of all topics mentioned in the oral traditions of a people—because such a corpus is so encompassing, reflects all aspects of current social

life, and expresses all culture[49]—it is interesting to find that the corpus of intentional historical accounts yields only a small number of topics. They may deal with origins, migrations, descent, wars (over land, women, other wealth), natural catastrophes, and not much more. The poverty of this repertory is in every case quite remarkable, but, given the fact that information is only transmitted when it is "significant" and that significance alters over time, this situation causes no surprise. The other result is that such a repertory becomes internally quite coherent. It deals with the concerns of leaders and elites. As A. Delivré convincingly has shown for the Merina kingdom in Madagascar, the repertoire is a blueprint of the political system, not as it is, but as it should be.[50] The repertory concerned itself with the central issues of authority, power, and legitimacy, and it included ethnographic oral description as recorded in the nineteenth century. Malagasy traditions reflected all elements which were crucial to society in its political dimension. The historical consciousness expressed in this body of tradition corresponded completely with the present-day concerns of the time when they were recorded. Malagasy accounts are a model of Malagasy political structure, and Delivré showed that in order to prove this one must look at the whole corpus of accounts, not at accounts in isolation. One then realizes that social memory acts on the whole corpus and not just on every single account separately.[51]

## (3) Homeostasis

The congruence between a society and its traditions led J. Goody to claim that this is the product of a dynamic homeostasis. At any given time traditions are perfectly congruent with the society. Any alteration in social organization or practice is immediately accompanied by a corresponding alteration in traditions. Therefore, the corpus of traditions constantly changes and cannot correspond to a past reality.[52] For Goody the difference between oral and literate society is this homeostasis plus the claim that culture is totally homogeneous in oral society and heterogeneous in a literate society. The latter finding is based on his claim that information available to people in oral societies is the same for everyone, whereas in literate societies varying information inputs exist, since some people will read certain material while others read different data.

What we said about congruence seems at first to support this sweeping thesis. However, Goody exaggerates his thesis, both in the sharpness of the opposition between "oral" and "literate" (a subject that I do not further pursue),[53] and in the claim for total homeostasis. In short there is congruence but there is no total congruence of content with the concerns of the present. Continuous selection of intentional historical accounts does not perfectly operate.[54] The presence of archaisms in various traditions gives homeostasis the lie.

Perhaps the most remarkable proof that homeostasis is far from perfect comes from the data assembled by that pillar of functionalism, R. Firth. In his *History and Traditions of Tikopia* he had already argued for a total congruence and hence homeostasis. But when he analyzed the relationship between claims for prestigious origins and actual status of the descent groups involved, he found no congruence at all.[55] The third ranking descent group of the highest ranking clan had the most prestigious origin, agreed to by all, and this was not even a group of chiefly rank. He concluded from this that "the more firmly established aspects of the social structure may not have, and may not need a reflection and legitimization in traditional tales" and "traditional tales may be not so much a reflection of the social structure itself as of organizational pressures within the social structure."[56] He sought the functional congruence elsewhere, maintaining that the claims rather than their acceptance must be taken into account and that traditions are instruments of social relationships. Claims give private status increments to the leaders of the group concerned, he stated. Past glory is used as a present social counter. But further on he concludes that origin tales are linked to the social structure, but not in a simple relationship.[57] This amounts to a denial of homeostasis. The reflections that follow confirm his unease: Accounts about past happenings are necessarily molded into forms that are dependent upon existing social relationships and therefore "must be" largely a projection of the present into the past. This is a statement of functionalist faith not proof. The whole research presented in the book belies it.

It is easy to pile up examples to show that homeostasis is not complete. Social change often leads to additions, not to suppression, leaving older variants intact. Items that tend to be suppressed leave traces. Kuba dynastic tradition tends to suppress irregular successions or succession struggles. So many traces of these remain, however, that one concludes that irregular succession was the norm.[58] Homeostasis theories cannot explain why history is valued more in some societies than others—why it is a principle of legitimacy to begin with. Beyond homeostasis, fundamental cultural options and differing worldviews must be taken into account, and they are not wholly conditioned by the present social organization. It is to questions of culture that the next chapters are devoted.

The basic flaw in Goody's view is the hidden analogy of societies to organisms or machines where every part must function in accordance with everything else. In fact this is only partially the case and one should talk about tendencies towards homeostasis, not of homeostasis as a radical process. A body of tradition therefore reflects both the past and the present. Because it reflects the present it is of interest to social scientists and these scholars have not yet given enough weight to this kind of evidence in their own studies. But despite the present there also is a past. The case of W. Van Binsbergen's Tunisian saints shows how the tradition explains relationships between shrines and their backers today, including the claim of the ʿArfawiya that they are superior. But it also includes the admission that they arrived later than the Ulâd ben Sâyyid. If the homeostasis were total the ʿArfawiya saint would be the earlier one. The story explains why the ʿArfawiya enjoy God's grace (baraka) more than the others, but an element of the past is essential to this legitimation and need not be distorted to legitimize.

The historian can overcome the inherent distortion caused by the impact of social organization, but only to a limited degree. One cannot reconstruct what has been eliminated or disentangle easily what has been telescoped through time. The elements surviving in the traditional record stem for the most part from the past and the imprint of the present can be assessed through fieldwork or through careful examination of social organizations of the time when the data were recorded. All the possibilities of distortion that have been mentioned in this chapter can be checked; where suspicious congruences are detected it is possible to see whether the tradition was altered and, if so, how. An assessment can at least be made.

## CHAPTER FIVE

# THE MESSAGE EXPRESSES CULTURE

All messages are part of a culture. They are expressed in the language of a culture and conceived, as well as understood, in the substantive cognitive terms of a culture. Hence, culture shapes all messages and we must take this into account when we interpret them. I first examine the impact of the cognitive aspect of culture, that is, the impact on a given message of what is generally and commonly known in a community. Then I turn to the modes of expression of a culture beyond the rules of language. I examine therefore the symbolic aspects of the message and discuss images, clichés, and the problems of their interpretation.

## I. The Substance of Culture

Culture can be defined as what is common in the minds of a given group of people; it refers to a community of society. People in a community share many ideas, values, and images, in short, representations which are collective to them and differ from others. The division of the color spectrum into recognized primary colors varies from language to language, from society to society.[1] This is not to argue that the contents of the mind of every individual in a given community are identical to those of every other individual. Idiosyncracies do exist. But the principles through which experience is internalized are common and most of what people hold to be true about reality is common as well. Such cultural contents are transmitted to children in the process of learning the language and in learning how to behave. Communication of oral tradition is part of the process of establishing collective representations.

J. Goody has argued that common culture is much more encompassing in oral societies than in literate societies, because one can only acquire contemporary, generally known materials in the former, and all learn them. In literate communities the acquisition of information is selective, since one person can turn to ancient books or manuscripts which others may not read, and they may read other material which the first person does not know.[2] This view is exaggerated. It underestimates the degree of uniformity of collective representations where writing is known. People, on the whole, read the same things—those which they are told are worthwhile reading. The content of their minds is more standardized than Goody believes. On the other hand, people in oral communities differ more in the contents of their minds than Goody holds. Idiosyncracies remain important. Interests, vocational and others, differ.[3] Nevertheless, collective representations remain fundamental in the minds of both literates and nonliterates.

## (1) Basic Concepts

Basic concepts are those by which perception, memory, experience, and their communication are regulated. They exist before perception and involve representations of time, space, number, reality, and cause. Insofar as they affect a sense of the past, those relating to space, time, historical "truth," and cause are discussed in turn.

### (a) Space

Every culture has representations concerning a universe and these involve spatial connotations. Like time, space is a relative notion in that it implies a spot in relation to other spots, as grammatical uses show. Within space some parts are more important than others and some are known while other, more distant parts are only vaguely known. The most important spaces were linked to the spot of creation, having temporal as well as spatial value. The classical example here is that of the Maya who divided space starting from a center in which they find themselves. They thought there had been four successive creations, each one more perfect than the preceding one. With each new creation the creatures of the preceding one were pushed outwards towards the periphery, the most perfect creation being the one in the spot where the Maya now live. So it was possible to seriously ask whether the inhabitants north of the Gulf of Mexico were not savage cannibals, the products of a previous creation.[4]

The views one has about space influence one's view of past happenings. Until the last century devout Christians visualized the Garden of Eden in Mesopotamia. Hence, the migrations of all peoples had to somehow stem from there. The thirteenth-century European maps of the world were disk shaped and had Jerusalem at the center. Redemption was translated into space. In Africa the direction of migrations and the explanations of cardinal points of orientation often are connected with origins. The Kuba, Fang, and Komo of Central Africa orient themselves by streams. Their major categories of space are "upstream" and "downstream" which Kuba and Fang also associate on the whole with east and west (i.e., the way the sun travels). For the Kuba the world began in a place where there was no orientation. The waters turned "round and round." This was obviously the most downstream place possible; dead souls go there, spirits lived there, etc. It is the sacred direction, hence all migrations had to go upstream from there, and this explains why they claim to have gone from the absolute upstream to the most downstream possible, the sea. On the whole the Komo were more like the Fang.[5]

The importance of orientations such as these can scarcely be exaggerated. Villages were laid out according to the cardinal points, ceremonies proceeded through space in a symbolically meaningful order, the inner arrangement of the house might be a microcosm, and so reference to space can always be suspected of having more than accidental meaning.

The concept of universe involved more than the earth; it encompassed the sky as well. The Ainu of Sakhalin, for example, divided the universe in the horizontal plane, the earth in a vertical plane, in which both the above and the below were distinguished from the earth, the above being sacred and the below mundane. On the surface of the earth they opposed the mountains and the sea to the shore. Orientation on the shore was east and north opposed to west and south. East and north were more sacred and shrines in the houses were located on that side. The shore as a whole was a mundane place while both mountains and sea were more sacred. Between those two the sea was more mundane than the mountains, and in either the distant was more sacred than the near. So the most important gods lived on top of the most interior mountains known.[6] Here then it was not only movement, but the very space in relation to other space which denoted superiority, sacredness, and humanness. Such hierarchies of space were implicit in all Ainu traditions.

It is therefore necessary to be aware of systems of orientation and spatial representations in general, both to understand the resonances and implications of statements about space and to understand how spatial movement could be expressed. North and south for the Kuba could only be left or right, it being understood that this was left and right for a person facing toward the spring of a river, not, as is usual in Europe, toward the mouth. And here again values were associated: right was superior, left inferior. Any movement could then only be described as either upstream, downstream, left, or right, and this in relation to rivers or river systems. In Burundi the most important direction was up or down, that is, up towards the top of a hill or mountain or down towards a river. But for the country as a whole the dominant "up" was where the court was, even if it resided in a low valley. Hence multiple misinterpretations could arise when "up" and "down" were used, whether the relationship was expressed in terms of the kingdom or in terms of the local orography. Finally, it should be kept in mind that distances were not measured in oral society but rather were expressed in qualitative terms or for short distances by approximation as "one day in distance," "over x ridges," and so on. Space was not usually thought of in quantitative terms.

(b) Time

Concepts of time are linked to those of space, as we saw in the Maya case or in traditions of origin. Time, as a concept, shares many characteristics with space. It is perceived as duration for a traveler. Such a time/space continuum is directly expressed in some languages by the use of the same term for distance in time or space, as in Bushong *kaany* and in many other Bantu languages.

In most worldviews the universe has time, because it was or is created. The direction of time is linked with "better" or "worse." The golden age lies before us or is long past. Qualitative notions of "long ago" or "almost now" correspond to the qualitative notions of "far away" and "nearby" for the Ainu with implications of more or less sacred. For the Ainu the universe has a limited lifetime. It will die and be reborn. Time is cyclical, yet time moves as a wave with a crest and a trough. A universe starts when the holy (*nupuru*) and the Gods dominate. It is born at its crest. After that there is only one other period: the long present, a time for humanity, mundaneness, and progressive decay. Therefore, the most sacred circumstance is the top of a mountain at creation, the most human, the present shoreline. Subdivisions of time such as years, moons, or the lifespans of people also move in waxing and waning halves, the phases of the moon being the exemplar. People move in the opposite direction of all other phenomena. Their youth is their waning, they are born at the nadir. Their old age is their waxing as they become less human and more holy, and they die at their crest.[7] Again, such a representation of time must be known before one can interpret Ainu messages involving time.

Conceptions of time in general can be of a timeless eternity, of cyclical times and of linear time, but no culture uses just one of these representations. Many use all three. In Christianity, Islam, and Judaism, the dominant time is linear. Time marches to a resolution of the world into an eternity that exists side by side with it. The dominant Maya time is cyclical and linear. Creations succeed each other, each similar to the preceding universe and yet different, for with each creation the succeeding universe becomes more perfect. In contrast, Ainu cycles are merely repetitive. The coexistence of linear and cyclical times in a given culture has sometimes been denied, as in Bali.[8] M. Bloch claimed that whereas ritual time was cyclical and nondurational, in practical life time was linear and durational. This does not hold up. Balinese hold a single concept of duration in both cyclical and linear time. Similarly, some Africanists have claimed that there were three times: the timelessness of creation, the cyclical time (which denies causality in the middle past) and linear time (which is causal for the recent past).[9] On closer inspection the claim holds for a notion of timelessness and creation, but linear and cyclical time coexist in a single concept of duration.[10] It is definitely not as if people thought that in some past everything began over and over again and that since a given date time no longer repeats itself. The qualitative conceptions of time vary from culture to culture and must be elicited separately in every case, all the more so as the concepts of time are crucial for any understanding of tradition.[11]

(c) Historical Truth
Historical truth is also a notion that is culture specific. The notion is important to the historian because it guarantees that past historical traditions, claimed to be "true," have or have not been faithfully transmitted. When G. Gossen reports that the Chamuleros (Maya Chiapas) believe that any coherent account about an event which has been retold several times is true the historian does not feel satisfied.[12] There is no element of faithful transmission here. Later, however, he cites a text which expands on the notion of truth. It explains that we know how the first people came to be because the ancestors saw it all and "when at last the ancestors died, they had already told their children how things were, long ago."[13] Truth among the Chamuleros involves both a witness and transmission.

In many cultures truth is what is being faithfully repeated as content and has been certified as true by the ancestors.[14] But sometimes truth does not include the notion that x and y really happened. When Trobrianders (New Guinea) hear assertions that run counter to their everyday ideas about natural laws, the words of the ancestors, while true, should still be backed up by a trace of the event visible in the landscape. Otherwise the tradition is true, but not factual. The Rundi for their part, even when they seem incredulous, as when they tell with glee about the Kingdom of Women, still, when all is said, accept that all this really happened.

Status and truth are sometimes related. In Mande land (Guinée, Mali) truth is appreciated according to the antiquity of the family of the professional who speaks: the older, the more truthful.[15] A correlation between truth and rank seems to occur in some stratified societies: the higher the rank of the speaker the truer what he says, even if he speaks about the past. For the Kuba, truth is guaranteed by the state councils. When chiefly tradition is to be related, the council rehearses first in secret session, the *kuum*, to establish once again what the truth is. Then a spokesman delivers the information to the public. The notion of truth itself is derived as to its form from the notion of "council" and "matter of council."[16] As a very old chief told me once, what once was true is now false and what was false is true. Kuba skeptics still accept this notion of truth. The same person who scoffed at the story of the creation of the first man (there could be no witness, so no one could know) accepted that king X killed the nine ethnic spirits. There were witnesses. It happened and the councils guarantee it.

Whereas many anthropologists and historians have realized the crucial value of the notions of space and time and have studied them in various cultures, similar information is lacking, in far too many cases, for the notion of historical truth. One cannot just assume that truth means faithful transmission of the content of a message. The historian must be on his guard; he cannot assume anything on this score, but must elucidate it for the culture he studies.

(d) Historical Causality and Change

Historical causality is a complex notion involving a link between phenomena over time. The earlier event or situation causes the later one. Western historians think of causes as multiple and of causality as continually operational: things change all the time; nothing ever remains the same over time, even when it seems to. Oral societies, however, tend to have a simpler notion of historical causality, one which negates gradual change altogether.

They tend to view institutions and techniques as unitary phenomena that came into existence fully fledged as they are in the present. In other words they operate with a notion of change that opposes the present to a single past and not to a variety of pasts. This attitude seems to be very widespread in oral societies. L. Lévy-Bruhl already noticed this *tendency* to overlook or negate a complex historical becoming.[17] We are inclined to explain it in the manner of Goody and Watt by reference to homeostasis.[18] People in oral societies go out from the present when they think about the past. Hence, an explanation of the type that institution A "appeared" at some time in the past suffices. Thus, under such and such a reign of a Merina king, the poison oracle appeared.[19] It is understood that it remained unchanged since then. An analysis of the Kuba notion of change shows that it literally means "to appear" while their notion of cause is "the base of the tree trunk," thus confirming the above.[20]

Often the initial past is seen as one where chaos existed. Some of the main institutions that exist today existed then in inverted form. The historical period begins with culture heroes who create order and invent or make institutions appear. J. Middleton has shown this for the Lugbara (Zaire/Uganda): in essence they create an initial past which is homeostatic to the present. It is the negative of the present, one of its possible contraries.[21]

In many, usually somewhat complex societies, historical causation is perceived as more complex. But causes are isolated. Complex chain reactions through time are not perceived. History is seen as a series of static states in which new items appear, but these are unconnected to each other. Each new appearance or invention is merely apportioned to a culture hero.

For it is another feature of the nature of causation as seen in oral societies that individuals are responsible for change. They create. New techniques, institutions, and activities "appear" to them. So history becomes a sequence of greater or lesser culture heroes. These are responsible for classes of invention so that a later one never alters anything already invented by an earlier one, but merely adds. The present in this view is the result of mere additive change in the past. Causality as a process of change does not exist in oral societies.

History as a succession of steady states created by successive leaders is the typical concept of causation in all African kingdoms. This conception of causality also explains why such traditions occur as anecdotes about king A or B and not as a consecutive narrative. Or, rather, perhaps it is because such traditions appear as anecdotes that the problem of causality as process never comes to the fore.

Along with these concepts of appearance and creation by an individual the idea of Fate appears. There is a Rundi tale connected with history in which a child brought about the ruin of his father the king.[22] They asked the mother then "What were you doing when these things happened?" She answers, "They happened, just as I was instructing the child in the way he should go; they had to happen." Diviners are common in Rundi oral traditions and their predictions about the future always come true. This reference to Fate leads us to a consideration of the cause of causes. These are always put in "ultimate reality," the reality that is religion and includes the unseen along with the visible world. In this sense consideration of causality carries us to a consideration of worldviews.

Once a historian has been alerted, the impact of basic concepts on the content of messages is not difficult to prove. When one considers bodies of recorded tradition, recurrences and apparent oddities help to clarify what is meant by space, time, truth, cause, and number. The latter also has particular cultural aspects. There are perfect numbers. Among ourselves three can mean perfection just as four does among the Maya or Yoruba (Nigeria). There are numbers standing for "many" as does six among the Ainu. Intervals between numbers are not really equal, in part because ratios differ. The distance between zero and one is of a different order altogether than any other; one to two doubles and is hence more than ninety-six to ninety-seven. Most peoples who have a complex numerology are literate. For low numbers equivalents can be found among oral people as well. The European theory of numbers is not universal and hence historians do well to ask themselves whether numbers cited are to be taken literally or in the sense of a particular number theory. And just as space, time, and cause are, so number is linked to a wider worldview. Perfect numbers are religious numbers and so are sinister numbers, the numbers of ill luck.

## (2) Worldview

(a) Finding Worldviews
Worldview is a representation of ultimate reality in all its aspects visible and invisible. It includes views about the creation of the world, about the kinds of beings that are in it and their taxonomies, on its layout, and on its functioning. There probably is no oral society in which this complex set of representations forms a single system worked out in a noncontradictory way which accounts for everything in relation to everything else.[23] Moreover, worldviews are obvious. Everyone knows them and the main principles are not often talked about, precisely for this reason. It will therefore be difficult for outsiders to discover the impact of worldviews on messages because knowledge of them is supposedly known. The first question then is to know how an outsider can discover a worldview. There are several avenues. One can inquire into religion and learn through discussion and observation what invisible entities people believe in and what their relationships are. Often these have not been worked out. For instance, in most of Africa the relationship between a Creator God and the existence of witches has not been thought about.

The second way is to study traditions of origin: how the world began, how people were created, and how they became as they are now. Other stories of origin deal with a single item, such as a custom or practice, and are etiological stories answering questions like why we never hit a dog or why we have fire. The main accounts of genesis pose no problems. They reflect the worldview directly. However, etiological stories are not so unambiguous. At some point we no longer know whether people take them seriously or not. Thus African tales about the dog as bringer of fire range from some which clearly are believed true to some that are just elements in a tale.[24] How does one find out whether such a story belongs to the worldview or not? In the field one can ask, and doubts of this sort are easily resolved. Otherwise caution is indicated, and anecdotal stories of an etiological nature should be handled with diffidence.

One can usually compare traditions of origin to other messages and gradually confirm particular worldviews, but the worldview thus given often does not link up with existing folk taxonomies. Yet such classifications exist everywhere, encompassing plants, animals, people, and even literary genres and disease types.[25] They reflect a whole folk science which must be elicited by detailed and repeated questioning. A taxonomy is rarely so conscious in the mind as to be a topic for a simple message. People often have difficulty expressing it in a single statement. Studies of ritual and of practices where items are in relationship to each other as inclusive or exclusive of sets help us further, but there are pitfalls in this research. For instance, one will observe that Kuba oracle boards display figures of a person, a dog, a warthog, or a crocodile. The person represents a nature spirit; the other animals are its domestic animals. They do not form a taxonomic set. The warthog is there because it is the spirit's dog, the dog because it can see into the unknown, which people cannot, the crocodile because it is the king of the water, and spirits are of the water. The explanations are all different, but all these animals obey nature spirits, except for the dog who merely "sees" (i.e., smells) what the nature spirit wants.

One can pile example on example to show both how complex worldviews can be and how difficult it is to prove that any particular explanation fully corresponds to the worldview of a community. The dangers here are threefold. First, one easily confuses symbol and reality. The lion is a symbol of kingship but has nothing to do with kings in reality—except among the Tio of Brazzaville, where it is held that kings can really command lions.[26] But the Kuba warthog *really* is the dog of the nature spirit and not just a symbolic image. Secondly, favored and gifted informants can create a much more systematic and broader worldview over time than existed hitherto. This is their own idiosyncratic culture and no longer the collective representation of the community. How is one to show the difference between the two? Thirdly, logical connections made by researchers, who often cannot help making them, are often not part of the worldview, yet when they are put forward most members of the culture may well accept them. One can use implicit categories of grammar or meaning to bring out unconscious principles and often taxonomies. Componential analysis does this for kinship terminology,[27] but we know well enough that this can be nonsense. Do Germans really look upon children as "things" and "time" as a woman because their grammatical genders label them as such? Once again, how do we prove that such patterns belong to a worldview, when people may not be fully aware of them?

In practice one can only say that there should be evidence beyond the demonstration of a pattern itself, either from the fund of oral tradition or—and this is often a very neglected angle of study—from what children are taught, when they ask questions. We should limit worldview to representations that are held collectively and are not unconscious. It is assumed that everyone knows them. Hence they are not often expressed, except to children and as commentary to explain traditions or usages.

The historian in the field studies the traditions of origin on this point and asks for explanations or makes prudent connections himself. Once I am told that the Kuba visualize the creation of the world as if it were a rolled-up mat thrown into a void by the Creator so that it unfolded as a huge rectangle but in a tilted way, I can understand why the main directions are upstream and downstream. Once I am told that people were created in the perfect downstream, at the bottom of the earth-mat, I understand why all migrations go upwards. I can accept all this because I have been told these stories many times over, unlike the story of the personality of numbers, a numerology that one man developed and one man only. Others approved of it, but they approved of a speculation that they did not know and that had no effect on messages from others. This means though that grasping the ramifications of a worldview will be gradual and that all of its effects on messages are not quickly understood. It also explains why, ideally, communication between a field-worker and the communities he worked with should continue for long time spans, so that it is possible to return for further information.

### (b) Effects of Worldviews

The effects of worldviews are the most important when one deals with traditions of origin themselves. Most of what one is told reflects no remembrance of times long past, but simply representations of the world. It is for this reason that accounts of original migrations often cannot be trusted simply because people affirm them. Even when there are detailed accounts of the place people came from, we still have to be cautious. Some Kuba told me that they came from the sea, that there was but one shore, that there were waves, that it was so wide that no bird could cross it, and that in their life near the sea they met whites in armor and on horseback. All these elements that seemed to prove their point did not do so. They had taken them over as "revelation." The main traditions dealt with an origin at the most downstream place possible (also a place of chaos) . When the Imbangala reached them from the eighteenth century onwards, here was confirmation! It had to be true, and it was added.[28]

Additions to historical messages are often due to the need to explain them in terms of the worldview. In the Hopi example cited (chapter one), the additions to the original report about the Navaho ambush dealt with its meaning and its motivation. The Hopi major events are predestined, but individuals decide how and when they will take place. So one had to add an explanation as to why the Hopi involved innocent companions. The raid was no longer an accident. Other details were also made more meaningful. Animal omens warned repeatedly about the impending catastrophe. The white man to whom the Hopi traveled was identified with the primeval man in the Hopi worldview of the time. The other added or changed elements were destined to turn the hero of the story into an example for young Hopi to follow —and even here the model for heroism is taken from an incident in the creation of the world.[29] The example shows how thoroughgoing and substantial the additions or other transformations can be, just in order to make the message more "meaningful," more consonant with Hopi worldviews. One understands how it happened. Speculations about the why of this ambush turned into accepted fact of the type "it must have been so!"

## II. IMAGES AND CLICHÉS AS COLLECTIVE REPRESENTATIONS

The collective representations of a culture include not only substantive matter, data of cognition, but also imagery. To the historian it is important to understand not only intended meanings as they have been discussed in chapter three, but also what can be called the context of meaning: the imagery and its impact. I examine this subject now, starting with images and then proceeding to complex stereotype and other clichés.

## *(1) Images*

Every culture has its imagery, collectively held and understood by all. Thus the equivalence of a banana tree and fecundity is quite general in the rainforest of equatorial Africa and is expressed in rituals, as is the equivalence of bulls with leaders in many parts of eastern and southern Africa. The image adds to a message a context of emotional value. It adds resonance. When in Rwanda or Burundi the verb *kuvumeera*, which designates the lowing of bulls, is used to describe the utterances of kings, the image resonates. It recalls the form of utterance of the mediums of the Kiranga/Ryangombe cult, who imitate the lowing of bulls, and it recalls much less consciously ideas associated with fertility. The use of this verb in a message, so Rwandans say, always evokes strong emotions. The emotions are sustained by the resonances to authority, power, and manhood. To Rwandans there is no question of emotion; to historians from another culture it may be necessary to indicate what type of emotion is generated here and why. It requires a thorough knowledge of a culture to be able to do this. One must compare the image with other places where it occurs in tradition or in ritual and eventually examine its semantic connotation. One consciously pursues the resonances and evocations which occur spontaneously in the audience which hears the message. The problem is now to avoid overinterpretation. Hence it is important that direct evidence of the existence of an impact on the audience be given.

Images can also be used as aids to reasoning, to make abstract notions concrete by use of analogy. The inhabitants of Roti (Indonesia) visualize their kinship system in terms of local flora and do so much more systematically than we do with our "genealogical tree."[30] The people around Lake Mayi Ndombe (Zaire) think of kinship models as banana trees, using the analogy very systematically: the community is the plantation, divided into smaller articulated groups that are trees, branches, and hands, while individuals are bananas.[31] Kinship systems are visualized as the human body from finger to trunk by the Fang (Gabon/Cameroon).[32] One thinks in terms of kinship with the help of the chosen analogy, while the link between the abstract ideas, the folk model of kinship, and the concrete image is essentially arbitrary, being determined by the culture. The culture decides whether a tree, a banana tree, a human body, a network of rivers, or some other simile will be used. Moreover, the image still has emotional resonances and the simile may be pursued in other contexts. For instance, banana tree products are much used in rituals around Mayi Ndombe and symbolize not only kinship but also fecundity in general. They are powerful positive symbols. It is not too difficult for researchers to discover this use of imagery, as it is often carried over into semantic usage, and many informants will use the same image when they explain the folk model of kinship. Use of the same imagery in other contexts helps to confirm the analogy.

Images have the property of expressing what may be complex relationships, situations, or trains of thought in a dense, concrete form, immediately grasped on an emotional and concrete level. The image "banana" immediately relates the fruit to people, to collectivities, to a favorable demography. There is a condensation of social relationships and emotions linked to them. Similarly, the *kuvumeera* image in Rwanda did recall royalty, cattle contracts, and social inequality as well as authority, power, and manhood. It is this property that comes especially into play in complex images.

## (2) Clichés

In the literature, the term cliché designates various realities. The first is as a synonym for topos or stereotype. In this sense clichés are stock phrases or *Wandersagen*;[33] they are statements or episodes, indeed even narrative plots, that recur in other traditions of the same or different genres in the same or different cultures. The African stories about the foreign hunter who founds a kingdom are an instance.[34] In time a second sense of cliché developed: it designates a highly compressed and deceptively simple statement of meaning that refers to a much more complex reality. Clichés are deliberate and purposeful simplifications.[35] Other authors use the term much more loosely as a complex image or set of images in which the action that takes place also is symbolic.

The only element common to these definitions is that clichés must be interpreted symbolically because they cannot be accepted as they stand. Various stands—obvious, as in the violation of laws of nature, or not obvious—tell us that the intended meaning is not acceptable. As R. Firth, discussing Tikopia tradition, has it, "Many of the incidents are unacceptable as they stand. They *must* be reinterpreted if they are to serve as data for history." And he goes on: "But what are to be the principles of such interpretations?"[36] This indeed is the core question, one to which he cannot provide an answer.

The following examples show that finding clichés is not difficult when the imagery is very complex or often recurs. On the other hand, deceptively simple imagery which occurs just once, as a *hapax legomenon*, may be quite difficult to find. In the Hopi story already cited the omens can be seen as symbols because omens occur very often in Hopi narratives and because the coincidence seems too strong to be believed. The hare that was Hani's totem animal conveniently appears and erases the Hopi tracks so that the Navaho abandon their pursuit. It is a quite different matter from Imbangala (Angola) traditions that say that their first king, Kinguri, died in such and such a spectacular way. At first glance this is not a cliché, but the name for the king is also the title for his office, so the statement could mean that the Imbangala abolished this type of kingship, and J. Miller interpreted it as such.[37] In reality there is no way of deciding whether the tradition really referred to the death of the man Kinguri rather than to the abolition of his office. We just do not know whether this is a symbolic statement or not.

More complex imagery is easily distinguished as symbolic. The Tagish (Canada) tradition about the 1898 Gold Rush is a case in point. This tells how the white prospector and his Tagish brother-in-law Skokum Joe found gold. The Tagish also say that Jim met Wealth Woman, she who defecates gold balls, and that he visited the Master of the Frogs. Wealth Woman and the Master of the Frogs are stereotypical in Tagish stories about "long ago"; they are also miraculous. The first cliché is used here as condensation of what the Gold Rush stood for.[38] A similarly powerful cliché is detected both as a stereotype and as something miraculous in several Tlingit (Canada) accounts about the arrival of the first European ships in 1786 and thereafter. It is told for various encounters in various ports as a regular *Wandersage*. The first part tells how the ship arrived and how the Tlingit, looking at it through magically protective tubes, thought it was Raven, while the crew were the crows attending Raven. For them the Creator is a raven and in their oral art Raven is the central figure in accounts of creation. This part of the story summarizes the significance of the event of the arrival of such hitherto unheard of creatures, by reference to traditions of origin, where such matters really belong. Emotionally the image is correct and remained so as Europeans, in the course of time, altered the Tlingit way of life ever after.[39] Both because it is a *Wandersage*—it occurs even among the Haida neighbors of the Tlingit—and because of the obvious connection with accounts of Genesis, it is clear that we cannot take this literally. It is a cliché and it must be interpreted. But how?

## (3) Interpreting Clichés: The Mbegha Case

The interpretation of clichés is the most difficult task students of oral tradition face because such interpretations can occur at various levels. Often we find a sociological explanation to account for the meaning of the cliché in the present, and a historical explanation to explain for what it stands. Neither is exclusive from the other. An exemplary interpretation of this type by S. Feierman deals with the Mbegha account.[40] The plot is stereotypical: Mbegha (hunter) founds the kingdom of Shambaa (Tanzania). Mbegha lived as a hunter of bushpigs to the south of Shambaa country. He had been cast out by his community because he was mystically dangerous. In a settlement where he found a refuge he teamed up with the son of the chief, but during a joint hunt this person was killed and Mbegha fled again. Eventually a Shambaa settlement discovered him and he began exchanging meat for their agricultural produce. Because he was generous and efficient in killing the bushpigs which prey on the Shambaa fields, he was welcome and, traveling through the country, finally reached what would be his later capital, Vugha. One night he killed a lion and the next day the Shambaa made him chief at Vugha.[41] His skill at arbitrating disputes between them also led them to take this step.

Feierman first points out that the structure of the account parallels a rite of passage. Mbegha changed all his statuses at once. He identifies the set of relationships hero-as-outcast and hero-as-king on the one hand and the set of relationships king and subjects on the other. The elucidation of each feature in each half of the set and its relationship to the other half of the set decodes the whole. For instance, Mbegha is hunter, the Shambaa are farmers. Hunting is man's work, farming woman's work, and to the Shambaa in general these activities stand for masculinity and femininity. Hence Mbegha is powerful, the Shambaa dominated. Feierman adduced at each step explicit ethnographic support: from commonly known imagery among the Shambaa, from imagery in ritual or everyday practice, and from direct statements corroborated by other informants. The images are Shambaa images. Any researcher retracing his steps can arrive at the same results. The procedure of interpretation is valid because it is replicable and can be falsified.

Feierman goes on to show how the overall cliché represents an ideological statement about kingship and order in society today. He then points to fragments of data which play no role in this ideological statement and may be bits about a genuine succession of events. Even the images contain the assertion that a man Mbegha came from elsewhere and founded the Shambaa kingdom. He may have come from the south, following the route described. A fair number of other historical elements also remain.[42]

Feierman convinces, yet there is still something lacking. He does not systematically show how over time such an account has grown out of a matter of fact recounting of the foundation of the kingdom. Nevertheless, he observes that the Shambaa and their neighbors tell a story about a primeval ancestor, who is still revered. This was Sheuta ("Father of the bow"), a foreign hunter with magical powers who became chief in Shambaa.[43] The Mbegha account was therefore patterned after this pre-existing one. The imagery in the Mbegha story is very widespread in East Africa and presumably older than the foundation of the Shambaa kingdom, which dates from the eighteenth century only. So the materials were there to fashion the account, but Feierman does not pursue it and tell us why and how this happened. To my mind the process can be sketched as a gradual adding and sharpening of images by various performers, to unify the story and to heighten its emotional response. The process does not differ all that much from the development of core images by the performer of tales.

## (4) The Validity of Interpretations and Implicit Meaning

Different scholars have interpreted clichés in very different ways. Feierman's interpretation was sociological—almost Weberian. His conclusions about contrasts between ruler and ruled and about the unregulated aspect of kinship (Mbegha) versus the regulated aspect of kingship (Mbegha as king) are not the only possible interpretations. His claim, which sounds very reasonable, that this account led the Shambaa to express a theory of kingship, is not really proven. In an analogous case R. Willis develops the oppositions ruler-ruled and men-women in a different sociological direction from the one taken by Feierman.

He finds a reflection of exploiters versus exploited, of dominant strata and dominated groups.[44] One could also have found this for the Shambaa material. Structuralist interpretations range further afield. They are freer because they are not constrained by the requirement that the imagery be well known in the society from which their "text" comes. Contrasts between the "wild" and "tame" aspects of kinship easily turn into contrasts about nature and culture. Others such as Miller do not try to explain the cliché in terms of its present-day meaning, but think that it contains information about the past in a very condensed form. He tells us about communal charms as if the names for these charms referred to successive political regimes so that the period of *lunga* government preceded that of *ngola* government.[45] Whereas the other examples said nothing about implicit meaning (that is, a meaning beyond the explicit one intended by the performers and creators of such accounts), Miller does. He holds that his interpretation is more than an interpretation. It reveals the implicit meaning, something that was put there on purpose by the originators of this tradition.

Interpretations can be construed as the interpreter of a text wishes to construe them. They are false only when they are internally inconsistent or when they contradict the explicit or implicit meanings of the text. Distinctions between interpretation, explicit and implicit meaning are familiar to literary critics. A novel has an intended explicit meaning, which critics interpret. But only a few of their interpretations correspond to the intentions of the author when he wrote his novel. Those have revealed the implicit meaning of the author. All others are *Hineininterpretierungen*, meanings a reader can discover, but that were not put into the text on purpose.

What we must discover is the implicit meaning of clichés. It alone has a special kind of validity. It alone was intended to be part of the message. How do we show that a given interpretation reveals the intended implicit meaning? We must start with the messages themselves, and we must convincingly describe how, by which process, a traditional message happens in the end to be expressed by this cliché in this way. So we interpret but we demonstrate the plausibility of our interpretation as implicit meaning. We can never prove it, because we lack sequences of different utterances of the message at different periods of the development. We can only make a plausible, convincing suggestion.

In the Hopi case the forces which altered the reminiscences and transformed them into group accounts were designed to render the account more meaningful to the community. This was done through the provision of motivation, the integration of the account into a corpus of accounts and by aesthetic elaboration. These are, I submit, the forces that will always act to alter messages over time, and, apart from the aesthetic elaboration, it is the working of mnemonic dynamics that provokes the changes.

By these principles we could defend Feierman's interpretations by arguing that the basic story was embellished to provide more meaning and that the provision of meaning amounted to a continuing reflection by a series of performers about the meaning of kingship. The mechanics of embellishment would be those used in tales, where core images are expanded.[46] The notion that Mbegha was a hunter is expanded by saying that he hunted bushpigs (which most hunters do), while that of the farmers is rendered more concrete by saying that they farmed root crops. The meaning of the plant-for-meat exchange agreed between them thus becomes much more significant because bushpigs are the biggest danger for fields of root crops: the animals just love them. Hence the hunter becomes protector and the exchange becomes a true symbiosis. Other images in this account can then be explained in an analogous way, and the shapes the messages had when Feierman gathered them become understandable. One could then have argued that the interpretation had revealed the implicit meaning of the account. It is now more than just one interpretation among many.

Guidelines for finding an implicit meaning can now be proposed:

(1) Compare the message with other accounts, tales, or traditions to see whether one is dealing with stereotypes or not. Since they recur, stereotypes, especially *Wandersagen*, are easy to find. Their implicit meaning is often clear because the stereo-

type occurs in different settings which make that evident. Most stereotypes give a motivation or develop a concept into a strong emotional image. The Tower of Babel explains why peoples are different from each other. The tale of the tyrannical king who kills slaves whenever he gets up from his throne tells us what tyranny is.

(2) Pursue the ways in which the core images of the narrative have been expanded (as in the hunter example, above) and determine what the core plot of the narrative is. What is the gist of the information? Check to see if the core plot itself is a stereotype or not. If it is not, we can accept it as the implicit meaning. If it is, as in the Mbegha case, we can only show how it could be this way (the Sheuta story) and must be content as Feierman was with the details that may reflect past events.

(3) Imagery (or cliché) can only be elucidated in so far as these images are commonly known in the culture studied, whether they occur elsewhere in oral art, in ritual, in speech and are a piece of collective representation. The imagery should at least be obvious to most people in a community. The study of schooling in symbolic discourse, which boys and/or girls undergo in many societies, usually in so-called initiation schools, is of help here. The interpretation of a single informant is not acceptable.

(4) The elucidation of implicit meaning must tell us how the original tradition was probably altered to arrive at the message studied. Even if proof cannot be attained here, verisimilitude remains an important element allowing one to choose which of several interpretations comes closest to the implicit meaning.

(5) Not all stereotypes have implicit meaning that differs from their explicit meaning. They may be intended literally by the composers or performers of a tradition. Thus, a frequent stereotype in the great lakes area of Africa is that a successor to the throne was spirited away as a child only to return later and claim the kingdom. This story usually covers up a conquest and original information about the conquest was falsified in this way to provide for legitimacy. But, in Burundi around 1900, a certain Kilima used this ploy to claim the throne, obviously because

many Rundi believed the stereotype in earlier accounts to be true. This stereotype hides a falsification. Its implicit meaning is *not* conquest. That is its explicit meaning. People should believe that king X was spirited away as a child.

(6) One should never *a priori* assume that a stereotype always has the same meaning. Images are multivocal and ambiguous. Their meaning becomes apparent within a specific context, which they color and by which they are colored. The same holds for stereotypes. This does not contradict guideline (1). Different settings do help to find implicit meaning because the different possible meanings of an image-range constitute a single symbolic field.

(7) Sometimes it is impossible to determine whether an explicit meaning is the implicit meaning or not. Thus J. Miller sees in the dramatic account of the demise of King Kinguri a cliché about the abolition of kingship. But Kinguri may mean "kingship" or "the man Kinguri." We will never know what the word means in this context. On balance it would be prudent to stick to the understanding of the account as dealing with the death of the real man Kinguri. For:

(8) We should never assume that the explicit meaning is not the implicit meaning also, unless there are signs to the contrary, such as the obvious, incontrovertible presence of imagery.

These guidelines are not a guarantee that all clichés will yield their implicit meanings, even if one knows that a statement definitely is a cliché. In practice the determination of implicit meaning remains fraught with difficulties. In any case, even in the best circumstances, proof cannot be absolutely provided. The cliché may be so opaque, so ambiguous, and so unique that nothing can be said about it. The greatest risk of all is to "decode" explicit meanings at all costs.

With this it seems that we have arrived at the end of the rules of evidence. If messages were like written documents, this would be true, but oral messages are not like documents. They are not permanent and given once and for all as documents are. They are a product of memory. What this means to the historian is the subject of the next chapter.

## CHAPTER SIX

# TRADITION AS INFORMATION
# REMEMBERED

In the last chapters I have applied the standard rules of evidence to oral messages. However, such rules were developed for the study of written texts, and implicit in them is the condition that messages be stable and permanent, not fluid or evanescent as oral messages are. The main consequence with which I deal in this chapter is that most information relating to oral traditions is not available in discrete packages, but is drawn from a single pool—a pool which only exists in memories. To cope with this, we must go beyond the usual rules of evidence.

As opposed to all other sources, oral tradition consists of information existing in memory. It is in memory most of the time, and only now and then are those parts recalled which the needs of the moment require. This information forms a vast pool, one that encompasses the whole of inherited culture—for culture is what is in the mind. It is a pool that is essential to the continuity of culture and the reproduction of society from generation to generation. Traditions in memory are only distinguished from other more recent information by the conviction that they stemmed from previous generations, just as memory itself is only distinguished from other information by the conviction that the item is remembered, not dreamt or fantasized. The convictions can on occasion be erroneous, but by and large they hold up well. Furthermore, memory is not an inert storage system like a tape recorder or a computer. Remembering is an activity, a re-creation of what once was. It uses for this purpose not just this or that bit of information, but everything available

147

in the information pool that is needed in this circumstance, reshaped as needed for this particular re-creation.[1]

It follows from this characteristic of oral tradition as information remembered that there is a corpus of information in memory wholly different from a corpus of written documents. The information here is inchoate, following channels which are completely different from flows of information between written documents. The consequences of this situation are presented in the first section of this chapter. The effects of the dynamics of memory acting on the corpus form the topic of the second section. I conclude by discussing the effects on chronology of a process in which inchoate memories cannot be dated and messages remain ephemeral.

## I. THE CORPUS AS A POOL OF INFORMATION

In this section I deal with the corpus of oral traditions in memory and not merely with the body of recorded messages that relates to an oral tradition. We want to know exactly what it is and how information flows in such a corpus. This is crucial in considering the extent of the independence of oral messages from various origins. If sources are independent and confirm each other, the events or situations confirmed can be taken as proven. The chances that they would agree by accident are virtually nil. Hence the agreement between the sources can only be due to the fact that such events really took place or such situations existed. Independent confirmation is conclusive proof in history.

### (1) What Is the Corpus?

(a) The Corpus Is Collective

The corpus of remembered information is first what a single person remembers in his mind. It is not entirely homogeneous information in so far as items learned by rote do not mix with others and do not absorb other information known to a person, while any other form of expression can draw on the whole pool of information. In addition, the mental tags that label information as traditional or not seem to be tied to the particular information needed as much as to how it came to be known. Thus if the information concerns a situation or event that is older than the lifetime of the person involved, it is tagged traditional. It does not matter whether the information was learned from a member of a previous generation or from a contemporary. In any case the tag also refers to a memory of memory, i.e., one of something heard from somebody else. Hence inputs into reality are not confined to material heard from members of previous generations, but may include speculation and commentaries about the past from contemporaries.[2] Information is acquired normally by assistance at performances, but this channel is not the only one. Bits of history are also transmitted during casual conversations so that history as gossip is perhaps as important a source as performances are.[3] This means that information that stems from non-oral sources, from writings or from foreign oral sources is also an input which will no longer be differentiated from other knowledge about the past. In the pool all information about a given topic will be fused.

The corpus is more than what a single person remembers because the information is a memory, that is, it does not go only from one person to another. Performances are held for audiences, not for single auditors, and historical gossip gets around as any other gossip does. So in practice the corpus becomes what is known to a community or to a society in the same way that culture is so defined. It will consist then of what A knows in a community, what B knows, and what N knows. Most of their knowledge overlaps—is "common knowledge"—and A, B, and N belong to one community or social network. They do frequently communicate one with the other and in practice pool their information on any matter.[4] The intensity and frequency of flows of information vary with the ways of life of different peoples. Locality may be a primary unit of culture where agriculturists have founded very stable villages. It is less so where shifting cultivators not only move their villages every decade or so, but split into several new groups or fuse wholly or partly with other settlements.[5] Residence is less important than range and flux among hunters, gatherers, or pastoralists. In kingdoms, the bulk of the corpus is maintained at the capital. From there it will affect all other places because the ruling group is the reference group for all others, who look up to it, and its culture is the dominant culture, which imposes itself on others and is often eagerly accepted. In practice then the structure and social dynamics behind the corpus vary, but it is always a communal social pool of information and the memory is communal. A good example of the social network behind a corpus is the royal Kuba court. Of forty-eight persons whose knowledge of traditions was recorded, only six could not be demonstrably tied in with the court, while all the rest were linked to each other, sometimes in cross ways, such as B derives from A and D from C. But D has been influenced by A and B by C. The information pools of B and D are practically identical. All written versions of royal traditions since 1885 also fit in this network. And I am certain that with further research the last six informants would also have been linked to the rest.

(b) Properties of the Corpus

As a body of information the corpus is always open in the same sense that a semantic corpus, a dictionary, is never totally closed.[6] The knowledge of different communities within a common society overlaps to a great extent because there is social intercourse, such as marriage and change of residence. However, it is not identical. Still, in practice, because information flows so readily in conversation the culture of the whole society can be seen as a common corpus. Contacts go beyond either from center to center by trade or by social osmosis across the boundaries from one corpus to another. One cannot find a firm boundary of one corpus and then step into another, unless one finds sharp language boundaries which prevent easy communication.

Such a situation does not make certain that the information will be distributed homogeneously within the pool. One could not deduce that any member will know exactly what any other knows. Some people have more interests, others less. Thus ex-

perts, the so-called encyclopedic informants or men of memory
or oral historians, know more than any other because they systematically have pursued historical information all across the
pool, often out of sheer curiosity. Other experts know esoteric
information. They are influenced by the generally known data,
but keep part of their information out of general circulation.
Among the Lovedu (South Africa), paternity of the heirs to the
throne is a secret. The throne was inherited by females through
females only. The secret could not be violated on penalty of
death. Clandestine genealogies of the descendents of queens and
their genitors exist nevertheless.[7] One notes also that officially
controlled information does not mean that it is unknown. To the
contrary, it is known to all, but can only be propagated by
some, presumably to stamp out competing information or to
prevent it from developing, if not merely for reasons of prestige.
Even different types of historical information are not kept
separate from each other. It is true that memorized speech and
the information it contains influence other knowledge, but
memorized speech cannot itself absorb other information. Yet in
practice when we look at the Kuba clan slogan for Ndoong (cited
in chapter two), it is clear that interpolation—i.e., addition of information—has been frequent and that one can proceed through
incremental change in versions from a slogan for Ndoong to one
for Bieng, for Kweemy and for the rain, if the units of memorized
speech are small enough.

   Yet there is a real boundary in the corpus, mostly consisting
of historical accounts, historical gossip, or other commentary
which one often finds aggregated in the mind of local people—
relevant poetry, proverbs, songs, epic, and historical tales. This
enumeration already shows that the boundary is relative, that
information does in fact pass from the world of fiction into the
world of fact. Elsewhere I have shown how this is obvious in
early traditions from Burundi.[8] Nevertheless, the flow of information is not unbounded. By and large, the body of "truth" is
distinct from the other, even if the only means for the performer
to know whether information is true or not is once again his
memory that is conditioned by the contents of the information
more than by other means. Still, this subcorpus will exchange

and absorb information in the same way as the whole corpus does.

## (2) Information Flows

Information flows are part of communication within every community. Formal performances and informal gossip are the main channels for them, but any gathering can be such a channel. Discussions in judicial courts, assemblies, rituals or funeral gatherings are all channels that can be important from this point of view. It is banal to state that no community or society can survive without communication. Equally true is that it cannot survive without exchange and mutual checking of information, including information from oral traditions. Hence the flow of information is not to be explained. But such a flow brings with it what historians have called "feedback," that is, the alterations brought about in one message by information acquired from others. The consequences of this are first examined with regard to a single society and then for several societies.

(a) In a Single Society
It is not unusual for one person to know a whole set of traditions, including contradictory versions when these exist, and he can create a new one by combining them into one. The Shi (Zaire) narrator Mpara did just this in his explanation about the history of the title holder NaRhana, a chief at the court of the Ngweshe king. NaRhana was for him both a subordinate chief of Ngweshe and also an independent chief.[9] Sigwalt is able to trace the inputs into the compromise stories, and to use them to show that changes in these charter myths about ritual offices reflect to some extent political changes of the nineteenth century. So the matter does not end with declaring that version x is contaminated, but explains why it exists and at the same time uncovers a ritual and political dynamic. It makes plain that one part, the part one may call the palimpsest (or older surviving portion), refers to an older situation.

The case of the encyclopedic informant belongs here as well. What is one to do with the accounts he or she gives? They relate to tradition only in the sense that they come out of the subcorpus dealing with "truth" from the corpus to which the informant belongs. He or she has taken pains to gain as much information as possible and went beyond the usual limits of information. Historians should gather the extent of the contacts of such persons from their life history and in this way establish the real scope of information which they controlled. One should then handle an account given by such persons as any other traditional account, keeping the social and geographical span of the information base in mind as well as the special interests which lead these persons to reconstruct histories which do not only reflect the social needs of the present, but tend to grapple with what is thought to be the reality of the past.

A tradition is known to many persons and each of them can always complete his information from others. This makes for difficulties when one attempts to establish a text or a testimony because in between two performances or interviews it is always possible to get additional information which, when fused with the first, alters the testimony. At the outset of my stay among the Kuba I was given a short list of kings by Mikwepy. A day or two later he gave a much more extended one. In the meanwhile he had been getting information from his uncle Mbop. In this circumstance it was much better to deal directly with Mbop, who turned out to be a man of memory. But this is not so in all cases, for the first person may have bits of information the second one does not have. What matters most is to realize how widely known a tradition is and to view renderings of it as being backed up by the collective memory of the group who knows.

Just as with persons, so with local communities. There, several versions of a tradition as well as a pool of many traditions are kept and may influence one another. What is perhaps special in this context is the relationship of this community to any local landmarks. These help them to remind themselves of the relevant account more often than other people elsewhere, or accounts may even be known which people further away do not really know well. Thus a mound at Mpiina Ntsa (Brazzaville) is said to be a single mound by outsiders who know vaguely of a tie with early Tio kings. Locally, several mounds are distinguished and several personages are linked to them. Near the royal capitals of Central Burundi people remember better what happened there c. 1900 than others do elsewhere.[10] Of course that does not necessarily mean that such accounts are truer. They are more susceptible to iconatrophy. They are different, but they should be heard.

Yet even in a small community knowledge is not necessarily, indeed not usually, quite uniform. There may be little to prevent information from flowing freely, but the interest or background knowledge varies, so that in practice the mixing of memories is not perfect. Specialists such as iron smelters or medicine men hold information about their crafts that is simply not accessible to others by virtue of its complexity, and it may be esoteric as well. Hunters know their landscapes and memories of associated incidents much better than farmers. There may also be some hindrance in transmission across class or caste boundaries, because different people do not often mix. Nobles may not know slave traditions, although the reverse often is not true. Social hierarchy leads to one-directional flows.

In the same way, information-flows between localities vary by the frequency and the type of relationship that exist among people living in them. Kinship grouping, social status, technical specialty, marriage relationships, trade patterns, ritual geography—all explain variation in this flow.

## (b) In Several Societies

People in one community or society are in relation with outsiders and inputs from elsewhere are by no means barred, so that the amount of information a person has, a community holds, or a society remembers, is constantly in flux. Some items that have lost relevance are forgotten. For instance, most of the life histories of deceased members are lost, while other information comes in from elsewhere. Folklorists have long known that tales can spread over enormous distances and motif indexes of tales prove it.[11] While it is true that some motifs are invented independently in different parts of the world, in most cases diffusion explains the distribution. What holds for tales is also true for other information. Two Kuba examples illustrate this well. The slogan of a Kuba king "It is not to his own house, but to other people's, that he sets fire" is not particularly appropriate. The same slogan exists among the Lulua, neighbors who speak a different language, and there it is associated with the name Losho antande. The Kuba slogan is a translation of the Lulua one, which is appropriate, since the name Losho antande ("fire of the village") is explained by it.[12] Among the Lulua and Luba of Kasai exist stories about "the little old woman" trickster. In their language "little old person" is *kakashi kakulu*. Some Kuba groups turned this into Kash aKol and made her the ancestress of founding genealogies.[13] As the examples show, different languages are no barrier to diffusion, although they certainly can lead to misunderstanding.

### (i) Wandersagen

The best known cases of diffusion are *Wandersagen* and tales. In chapter three I gave the example of the pit hidden under a mat. This was not independently invented from one end of the savanna kingdoms of Central Africa to the other.[14] A connection with one of the major kingdoms does not explain this diffusion. The story vividly tells how and why chiefs broke with their paramounts, and can be applied to all such cases—the explanation for its success. Again the diffusion of the Tower of Babel story in Africa and elsewhere can scarcely be due to independent invention.[15] That such information can travel far and fast is shown *inter alia* by the diffusion of biblical tales far ahead of any mission. Thus we find that the story of Noah in his drunkenness was known to the Kuba of Kasai and the Lunda of Shaba by the onset of this century and probably long before. The only possible source for it were the missions in the kingdom of Kongo (after 1491) and more than likely the mission at Ocanga, placed at the head of a trading route in the general direction of Kasai (mentions 1595 to 1640).[16]

One may well ask why information is borrowed. In the case of *Wandersagen* it may be because the image expresses a motivation, but it is also because the image makes a concept quite concrete. The king who sits on his throne between two prone

slaves and who holds a spear in each hand with the point on
their backs, so that when he rises, pulling himself up by the
spears, he kills the slaves, is a powerful image of a tyrant.
The image of the village that was so big that they had to tie bells
around the necks of little children to find them again well renders
the idea of a town.[17] Sometimes the borrowing also occurs
because the information fits with what was already known. It
is a "revelation." The Kuba held that they came from downstream. When Imbangala (Angola) traders from the eighteenth
century onwards told them about the sea and its marvels, it
fleshed out the image of their place of origin. It was new information about a point known. Sometimes the information
just fits *present* relations which soon will become a past. The
same Imbangala borrowed the account of their first king,
Kinguri, coming from Lunda in detailed stages; while it benefited their trading relations to the Lunda, it explained the new
world thus opened to them and the meaning of the very trading
route to Lunda.[18]

### (ii) Feedback

The attention to and sometimes eagerness for information is
not to be blocked by its ultimate origin. When the content of
writings comes to be known, people who hear them adopt them,
as the Noah case shows. When writing came to be practiced in a
society, oral traditions did not die out as long as literacy was not
general.[19] Rather, people incorporated them into their traditions
just as some literate persons incorporated traditions into
writings. The transmission became mixed and could remain so
for centuries. D. Henige, who has most forcefully drawn attention to the input of written material into oral traditions, reserves
the term "feedback" for this process.[20] After reviewing evidence
from around the world he concluded that "uncontaminated oral
tradition simply does not exist any more, except possibly in the
most remote areas of Amazonia, the Philippines or New
Guinea." Historians should be aware of possible mixed transmissions and loans from written sources, and it behooves them
to carefully examine all the writings that were available to

the communities studied and especially those that concerned them.

What is true for writing is also true for other sources. Archaeological sites also can be integrated into oral information or seen as a further expansion of them. Sites which the Rwandese and people from northern Burundi recognized as belonging to people who were there before them were linked to the Renge population. Renge was just a name for the last known population before the present one. Speculation linked the huge earthworks of Bigo in Uganda to a capital of an early kingdom, although the link with the so-called Cwezi kingdom took shape only after speculation by writers about the Cwezi had fed back into tradition and from both the writings and the oral data to the Bigo site.[21] Archaeologists then should be as wary of feedback as students of oral history.

Feedback from other sources such as monuments, language, and even the rationale of customs also occurred. Speculation about the why of a landscape, a monument, a name, or a custom sometimes became so convincing that it was accepted as truth and added to the information from tradition, in which the original datum now became proof of the truth of the information. The Kuba of a nearby village show a depression which they said was caused by the dancing people after the nomination of the first king. One could see that it was true because the depression is there. In fact the dancing bit first entered into the relevant account *as an addition*, once the "explanation" for the depression had been found.

(c) Capturing the Information Flows

One result of a better understanding of what a corpus is and how it contains information is that this can now be used to plan the collection of information. In cases where traditions are being collected that anyone can tell and know, the problem is to know where to begin and where to stop. In principle all known versions of a tradition should be collected, but it is obviously impossible to gather all the performances, even less all potential performances. One can, however, establish, after some pilot trials, what the main factors of contemporary variation are. In general one will take into account what the frequency and density of intercommunity relationships were, what their nature was (trade, religion, kin, marriage, political, etc.), and where the historical sites were located. In addition, relevant specialties and nonlocal groups such as kinship groupings, classes, and age grades also are taken note of. A pilot study across these categories will indicate which general patterns of variation (for instance, in tales) occurred as well as which patterns were limited to particular traditional types. In this way an understanding of the corpus helps the collection of data. This is also essential to answer a key question: How independent are the sources?

## (3) The Interdependence of Traditions

On the basis of his experience with the Ilongot in the Phillipines, R. Rosaldo claimed that "oral sources can best be interpreted by using convergent lines of evidence, and not through internal criticism of single testimonies. This principle involves assembling all the possible reports on a single incident."[22] Again, P. Thompson, in his *The Voice of the Past*, recommends mass collection of similar data, so that the interview almost becomes a questionnaire. The results cross-check one another, and we need no further rules of evidence. This reminds one of a dispute between "Ancients and Moderns." Historians of the contemporary world drown in documents. They have such masses that they find it is best to go over the contents of each document and to look for confirmation or contraindications. The problems sort themselves out. All they need from the rules of evidence is what applies to whole classes of data: vital records, censuses, police records, and others. This approach works for most cases most of the time. Their sources are independent and can confirm or contradict. Medievalists and ancient historians, however, have very few documents and have to wring the last ounce of information out of them. So they apply the rules of evidence, especially those of internal critique, to the hilt. Oral historians working with a relatively recent past, in which the majority of data stem from narrative reminiscences, which are not yet standardized nor widely spread as information throughout the community, can use the approach recommended by Thompson and Rosaldo—up to a point. But most research dealing with oral tradition cannot, because the sources are no longer independent. They do not "confirm."

The pool of information kept in memory and its relatively free flow mean that we cannot assume that the testimony of two different informants from the same community or even society is really independent. This is very important. In history, proof is given only when two independent sources confirm the same event or situation,[23] but this proof cannot be given under most conditions from oral sources alone. Independent confirmation is proof because the chances of two accounts relating the same event or situation by accident are almost nil. If they do, it must be because the data were really there. If only one witness is available, the event or situation may have been invented, or misrepresented beyond recognition. From what we have just stated, it is not possible to do this with oral tradition wherever a corpus exists and information flows are unstemmed (i.e., in most cases). Feedback and contamination are the norm. The further one goes away from the present the more this rule holds. It holds already for most renderings purporting to deal with the past beyond the lives of the living elders in a community.

This becomes true to such a degree that when one does find converging evidence in such traditions one must assume that they are dependent on each other, that they are renderings of a single tradition. A. Delivré first proposed this rule after his study of Malagasy traditions.[24] No one will consider the three synoptic Gospels as independent sources, even though they have different authors. The resemblances between them are too great, both overall and in detail, to conclude anything else but that they stemmed from one single oral milieu, from one corpus in one community. Once this is realized, it is easy to see that it also applies to John, the fourth Gospel, in those parts that agree with the others. This situation is the norm with oral traditions. We should merely add that to give proof of independence is to prove a negative, a nonevent, which is in any case notoriously difficult. Except for the rarest of cases, we will find that messages from oral tradition are interdependent, when they relate to the same events or situations. We dare not even claim that unconscious evidence can confirm conscious and intentional history, as in the case of Pueblo Indians entering the house through the roof. It is probable that the conscious account borrowed this detail from a tale where it was noticed or the reverse: a smart performer creating *couleur locale*. In such an instance we would rather remove the item from our list of unconscious evidence.

What is there then to do? The historian should attempt to complete his oral sources by outside sources that can be checked and certified as independent. This means that oral tradition is to be used in conjunction with writings, archaeology, linguistic or even ethnographic evidence, etc. It can confirm the other sources and be confirmed by it. This does not mean then that a written source is *a priori* better than an oral one. It does not mean that oral sources are useless when they are confirmed by writing, because in this case, the written document is also confirmed by the oral data. It means that, when a written document and a tradition converge, both are part of the proof. The evidence now is of a wholly different order of plausibility than if just one of the two were available.

As long as traditions are not independently confirmed the evidence they present can best be described as "on probation." Such evidence is not worthless. It has a certain plausibility and forms a hypothesis that should be tested first, before any other hypothesis is considered. A body of tradition thus becomes an agenda for research.[25]

## II. The Corpus as Remembered over Time

Memory constantly acts unconsciously and perhaps very slowly on the dormant data it contains. But the activity of recall and the encoding into memory of what one hears are obviously the main moments when the dynamics of memory operate. Traditions are memories of memories. For each rendering they must be presented and they are then encoded again by listeners as well as by performers. Traditions presuppose the slow remodeling of memory as well as reasonably frequent, more dynamic reorganizations. That this is collective memory is important. To a point all memory is collective,[26] but memories of traditions are especially so since different people hear a single rendering and may or may not render it later themselves. Indeed the earlier performer often is the later listener. This collective character is important also in that it implies a faster pace of remolding of dormant data in memory. Memory changes over time, even when dormant, because of the constant input of new items in memory which must coexist with older material and force its reappraisal, its reorganization, and, in the case of repetitive events, its disappearance. Such inputs are greater in collective memory than in individual memory, at least with regard to tradition. The memory of oral tradition is more dynamic at all times than individual memory.

This has effects on the corpus. We should first remember that the corpus is not truly homogeneous over time. In the first chapter, I described how several modes of transmission exist. Memorized speech should be remembered by rote and is affected differently by the dynamics of memory than the subset dealing with truth, where faithfulness, however defined, is a condition of reproduction. Narrative without this condition will alter differently (and faster). Then there are the cumulative genres such as lists, the memory of rituals that are added to over time, and genealogies. These can only be composite and *have to change* over time in order to be correct. At any moment in time the corpus of any community is in fact not totally homogeneous either. Information over time therefore tends to flow differently in different channels even though cross flow to other channels is common at all times, hindered only here and there by the partial barriers of esoteric knowledge, genre, and the like. This reminder is useful at this point because the first topic to be discussed here is structuralism, and structuralists assume that in addition to its large size the corpus (of narrative at least) is totally homogeneous.

I must first discuss the structuralist belief that the effects of structuring in tradition, which are quite visible, are due, not to the dynamics of memory, but to other processes they ascribe to the human mind. Only when the claims and procedures of structuralism have been considered can I then turn to structuring and its consequences, and how historians can cope with them.

## (1) The Fallacy of Structuralism

(a) Assumptions and Theory

Structuralists hold that structuring is found in bodies of narratives because the human mind, at least the untutored mind, makes myths (symbolic constructs) when it is not otherwise engaged.[27] The corpus or pool for such thought is very large and completely homogeneous, so that C. Lévi-Strauss can find a portion of a symbolic train of reasoning in California or Oregon and another in Central Brazil. The pool is only limited by the necessity of some common historical origin, and all American Indians have a common origin. The human mind communicates hidden messages through structured symbolism which are painful basic truths about the human condition, literally matters of life and death, nature and culture. Such a symbolic message always starts by posing a fundamental painful paradox through opposition, and then proceeds to lessen the gap between its terms by proposing other sets of opposition which are linked by transformation to the first. Thus cooked food :: raw food is a transformation of nature :: culture. In the end the oppositions are not abolished but minimized, and mediating images appear. Thus "grilled meat" may be a mediator perhaps itself opposed to "fried slices of cassava."[28] Such myths reach no conclusion because there is no true solution for the grand human conundrums. The reason that this whole communication must remain veiled is that it would be too painful for conscious discussion. This is a Freudian explanation. Structuralists, then, deal with messages of the unconscious and have links with artistic movements in literature and painting that attempt to tap the unconscious. They conceive the mind by analogy to be a machine, they work with a binary code of opposites, and they do not link symbolizing to human memory at all.

Critics will point out at this level that corpuses are not as homogeneous as was thought, that the Freudian analogy of the human mind as a machine that could generate excess energy which had to be disposed of has now been disproved, and, since the analogy is basic, that its conclusions are now invalid as they stand. Symbolizing is best explained as a use of mnemonic capacity and coding in creative ways.[29] Items will now be recalled not according to cues or tags as the mnemonic code would require, but according to other properties of the tags, for instance, by color, fragrance, or some other accessory property. Symbolizing is an activity just as remembering is, but an activity aimed not at recall but at the generation of new knowledge through reasoning by analogy. Critics reject the rigid logic that flows from the concatenation of opposites and which according to Lévi-Strauss shows the laws of human thought. They claim that Lévi-Strauss has not proved this in his work, nor has any other structuralist succeeded in doing so. They claim that the operational procedures of structuralists rest only on associations made by the researcher and valid only for him. The procedures are not scientific, as they cannot be replicated—or falsified—by others.[30] We must therefore examine the procedure of structural analysis more closely, to establish whether this critique is justified. If it is, then structuralism fails, whatever its assumptions.

(b) Procedure of Analysis

As a set of operations the procedures involved use only oppositions, excluding all other properties of relationships construed by the mind.[31] They can be presented as follows:

(1) Set up oppositions between symbols in a text so that their *relationship* yields a meaning. The closer the overall similiarity between the images opposed, the clearer the relationship and the more elegant the meaning. Thus "cat":"wild cat" is much better than "pig":"hippopotamus" even though both refer to the opposition domestic/wild.

(2) Set up equivalences between oppositions so that a:b and c:d can now be written as a:c :: b:d. Thus nature:wild cat :: culture:cat or more creatively: hippopotamus:wild cat :: pig:cat.

(3) Parallels of equivalences yield transformations. If a:c :: b:d but e:f :: b:d then a:c can be replaced by e:f. Fowl:guinea fowl :: pig:hippopotamus as cat:wild cat :: pig:hippopotamus, since all oppose domestic animals to wild animals of the same categories.

(4) Use one or more different narratives to build up sequences of oppositions through transformation that will yield new lines of inquiry—fowls differ from cats as birds from mammals—and establish lines where mediating oppositions occur. If this analysis dealt with the Tio of Brazzaville, we would introduce the crane *nkwũũ* in the wild with its wings intact opposed to *nkwũũ* in the village with its wings cropped, waiting to be eaten—domestic for a time—and oppose it to fowl:guinea fowl. In Europe we might go from opposition between marine fish:sweet water fish to oppose further: fish in pond:fish in aquarium, for example.

The end product of such analyses should be the full explanation of the text chosen first and ideally of all the narratives in the corpus. During analysis the corpus remains open and one can draw on symbols from other realms such as ritual or art.

Given the above and the practice by structuralists, the limiting rules of these procedures are:

(1) Comparison involves only oppositions.

(2) No triads or higher order sets are allowed, only binary opposition.

(3) All equations ·must be symmetrical. Elegance dictates the choice between opposites and between sets of equivalences.

(4) Any opposition or transformation that denies an opposition or contradicts the basic paradox is *ipso facto* invalid. Thus, sun:Venus :: great fire:small fire and moon:Venus :: great fire:small fire, but sun = moon is invalid.

(5) All data must stem from a single historical whole.[32]

It should be noticed that connections between images can be made on the basis of properties of the signifiers (images) or through the signifieds (meanings). In addition, there is no limit to the choice of symbols in a narrative; one may very well choose images that are not obvious and predominant in a narrative.

Reasoning in structural analysis is by analogy and aims to convince as the progression requirements in procedures indicate.

Analogical reasoning is neither truly deductive nor hypothetico-deductive. The procedures are not replicable. For instance, the North American Indian tale of the Star Husband has been analyzed seven times with seven different results.[33] The procedures lead to no clear point and do not bring problems into focus. This is shown by a reexamination of the famous story of Asdiwal, famous because it was the first demonstration of structuralist analysis by Lévi-Strauss. It is said to lack ethnographic evidence about the Tsimshian (Northwest Canada) so that unwarranted generalizations occur. Data are occasionally misrepresented, the analysis fails to account for the data, and readers do not know what the author precisely asserts, nor what he wants to prove.[34] Furthermore, analyses proceed from a *text*, one version of a message being equal to any other. This can be defended, but the examination of one version to the exclusion of others is not defensible. Last, but not least, the analyses cannot be falsified because ethnographic validity is irrelevant, the discourse being unconscious. Whether members of the culture involved approve or not is irrelevant. All that can be verified is whether the images used actually occur in the text. What one makes of them is arbitrary and cannot be falsified.

Beyond the critique one can make of the assumptions and goals of structuralism, its procedures are also invalid. They are neither replicable nor falsifiable and therefore they cannot be scholarly. Despite their pseudological presentation such analyses are in fact creative discourses, valid only to the mind that creates them, aiming at conviction not at proof.[35]

## (2) Structuring

Just as any message is structured, if only for the needs of communication, so too are bodies of tradition. The very existence of cycles in tales is an indication of this. Thus we have the cycle of the fox in Europe, Raven in Northwest America, and the hare in East Africa. These characters have attracted all sorts of tales that involved other characters, animals or not. Human tricksters—such as Samandari in Burundi, Tooml Lakwey among the Kuba, and Tyl Uilenspiegel in the Netherlands and Germany—also have become the focus of cycles. In epic a central figure is the magnet that attracts anecdotal scrap metal from everywhere. These are all clear examples of reorganization of information in the mind.

Structuring is, however, particularly clear in the subcorpus of historical accounts, where it has often been demonstrated.[36] One wonders how this is possible, as individual anecdotes in such accounts are performed separately, never as one big account, unlike the epic, where general performances are common. So how can structuration occur? The case of Rwanda helps to make the point. Here the adventures of different kings are all separate anecdotes. For many kings there are different anecdotes which are not performed as one account.[37] Yet all of the *ibitéekerezo* together are structured, first by reign—the implied sequence—and then by type of king. Royal names succeed one another in a cycle of four and to each name is attributed a special fate: Thus, A conquers, B is unlucky, C prospers, and D is a legislator. The attribution of regnal names and part of the stereotyping are precolonial, since they occur in dynastic poetry, which can be assigned to the eighteenth century at the latest, and they are reflected in the royal rituals.[38] So despite the mode of performing there is a consciousness of all these accounts as a whole, and dynastic poetry does handle them as a whole. Structuring is a fact, and it is shown that people reflect on the whole amount of information they have and not just one that is given in any performance. This is so even when they resist performances that will develop the whole cycle at once, and even though they do not recall at any one moment all of the information from all of the accounts.

Is this due to a mystical property of the mind seeking its own discourse? Hardly. It results from the dynamics of memory, from the continuing activity of collective memory as new inputs occur, and as material is remembered, transmitted, and remembered again.[39] There is no single collective brain at work here, but there is a collective memory and it is at work. As E. Leach demonstrated with regard to the Tudor dynasty in Britain, it works by selection. He showed how a student could remember the succession by opposing the figures of Henry VII and Elizabeth and then fitting in Edward, Mary, and Henry VIII. He hits the nail on the head when he states that a myth is the sum of the development of historical tradition.[40] He shows, not that all students of Tudor rulers would do this, but rather what sorts of principles of selection are involved.

That this structuring has to do with memory is directly shown by the observation that recent material—disconnected historical gossip, reminiscences, and the like—is much less subject to structuring than materials that are old in the collective memory.

The importance of restructuring to historians should be obvious. Data are discarded, meaning is added to other data, secondary causations are denied, and time sequences severed. Material can be transposed from one setting to another, rearranged "logically" by topic, or condensed. Just the listing of the effects of such a process shows how important it is to understand how the process operates, what its signs are, what it touches, and what it leaves untouched.

## (3) Structuring of Narrative Accounts

Restructuring affects narratives most, and it affects the subcorpus of historical accounts (narratives deemed to be true) most because such accounts are all part of the same discourse. Logically such traditions belong together and they are together in memory. A first task of any study is to establish how far structuring has gone. Disconnected short items of rather recent information are untouched. Historical gossip is typical of this. It remains atomized in a mass of short, matter of fact utterances—such as "X married Y" or "village A was once on yonder ridge" —and most of it deals with small groups only and with a time not very far from the present. Most of this information may be discarded from memory several generations later. It is definitely not structured. The second task is to examine the different versions in the body of recorded accounts. Where versions are few and standardized, as in most traditions of genesis, the mnemonic process has gone a long way, especially when the tradition is widely known. The narrative has reached the point where stability reveals that structuring has achieved its purpose: to make the account most significant and most memorable. When versions flourish, and not for obvious social uses only, it means that mnemonic processes are still at work and so far have only had a limited impact on the tradition. Indeed it is often possible to see in what direction the achievement of greater significance through structuring will lie. Lastly, an assessment of restructuring will take into account how long the tradition supposedly has been memorized. This will be imprecise, both because the measurement of time is far from perfect and because the dynamics of memory do not work at a steady pace. But there exists a rough and ready correspondence. One will expect traditions that purport to be five generations old or more to be more affected by the dynamics of memory than those that refer only to two generations ago. There may or may not be a threshold for ruthless restructuring of a given account.

We saw that the Hopi example in chapter one was restructured half a century or so after the event, but we don't know how it would look a century later. One can, however, reasonably suspect that a major process of selection and structuration occurs in the first and second generations of transmission, when most information is discarded and the selected remnant integrated with older traditions. Another Hopi tradition supports the notion that structuring is very slow after the initial period. Narratives about the coming of the Spaniards in the 1630s were only recorded in 1902 and later. Comparison with the written records of the seventeenth century shows that they have been restructured in the same way and to about the same extent that the tale about the Navaho raid was restructured. It looks as if structuring stopped here a generation after 1680 when the last events mentioned in the narratives occurred.[41]

Structuring is recognized when definite patterns appear in the subcorpus. One which exists nearly everywhere is the existence of a "floating gap." There are many accounts for very recent times, tapering off as one goes farther back until one reaches times of origin for which, once again, there are many accounts.

This profile has been compared to an hourglass. At the junction of times of origin and the very sparse subsequent records, there usually is a chronological gap. It is called "floating" because over time it tends to advance towards the present, that is, the oldest accounts of later times tend to be forgotten or else amalgamated with later or earlier materials. The presence of founding heroes is another sign of structuring. So is the presence of epochs—the imposition of units of sequence, such as reigns in kingdoms, a succession of different creations, or any other. The clearest patterning occurs when different figures with different attributes follow each other in order, and/or when anecdotes are grouped by topic, each topic forming a set or alternating with others in the record.

Consider, for instance, the traditions of Buganda: The first king, Kintu ("the thing"), comes from the east and from heaven, founds the kingdom, and ultimately disappears from remorse over having killed a lover of his wife. One of his two sons disappears as well. His remaining son, Cwa, succeeds to the throne, falsely charges his own son Kalemera of adultery with his wife, and sends Kalemera into exile to the west. Returning from exile, Kalemera dies on the journey. Meanwhile, Cwa also disappears, fearing a return of Kintu. The Ganda then appoint a regent and later another, but when they hear about Kalemera's son, born in exile in the west, they accept him. This is Kimera. Kimera creates offices and an administration, and lives in a number of capitals. He sends someone to the east on an expedition for cattle. The man dies on the road, and his son, holding King Kimera responsible, kills him. The murderer, Tembo, becomes king. Tembo's sister becomes pregnant by the person who would be the next king, thus tying this in with the next reign. After his sister's adventures, Tembo becomes a lunatic and dies.

Notice first how in each sequence, for each king, there is a link to the successor. The whole of this, and indeed four more reigns, fit into one coherent narrative. Notice the pattern. The most obvious is Kintu from the east, founder of the kingdom, who disappeared, and Kimera from the west, founder of the institutions of the kingdom, who was killed. The sequence of

Kintu runs to the arrival of Kimera, for he plays a role in the end of Cwa's reign. Cwa parallels Kintu in the adultery stories: one real adultery, the other a false one; one a disappearance caused by adultery, the other a disappearance unconnected to adultery. It is also obvious that Tembo parallels Kimera. Kimera was a rightful heir in exile who became king; Tembo was a rebel. Kimera was murdered; Tembo becomes mad. If we just look at the end of reign, we find Kintu and Cwa disappear, the regents are deposed, Kimera is murdered, Tembo becomes mad, his successor retires in old age, and the next one is killed by an illness from the sky. The old predecessor returns and dies in office of extreme old age. The next two kings are both killed in war in parallel circumstances, and, with the death of the second ruler, the first dynasty ends.

R. Atkinson followed up these patterns and others (illicit sex is prominent in many anecdotes) and documents the full extent of the structuring. Unfortunately, he interprets the content away in structuralist fashion.[42] The actual unraveling of the processes that have been at work here, if still possible, remains to be done. While we can see that severe selection has occurred because so few topics remain, we cannot say more. Historically, so far all we know from this is that there was a first dynasty unrelated to the next one and that the land was defeated by attacks from the west. That all the topics have to do with the nature of royal power and with succession to royal office is clear, but it is little. More study could probably better clarify the principles of selection. In this case some of the narrative unification of these accounts may have occurred as the result of a mixed transmission involving writing and tradition. It is unclear how much of all of this was, formerly, performed at one session.

The example makes the point as to how structuring can be recognized by patterns. What happens is selection and reordering. The selection occurs on the basis of what is important in the *present* (i.e.,the time when selection occurs) social and cultural environment, and this can and should be expected to change over time, forcing further rearrangements. Thus, in passing remarks F. Eggan notes that the Hopi reworked some traditions after c. 1856 when the Horn phratry had ousted the Snake phratry from rule at First Mesa. The Horn phratry now moved to third or fourth place in the origin story of the arrival of clans, and their mythical arrival was dramatized. They brought the Flute ceremony and hence control over rain, a skill of great value in the arid lands of the Hopi.[43]

The restructuring itself involves regrouping data by topic through fusion, as when all inventions are attributed to cultural heroes,[44] or involves patterned redistribution, as in the case of the early Ganda royal adultery motifs. Sequential order is imposed and the ordering made easier to remember by patterning successive accounts in one of the basic ways in which the mind patterns—by oppositions, or by strong sequential association. Well-known properties of memory come into play as well. The most important one is that memory of a concrete item is much better than of an abstract item. A concrete item can be visualized and hence can be doubly coded where otherwise only one bond exists.[45] It is easier to remember images or clichés than the concepts they stand for. This may explain why images and clichés become more and more prominent over time. Another reason for this is that images allow greater condensation of material than any other means do: they are the ultimate in fusion. Repetition and irregularity are difficult to remember, the one because later incidents tend to fuse with earlier ones, while irregularity —as in the sequence of royal names—is illogical. Patterning will do away with them first, unless strong mnemonic countermeasures are taken, such as to attach the name of a successor to that of a predecessor. Numbers are a casualty in all this. They are both abstract and repetitive, so that they fare badly in all traditions and are stereotyped to numbers meaning "perfect," "many," "few," "sinister," etc. Finally there is the known tendency of the mind in memory to construct a coherent discourse.[46] This leads to structuring of the same topics over and over again so that they become more meaningful in terms of the worldview of the culture in question. The Ganda material cited is an excellent example. Everything hangs together with everything else. There are no loose ends anymore, and few topics (such as the mention of a cattle raid) remain haphazard at all. All in all the dynamic of memory acts so strongly on older traditions that they become excellent material for studies of human memory and of the workings of the mind.

## (4) Effects of Structuring

The effects of restructuring can be devastating to historical information. Temporal transpositions are frequent, fusion prevents one from disentangling the original elements that were fused, selection discards data, and secondary causes are eliminated by sequential reordering and by the operation of the cultural ideas of causality. What value, then, can such accounts still have for historians? First, it is good to realize that the picture I have sketched here is rather extreme. In reality, irregularities survive and are indications that certain anecdotes may well have a foundation in the past. Then, we should be careful in establishing patterns, and be certain that we do not create them where they do not exist. Where they do exist, they are not always due to the dynamics of memory. Founders of kingdoms tend to be strong personalities and warriors. Their successors tend to be organizers, administrators, and lawgivers. The Tudor example of a strong king with many wives (Henry VIII), succeeded by the feeble boy without wives (Edward), then by the weak woman with a powerful husband (Mary), and then by the strong queen with no husband (Elizabeth), is a real one! Even if it came to be simplified as strong king with wives is succeeded by strong queen without husband, we would lose some history, but the remainder would still be largely true. In short, one reasons that those attributes given to persons in a succession of accounts do correspond to some reality in the past for the key figures. That they have attracted episodes from other circumstances and influence one another by stressing similarities and contrasts, there is no doubt. But the interpretation a historian gives for each case must be grounded on the discussion of all the details of that case. Beyond this we should recognize that patterned data are weaker than any other in oral tradition and should not be used as underpinning for major historical reconstruction.

Careful examination of data allows one to recover quite an amount of evidence in the end.[47] After all, much can be said about Buganda, starting with the second dynasty, even if we can only say for the earlier period that some sort of chieftaincy then existed.

The main difficulty in coping with materials of this kind is one of balance. Just as it is easy to read nonexisting patterns into a record when one is bent on finding patterning, it is also easy to somehow recuperate every last bit of information which the accounts offer when one wants to fill voids of ignorance about the past. Consciously or not, one wants to prove, and the temptation to argue beyond what the evidence really warrants is equally strong in either direction. Lastly, I should remind the reader that the strong impacts of collective memory are typical for old bodies of material, but that these constitute only a small portion of extant oral traditions. The problem hardly appears for data that are less than a few generations old.

## III. Chronology and Information Remembered

Messages are ephemeral and traditions inchoate. Each culture has its own notions of time, and calendars do not exist in oral society. We cannot date the depth of a tradition in any direct way, we can only date the recording of a performance or of testimony by an informant. How then are we to establish chronology? Chronology is essential to history. History deals with chains of change, that is, not with change as a fact only, but with change as the result of preceding situations leading to later situations, change as a product of causality. The only law historians have is that what occurred later cannot have influenced what occurred earlier.[48] So history must have chronology. Chronology need not be based on an absolute calendar, it can be a relative sequence of events and situations only. But chronology there must be, if there is to be history. I examine in sequence, first, how time is measured in oral societies and therefore expressed in tradition, then, how memory deals with sequence, and, lastly, which oral sources could be used to establish chronology and how.

## (1) Measurement of Time

The cardinal directions of time everywhere are "before" and "after," and all grammars express this as a more or less important aspect of action. Absolute measurements of time on a uniform scale existed nowhere in oral society. Time was measured by the return of natural phenomena, by the occurrence of extraordinary events, by reference to human lifespan and reproduction, and by reference to the return of recurrent social events.

Ecological time deals with recurrent natural phenomena, such as the day, the moon, the season, and the year. An accurate count of such units did not go very far in the absence of writing or when mnemotechnic means were not used. These are repetitive durations and memory cannot cope well with their numbering. At best one remembered the two, three, or four seasons in a year and combined that memory with that of a few years past. One could be more precise and go further where months, days, or years were named, as lists are easier to cope with than mere numbers (they are less abstract). Naming these was not very common. In fact we have but a rare instance, that of the Himba of southern Angola.[49] For days we find the use of names where there were weeks, as the first to third or so day before or after a market, or another special recurrent day. The units were culturally determined. Some count the day as a twenty-four-hour period beginning at sundown, others as a twelve-hour day beginning at sunrise, others in still different ways. Seasons are not obvious either. The Ainu knew only two seasons a year, even though others in their neighborhood counted four.[50]

Ecological time was usually associated with some activity, although it need not be. In medieval Dutch the names of the months tell what the typical farming activities were. Subdivisions of day or night may not be obviously based on activities, such as the time to bring the cows home or the time to go to the fields, but they are linked to these, and only the time of sleep was eventually divided into a period or two that had no activity correlated.[51]

Extraordinary events, usually calamities which disrupted life, were a second mode of reckoning. One would say: before the drought, volcanic eruption, earthquake, epidemic, forest fire, comet, eclipse, or after. Each community had its own calendar of events, and historians usually can array them in relative order, often by comparison with genealogical data.[52] Sometimes such events were named, sometimes not.[53] When they were not named and calamities were recurrent, such as droughts or epidemics, they would be fused, and in later times remembrance would be of one eclipse or one drought instead of many. Even when they were named it was not always easy to place events exactly as before, or after. One could still confuse them. In the majority of cases the rough calendar made up by these did not reach far into the past, perhaps no further back than a generation or two. Cultural representations played their role. Here eclipses were omens, and there not. One famine might count and the next not. So without outside data one cannot *a priori* fix exactly what such events should have been in any community.

Then, and this is universal, there was calculation by age, relative age, and age of descendants, parents, or friends. This is the dating "When I was a young boy," "Between my marriage and the birth of my first child," etc. Such data organized in domestic genealogies allow one to designate and estimate time for a lifespan, but often in increasingly vaguer ways as one moves back in time. Beyond two or three generations this becomes "in the time of so-and-so" and even this reference is vague in relation to others.[54]

The fourth system was based on recurrent social events such as markets, boys' initiations, annual harvesting ritual, initiation of age grades and the like, investitures to office, and movements from one site to another where villagers practiced shifting cultivation. These could all be used for talking about time and measuring it, even though such units would represent disparate lengths of time (just as with those we have already described), except for the ecological ones. It was rare to actually calculate the length of any of these units. The Romans might say: "In the xth year of Emperor N when X and Y were consuls," but they had writing. In oral societies one avoided numbers to remember and usually the exact length of time of such units was not all that important. If it was, one would expect mnemotechnic counts to keep track.

As we have seen, to every social organization there corresponds a time frame. Such a frame could be as short as two generations or even one generation,[55] or attain a depth of thirty or even sixty generations (Polynesia, Hadiya, Fang), or be as long as a given kingdom lasted. Beyond the limits of structural time, however, there was no measurement of time possible, except to distinguish an era of creation or of origins from other times so as to link the measurement of time to the prevailing worldview.

## (2) Memory Organizes Sequences

Memory reorganizes the data it contains. It will put these in a sequential order which resembles an expression of measured duration but in fact is a creation of memory: the epoch. It places events or situations in one time frame or another and sometimes transposes them, which constitutes an anachronism. Epochs are sequences imposed by memory.[56] They are sets of traditions as they have been arranged in memory, even though often they look as if they are based on measurements of time current in society. For instance, in kingdoms most epochs are reigns. What makes these units epochs and shows mnemonic interference is the necessity for memory to relate all remembered accounts to an epoch; hence for a kingdom everything is expressed as "in the reign of so-and-so," for which, given the tendency to personalize, the ruler becomes very soon responsible. We then hear: "King so-and-so invented the cultivation of maize." So "epochs" tend to restructure.

In time epochs become too numerous and must be bundled together in fewer sequences. They must also relate to basic views about origins. Hence we have eras, and the last one is the only one that retains its subdivisions by epoch. Where there are but two eras, creation and historic time, they are not necessarily seen as successive. Among the Lugbara (Zaire/Uganda) and the Trobrianders (Melanesia) these durations exist side by side.[57] Indeed, a major personage in Lugbara creation is a British District Officer from the turn of the century. As an example of how epochs tend to become lost one can cite the three Rwandan eras: the first of creation, the second "of the belt," the third of "later kings." In the first two, names for epochs have been kept as names of rulers, but they are only symbolic and no Rwandan would recognize them as names for real rulers.[58] This becomes like a genealogy and is very similar to those cultures where genealogical trees have become a measure of epoch. In Polynesia as well as in Africa, they then begin with the era of creation to move over into our era, but often without any indication of change at all. In such cases there is no concept of separate eras.

Memory also causes anachronisms. In the reordering of topics accounts from a later period are placed with those of earlier times and vice versa.[59] A clear example is that of the Mbundu account of migration marked by events arranged according to where each occurred, regardless of the chronological order in which these events took place, because the main sequence arranged the places according to an imagined and false line of migrations.[60] Here sequencing is the cause of the anachronism. Often the epochs are in a correct order but accounts have been transposed from one to the other, as when the Assiniboine ascribe the introduction of the horse to the era of creation and not to the eighteenth century.

Aging of events or situations to make them more important is well known to Europeans, for whom time legitimizes and creates importance, so that the usual understanding of anachronism refers to items "ascending" through time. But as A. Delivré has best shown, there also exist "descending anachronisms" in which events or situations are made younger. In the dynamics of transposition the age credited to an item is usually less important than the proper bundling of items in an epoch. If the epoch is based on the term of office of a distinct person, the bundling relates to his or her personality. One may well suspect that unsuccessful wars in early Rwandan history have been moved from whatever reign they occurred in to one of a Mibambwe king. Kings with this regnal name were tragic figures who sacrificed themselves (who were injured) on the battlefield to gain ultimate victory through their sacrifice.[61] We cannot assume that the transposition always went from a later date to an earlier one.

In order to arrive at a relative chronology, all one can do is to test the consistency of the temporal progressions of data as given by the traditional accounts. If they are consistent, transpositions in sequences of epochs and eventual anachronisms will not be detected. If they are not, anachronisms can be spotted.[62] Delivré has used this technique tellingly for the corpus of Merina historical accounts. If, for instance, a certain king introduced the poison oracle as a practice, a later king cannot, without contradiction, be said to have done the same. The historian who knows that poison oracles are complex institutions knows that no single king-epoch could have introduced them in their now familiar form. The conquest of a province as reported must fit with the conquest of other provinces or an anachronism is suspected. Internal consistency does not however prove the absence of anachronisms. The whole consistent pattern may have developed as a principle of selection, retention, and ordering in the collective memory. When anachronisms are suspected they often cannot be proven. All the method can do is to raise the plausibility of a reconstruction. It does not prove.

## (3) Sources for Dating: Lists and Genealogies

When Djasjini, the Hopi man who was an eyewitness to the events he recounted, was asked when it happened he replied: "A long time ago, maybe a hundred years, who knows? It is not well to count the years, it makes us old."[63] Unfortunately, this attitude towards chronology is found in many oral cultures. In most circumstances precise indications of time are not valued and the only sources that do provide a chronology of sorts—lists and genealogies—are tied to specific social institutions or to the blueprint of social relationships which exists in the minds of members. Their existence does not presuppose any particular concern for chronology as a goal in itself.

Historians then can only use lists and genealogies to establish first relative sequence and eventually absolute chronology. Lists and genealogies are sources of a particular kind. They are cumulative, having never been composed at a particular moment. Whenever a change took place, it was supposed to be added to the source. Sometimes this occurred in a formal way, at least for lists of offices, when a new officer was installed. Thus the Kuba king and the female official *mbaan* gave a full recitation of their predecessors as part of the ceremonies of their installation. The other one hundred or so Kuba officials did not do so. Their informally remembered lists of predecessors were very short indeed when compared to that of the *mbaan*. As to genealogies, they were not performed, however important they might be. They were discussed when the need arose, invariably in practical circumstances where kinship or the degree of kinship mattered, and they were kept up to date besides by news or gossip as to who had been born and who had died. Recordkeeping of genealogies, and also of many lists, was then not nearly as meticulous as the historians who have to use them would like. These sources need therefore to be discussed further and, as lists and genealogies have different characteristics, I deal with them separately.

(a) Lists
J. Goody has convincingly shown that list keeping in general is a habit of literate people, a practice made easy by writing technology. It is not something that comes easily to oral cultures,[64] but oral lists are kept when they have a social meaning, though they are never very long. If they were, one would suspect backfeeding from writings. Among such lists, those of calamities are a special case. I do not know of any society in which they are kept. They are not used to make epochs, but people know about successions of calamities (named droughts, for instance), even though their sequence is not always secure. So historians have constructed such lists in sequential order by deriving chronological indications from their mention in connection with genealogies or other lists. They do so to use this material to establish crossties between different local relative sequences and thereby secure regional chronologies. Because calamities are not remembered as lists and in so far as they may be repetitive, confusions are frequent. One drought becomes two or two one depending

on the names given. If the same drought is given two different names in neighboring societies, it is often seen as two droughts by the historian who establishes the list. A second difficulty comes from the fact that droughts are not mnemonic sequences, that is, temporal tags attached to particular accounts. If a calamity is mentioned in an account, we can use it, but we cannot ask whether an event happened before or after a given calamity. When we do this, we invite the informant to speculate, because this is not in his tradition. In the best of cases the informant remembers an account that involves the calamity, and then, by the epoch structure of traditions, is able to place the calamity in relation to the other account about which he is asked. Even that can only be accepted if the whole reasoning involved is explained. As a rule then a list of calamities, even when in correct sequence, will only date the accounts in which they are a topic.

Among other lists we should mention first those of age grades. These are kept in societies where age grades are the basis of political organization so that particular age mates move from one set of roles and duties to the next as the result of initiations bringing them into the next age grade. In such a society lists of age grades make sense. The oldest living members will still remember those that were the oldest at the time when they went into their first initiation and even those of their own grandparents. When the initiation intervals are long this yields a chronology which can run over a century and a half.[65] The age grades being names, often according to principles which relate to their succession, are remembered in correct sequence. They are amenable to translation into an absolute chronology, once a date of initiation is known from writing. Then one can calculate backwards. This is possible because the initiations occur regularly—say, every eight years or so. Even if the regularity is not quite perfect, still the tie between initiation and a portion of a lifespan (a biological measurement) means that the intervals will not fluctuate widely.

The situation is not so favorable with other lists. Lists that are not used as epochs, such as the Kuba *mbaan* lists, are unimportant except perhaps for the first and last names: the first to establish the link with the office which was then created and the last to prove regular succession. In the middle, one can omit or add names, without any consequences resulting. Such lists tend to be unusable. No accounts are associated with them, and in many cases they simply cannot be trusted unless cross-checked (for instance, with genealogical data), to provide the true chronology. Lists that are used as measures of sequence, such as regnal lists, seem at first to offer better conditions. These are often bases for epochs and could be used for relative chronology, but their critical appraisal is necessary. First, it must be determined whether the order of names given can be trusted. This is most reliable when each name also refers to one next to it. Thus "B son of A" and "C son of B" establish solid links between names. When no such connection exists the links are less solid. How solid they are can be found by an examination of many versions of the lists involved, where discrepancies often appear. When the same name is repeated anywhere in a list transposition or even elision easily occurs. Transposition of blocks of names is not uncommon, especially in the middle part of a list, which is also the part most affected by variation.[66] In practice, comparison of versions usually allows one to establish a list which seems correct by finding out why other versions vary.

If the order is reliable, there still is a question as to the number of names. D. Henige, who wrote the standard work entitled *The Chronology of Oral Tradition*, has documented many reasons for lengthening or shortening such lists. They are often tampered with, and, because they are lists, they also tend to be unstable remembrances. The particular use of such lists, the prestige of time, the status or illustriousness of officers and the presence or absence of descendants are among the main reasons why such lists are consciously tampered with.[67] Tampering and instability in remembering, however, tend not to affect all versions equally, and in most cases it is possible to reestablish a minimum number of names with a fair plausibility.

Once a list has been found reliable as to number and order of names, and if it is used as a means of sequencing the tradition, it will serve for relative chronology. But despite many attempts to the contrary, it cannot be converted to absolute dating. The temporal units involved vary from a day to a century, that is, they encompass a whole human lifespan. With such variability it is illusory to even attempt to give averages, even though the nature of the office (hereditary, elected, a combination of both, primogeniture, ultimogeniture, succession by brothers, etc.) can give indications as to what one can expect by way of extremes for a given list. Over time these factors change themselves, and hence we cannot even calculate "weighted" averages over long periods of time. It is better to acknowledge imprecision and use the relative chronology as is, rather than to attempt a spurious attribution of precise absolute dates.

(b) Genealogies
Genealogies are among the most complex sources in existence. As taxonomies they are used all over the world for speculating about origins. As social charters, they validate relationships between groups in many societies, both centralized and uncentralized. They are therefore manipulated whenever such relationships change. One of the drawbacks of literacy for the Somali was that it became harder to adjust genealogies to the realities of the day.[68] They are only rarely expressed as a whole. Portions that are relevant are discussed in societies where genealogies are an ideological backbone of the social framework. They are sometimes constructed by consensus to solve or avoid a crisis.[69] In cases where genealogies had no practical uses of this sort they were rarely if ever discussed, as, for example, among the Abutia Ewe (Ghana). Most individuals would learn their links to relatives in their compounds in their youth. When elders died, their genealogical knowledge died with them, and genealogical links were reconstructed every generation. Patterns of naming might help, as persons are named after their grandparents or as teknonyms (renaming as "parent of X") were used. In such circumstances genealogies are therefore products of research and not given by the society.[70]

Even where genealogies are spontaneously given by informants or performed, it is still wise to ascertain the circumstances. Thus in 1958 I witnessed a father ask his son to recite his genealogy. The father was a nobleman in colonial Burundi,

where appointments and preferments had much to do with genealogical links as they appeared in the administrative records. I
would suspect backfeeding to have occurred there, not only with
regard to content, but in making genealogy a genre to be performed.

Still, fieldworkers reconstruct genealogies. For the last two
or three generations before that of the oldest members of a community, they may be reliable because they are not merely concerned with ascendancy and links, but can and do yield unpatterned records of births, marriages, and deaths, all at enormous
expense of effort. Such documents are in fact historical gossip
recaptured, and may be highly reliable (as has been argued for
Busoga),[71] especially because they can be crosschecked by
changes of residence, which are other data remembered in life
histories along with the demographic materials. As to deeper
genealogies, their aspect often gives a clue to which portions
could be used for dating. Wherever the family tree becomes
bushy instead of tracing only a stem, wherever it remains relatively unpatterned, it may well be valid, especially when the
various ancestral figures do not all become founders of social
groups now recognized as communities.

So portions of genealogies are of use. But are they used as
epochs by the people themselves? If so, they give a relative
chronology and this is true for most uncentralized societies.
They also are epoch markers for household and kin group histories in the near past. In other cases very little may be associated with the names on such lists. Even though they may have
chronological value, they offer no substance. In more centralized societies, dynastic genealogies are quite important, especially if they can be checked by the genealogies of collaterals and
contemporaries. In this way, for instance, events can be placed
with sufficient precision in the history of Rwanda, at least from
the eighteenth century onwards.[72]

Genealogies are based on biological intervals: the time between the birth of a person and that of his first child, first boy,
or first girl. Such intervals vary and are affected by age of marriage, fertility patterns, and other lesser factors. When we are
dealing with dynastic generations, patterns of succession be-

come important again; perhaps only children of a "principal" wife may come into account, or last-born children, or any child. The span can be as short as fifteen years between a woman and her eldest child. It can be as long as a lifetime when any child can succeed. The rules of most societies narrow this interval and in practice historians have used intervals between generations from about twenty-five to forty-five years, according to the influencing factors. They assumed that these did not vary over the total number of generations involved. In his major study, Henige has shown that when a sufficiently large number of cases are available one can indeed calculate averages for generations, but that in no case can these date any generation in particular. For instance, in France an average length of reign between 987 and 1793 is 24.4 years, but no king ruled for a period between 22 and 29 years.[73] So any automatic dating by average misdates every single French king! These are reigns and not generations, but the principle is the same. In practice the best one can do is to allot three or four generations (depending on the case) to a century and date individuals by reference to expressions that are precise in their vagueness. John lived around the turn of the nineteenth century, Jack in the first part of the seventeenth century, Francis in the middle of the eighteenth century. One can also use the first date given by an average calculation of a number of generations as an indication of the approximate time for the beginning of the series. The higher the number of generations the better. But even so, one never comes to a precision that would justify citing firm dates.

It is also understandable why synchronisms between persons who met each other cannot lead to synchronisms between generations or reigns. One example makes the point. Queen Victoria of Great Britain (1837–1901) was a contemporary of Emperor William II of Germany (1888–1918) and Napoleon III of France (1852–1870), but the reigns of the two latter do not even overlap. A synchronism between the first two reigns could confuse dates as far apart as 1837 and 1918.

What are we to conclude? Given the precariousness of measurements of time, the lack of importance attached to time, and the variability of intervals used to establish epochs in oral cultures, we can only arrive at a relative chronology. Only for the last century or so can better results be achieved. We must therefore date traditions by other means. We must date by written sources, archaeology, and physical means (astronomical, geological). The lack of reliable chronology in all but recent oral traditions remains one of its most severe limitations.

## CHAPTER SEVEN

# ORAL TRADITION ASSESSED

I have now discussed the impact of various artistic, social, cultural, and mnemonic factors on the contents of oral traditions. Now the time has come to conclude our journey and to give a general assessment of oral traditions as a source. Many readers will agree with Irwin, whose study of Liptako traditions (Upper Volta) concludes with the observation that the limitations of oral tradition are crucial. We must fully appreciate them, if we are to use such sources and if we are to assert about them that one can "truly vouch for the truth of a past series of events."[1] He was worried about the variability of the messages, the casualness of transmission, the possibility of feedback, the inherent biases of interpretation, and above all about the selectivity of his sources, ethnocentric and elite oriented as they were. On occasion he had to observe that there was no way to know which among competing versions one could choose, so none was really reliable. Once he seemed to say that the limitations were so severe that oral tradition could not be used by itself.[2] Yet he still maintains in the end that Liptako traditions have history to teach, and at least here there were no complaints about chronology.[3]

I discuss the limitations of oral tradition in general first. Then I can assert what the uniqueness of oral tradition as a source is, and why, because of this unique character, we cannot ignore tradition as a source whenever it is available.

## I. The Limitations of Oral Tradition and Outside Sources

In the last chapter I pointed out that lack of chronology and interdependence of sources are limitations that are truly characteristic of tradition. I consider these first. In chapter five the main limitation was the selectivity of the contents of tradition. These and the impact of form on content are true for all messages whether written or oral and so I consider them later. I conclude with a short consideration of the degree to which these limitations apply with regard to various traditions.

## (1) Chronology and Interdependence

The effects of a lack of chronology in most societies—barring Liptako, where the chronology is both absolute and reliable—can only be partially remedied by recourse to outside sources. This is easier said than done. The obvious sources that come to mind are outside written documents or archaeology. When there is a link between a site and an asserted event in oral tradition, dating could be obtained. Local tradition in northern Rwanda talking about the Ndorwa kingdom claims that the site was occupied by two different kings, although only one occupation was visible. Excavation showed this to be correct and dated the whole in the eighteenth century, which accorded with genealogical calculation.[4] Results are nearly always not this neat. In Buhaya (Tanzania), P. Schmidt dug on the spot where according to tradition the Tower of Babel had once stood and found an ironsmelting site from as far back as 500 B.C.[5] The memory of the site was kept but had no relation to the cliché of oral tradition. The Luba of Shaba and their neighbors, the Songye, argued that they all came from the area of Lake Kisale. There, especially at Sanga, several necropolises were uncovered, which began in the eighth century and continued without a break into the recent past. The people in them were "Luba," but this does not suffice to confirm that all Luba and Songye emigrated from there. It dates the tradition,[6] but such a link between tradition and site can be forged and merely rest on feedback from the site into the tradition. This is called iconatrophy. In southern Sudan, in Dinka territory, some sites are said to be remains of former Funj settlements, others remains of Luel settlements. "Funj" was only a label given to sites where pottery was found that was dissimilar from that of the present and "Luel" to sites whose pottery was similar to present wares and which were thought to have been settled by one's forebears. Both designations stemmed from oral tradition. Thus the sites were not a confirmation of the tradition, but rather another Pope Johanna case.[7] The difficulty of correlating oral data or written accounts with archaeological sites is well illustrated by the endeavors in Biblical archaeology to date the age of Abraham. There still exists no agreement at all on that question.[8]

Written sources also do not always obviously date or confirm oral traditions because the interests of the writers diverged so much from those of oral composers. A famous example is the past history of the kingdom of Benin (Nigeria). For several centuries prior to 1880 there is no mention of a king by name in the body of written records, and the same events are not mentioned in the body of oral traditions and in the written records. They only overlap marginally.[9] Sometimes one does obtain confirmation. The Ethiopian chronicle of Zara Ya<sup>c</sup> qob (1434–68) mentions a Hadiya leader Bamo, who sided with the emperor, against other Hadiya. Oral accounts place Boyamo at thirteen to seventeen generations ago and recall his ties to Zara Ya<sup>c</sup> qob.[10] As the names and the kinship relationships of relatives of Bamo correspond in both cases, it is the same man. The written record puts him in the framework of Christian-Muslim rivalry, as one would expect. Hadiya accounts put him in the perspective of rivalry between various Hadiya leaders and as a founding hero.[11] With written sources, as with archaeological sites, dating is sometimes possible and sometimes not.

Other events on which historians have pinned their hopes are reports of astronomical phenomena or calamities. The case of the New Guinea Highlands and the account of the "Time of Darkness," which refers to a volcanic eruption, is enlightening. After much research it was possible to determine the volcano involved and to date the ashes between 1640 and 1820 (barring a few years when the eruption could not have occurred). Yet it does not date anything, for the cataclysm occurred before a relative chronology begins in any of the traditions. All it does prove is that events from 180 to 340 years ago were not forgotten, although many researchers thought that collective memory here did not exceed a century. Associations of the eruption with the arrival of birds or plants can not be trusted because such topics are normal in stories that belong to the genre of tales of origin and early, prechronological time.[12] This vividly reminds the researcher that there must be at least an internal relative chronology if confirmation is to serve a purpose. The use of astronomical data, usually solar eclipses or comets, poses knotty problems. Such phenomena must be well described, and the link between the phenomenon and other events should not be construed as omens (as the star at Bethlehem and the eclipse during the Passion are to be construed). One should know to which eclipse reference is made—since eclipses recur irregularly, but recur—and why people would, if it is not the last recurrence, remember that episode and not later ones.[13] Nevertheless in some cases the correspondence holds, as for Halley's comet in 1835 and an eclipse of the sun in 1680, both remembered in Kuba traditions.[14] One cannot reject such links *a priori*, just as one cannot, given the case of Liptako or Sereer Saalum (Senegal), reject precise time measurement over very long periods.

On balance, then, absolute dating will not be as easily achieved as was once believed. The same holds for independent confirmation by other sources of events and situations described in traditions, as the examples above also show. There often is little overlap. Nevertheless, cases of overlap do occur from time to time where oral tradition confirms or completes written accounts. Thus in 1759 Franco-British rivalry in Maine (United States) involved the local Abenaki Indians, whose oral accounts were not written down before 1869. These confirm both French and British accounts and resolve at least one contradiction between the written versions.[15] When contradiction occurs, it is by no means always the written record which is to be believed, as Irwin has shown for a succession crisis in Liptako in 1890/ 1891.[16] Each case has to be evaluated on its relative merits. Confirmation or denial can also derive from other sources, especially from linguistics. Thus the peoples in Gabon are said to have all immigrated after the thirteenth century, barring only pygmies.[17] This cannot have been correct, because the Bantu languages spoken there must have been in Gabon for millennia. Or again: in western Zambia, in Barotseland, the Kololo are said to have immigrated c. 1840. They came, it was said, from south of the Limpopo. This is borne out by the Lozi language. It belongs to a group that has no closer relatives than the Sotho languages of Transvaal.[18]

Chronology and lack of independence are real problems for oral traditions. They can be overcome or alleviated in some cases by outside evidence, but because the contents of outside evidence tend not to be congruent with the contents of oral tradition such cases will remain the exception rather than the rule. One should still not give up hoping that outside sources will eventually be of assistance.

## (2) Selectivity and Interpretation

Selectivity, as we saw in chapter four, occurs mainly for social reasons. Some topics are worthwhile, others are not. Certain individuals or groups of people are interesting, others are not. The effects are loss of information and the creation of a profile of past history which is the historical consciousness of the *present*. There is no remedy for losses, but at least the profile can be fleshed out by the use of other sources. Interpretation, which we discussed in chapter five, is always combined with mnemonic effects and includes cultural selectivity. It, too, results in losses, and losses that become bigger the more remote events are from our times. Causal links tend to be reduced to rudiments, or general causes linked to worldview are introduced. A cultural profile results for all the traditions. They correspond to the *present* view of reality and of the world. Again, cultural profiles can be fleshed out by the use of other sources. All these factors turn traditions into something that is very much in the present, which it reflects. This has led some anthropologists, like T. O. Beidelman, to deny all evidential value to traditions. One cannot show that events recorded in traditions "actually occurred as recorded or whether these simply should have occurred in order for the past to conform with society as it exists today—or, at least, how it is thought to exist by those within it."[19]

Beidelman cannot realistically claim that in every generation people invent a brand new past for themselves and believe it to be the past. His position goes against the dynamics of oral tradition and against the principle of selectivity and interpretation. Selectivity implies discarding certain information one has about the past and from that pool of information keeping only what is still significant in the present. However, the information that is retained, still comes from the past. Interpretation means to alter information from the past to give it new meaning and as interpretation is more creative than selection it is also more dangerous, but not to the point that all is to be rejected. This is rather like the cleric in the seventeenth century who held that there never had been a Roman Empire at all, since none of the manuscripts about it were contemporary with the supposed Empire.

These characteristics of selectivity and interpretation are tied to all messages. Every person who speaks or writes chooses information, orders it, colors it. If one were to deny selectivity in written sources, how is it that European sources about Benin never have anything to say that crosscuts with the oral sources? How is it that oral history could develop as a field where sources from forgotten population layers explode the silence of written documents and balance the profile of society writings give us?[20]

Yet selectivity and interpretation weigh more heavily on oral tradition than on written sources. This is because, once a written source exists it becomes permanent, it is removed from time. It is no longer affected by selection or interpretation, as long as it survives. When it is copied, the copyist may reintroduce actual writing. Its past is the time it testifies about. It is contemporary when both overlap. For that reason historians appreciate contemporary documents more than any other. With oral traditions the processes of mnemonic or conscious selection and streamlining continue so that they show the impact of x generations of past-presents, which are experienced as a whole and can no longer be unraveled. As a result, the time depth of a tradition matters. If it is short, a tradition still resembles a written document from this point of view. The longer that time interval is, the less it resembles a written document. Using the example of George Washington, the man and the myth, P. Irwin brings out the fundamental difference between the two types of sources. Because there are writings extant from all the generations since George Washington, the development of a new cultural interpretation and of the selection process can be documented stage by stage. It never can be with oral tradition or when stages are lacking in documents.[21] We will never know how the epic of Alexander grew in the Middle East.

There are means to correct the biases. These are all pervasive and subtle, as I know from personal experience. When I wrote the history of the Kuba in 1963, I stuck closely to the sources, as one does with written materials.[22] I wrote a history of the Kuba as they saw their past c. 1950. It was valuable but biased. Later I used systematic linguistic comparison to elucidate other data about the Kuba past and rewrote Kuba history in 1978.[23] Economic history became much clearer, internal administrative growth in the kingdom took form, and the traditional accounts were filled out on other points as well. The struggles for succession are an instance. What I did not do was to reinterpret on the basis of hunches or supposedly valid generalizations about the development of kingdoms, economies, or religions. There are two lessons to be drawn from this case. First, that outside sources can be strong correctives of bias and, secondly, that more interpretation is needed from the historian than when he or she deals with full written records. One of the special difficulties with reconstructions drawn from oral traditions may then well be the value of the interpretations of the historian. This should be all the more reason to deposit one's raw materials.

## (3) Degree of Limitations

In the Kuba experience as in others it is quite clear that not all traditions are affected to the same extent. The body of recent oral tradition is quite rich, quite large, and very diverse, stemming from all the genres. Selection has not yet operated much, reinterpretation has not proceeded very far, relative chronology (mostly through a host of local genealogies) is still good, and sources have not yet become common to large numbers of people, so that a certain amount of independence still exists. Oral sources do not share the limitations of oral tradition, which we discussed here, and recent oral tradition—one or two generations beyond the eldest living members in a community—suffers only small damage. But as traditions are older, the problems become bigger, to be at their peak when one deals with traditions of origin. This is the reason why traditions of origin are usually chosen as examples when such effects are discussed, though they are not typical.

Different types of evidence and genres show different impacts. Unconscious testimony is not affected. We saw that this is common in tales. But they cannot be dated very far backwards. Memorized wording escapes these limitations, but then the glosses that are necessary to understand such sources do not. Poetry and song are excellent sources when they contain historical data and assert events or situations. Most of them, however, are allusive only. They tend not to be of a great age because, when they are no longer relevant, they are usually forgotten. A very few come to stand in the position of prayer formulas which cannot be changed, even if they are no longer understood. Historical gossip can deal in such small bits that they are not affected as long as they are remembered, but they, too, are usually not remembered very long. In sum, it is important to historians to differentiate between sources. All are not historical accounts remembered as such and given out as history, nor are all genealogies. Plotting items against time scales will show that the distortions resulting from the limitations of oral tradition apply to the smaller body of data, but only one that is older than a century or so. Hence it is wise to propose a reconstruction for the last period first, and to go from the present into the past. One can identify the situations and the problems these raise for, say, a century ago, when the mass of sources dried up, and use that knowledge in asking questions of earlier data, in identifying gaps of information, and in interpreting the data one has.

## II. The Uniqueness of Oral Tradition

### (1) As a Source

All traces from the past fall in two major categories according to a basic characteristic: whether they are messages or not. This is the most important feature of a source from the point of view of the rules of evidence. A pot, dug up from an ancient site, is not a message. It bears direct testimony to the age when it was made and used. An oral tradition, an inscription, and a charter are all messages. Messages are information that has been interpreted in the mind of one or more persons, contemporary to the events or situations in question, and has to be interpreted again through the mind of the person who receives them, in the last analysis the historian who uses them. Messages are therefore characterized by a double subjectivity, that of the sender(s) of the message and that of the receiver.[24] All other sources are evidence which has only to go through a single interpretation, that of the person who uses them for an historical reconstruction. Messages encompass written sources, iconographic sources, oral history, and oral tradition.

A first inclination is to consider those sources better which go through only a single interpretation, and to deplore the fact that messages must go through at least two interpretations. But there is in fact a safeguard which renders the apparently more subjective sources (the messages) often more objective than the apparently less subjective sources (the direct evidence). The first interpretation limits the scope for the second, whereas nothing limits the interpretation of direct evidence. This is due in part to the different means of communication: language as opposed to direct perception. The adventures of Ulysses or of the West African king Sundiata tell the receiver quite clearly that these epics deal with a person who is claimed to have done certain things, and there can be no mistake about the claim. A register of tax collections claims that tax was received from these persons to a certain amount. The numbers given cannot be confused with ritual numbers, but with direct evidence such grievous misinterpretations can happen. Archaeologists in Tripolitania identified structures from the Roman age as "monuments of some prehistoric cult" before later authors came to the more plausible and consistent interpretation that they are oil presses.[25] Such drastic variability in interpretation is not possible and should not be allowed when it comes to messages.

Oral traditions are messages. Even though one must search for symbolic significance and intended meaning, one is never allowed to interpret them without any concrete reference to the message itself. The structuralists failed to do that and thereby disregarded the cornerstone of all rules of evidence. They suppressed the first subjectivity to give wider scope to the subjectivity of the present. They abandoned language as a mode of communication to favor a supposedly less-conscious, infralinguistic mode, and so they made cult monuments out of oilpresses often enough.

Oral and written sources differ with regard to the subjectivity of the encoder of the message. Oral sources are intangible, written sources are tangible. Tangible sources survive unaltered through time and are defined by their properties as objects. If they can be dated, they testify directly to the time of their manufacture. In this, a written source participates in the advantage of an archaeological source or an ancient monument. Nothing has altered the source since it was made, and because written sources are the only ones which are both messages and artifacts, the subjectivity of the encoder of the message is clear and unaltered since the time of writing. Copyists can add or subtract from the original message and add yet another interpretation to the message, but even there the sum of interpretations ends at the date of writing. Hence the concern of scholars with originals and contemporary, "first hand" written data. Here subjectivity is reduced to a minimum: an interpretation encoding the message at the time of the event and an interpretation of the decoder, the historian.

When sources are intangible, such as oral tradition, ethnography or linguistic sources, they must be reproduced from the time of their first appearance until they are recorded. Oral history and oral tradition are the only ones among them which are also messages. That means that they accumulate interpretations as they are being transmitted. There is no longer an original encoding interpretation and a decoding one, but there are many encoding and decoding interpretations. If we represent the situation with regard to writing as EP ---- DP (encoding, decoding persons) with oral tradition we have EP, EP'-EP$^n$ ----DP.

One could whimsically argue that, since encoding paradoxically assures more objectivity than if there is just the interpretation of the modern scholar, the more encoding there is, the greater the objectivity. This is not so, as the analogy with original documents and copies shows, and we have discussed the disturbing effects of mnemonic activity. Nevertheless, one should keep in mind that the first encoded message limits the decoder's interpretation. Hence, and however much various successive encoders have altered original messages through selection or interpretation, they were also restrained by the previous interpretations. Such interpretations are therefore cumulative. The one a researcher is confronted with is to a degree a collective interpretation. It is the product of a continuing reflection about the past, the goal of which was not to find out "what really happened," but to establish what in the past, believed to be real, was relevant to the present.

It follows that oral traditions are not just a source about the past, but a historiology (one dare not write historiography!) of the past, an account of how people have interpreted it. As such oral tradition is not only a raw source. It is a hypothesis, similar to the historian's own interpretation of the past. Therefore oral traditions should be treated as hypotheses, and as the first hypothesis the modern scholar must test before he or she considers others. To consider them first means not to accept them literally, uncritically. It means to give them the attention they deserve, to take pains to prove or disprove them systematically for each case on its own merits. It is not enough to say that, in general, genealogies are telescoped; one must adduce reasons why this one would or would not be. It is not enough to say that a particular king, who was supposedly a great warrior, is really a culture hero figure, that he attracted to his name the glorious campaigns of other kings. One must prove that it was so, and not merely assume. In short, the historian must justify his interpretation. Why should it be better than the local one? That is the question he must address. He must continue the historiological process that has been underway. This by no means is to say that the historian's interpretations should be literal, but only that they should at least be more believable than the already existing oral hypothesis.[26]

## (2) As Inside Information

In applying the rules of evidence to oral traditions we have constantly questioned the reliability of the information they yield. Superficially, this leads to gloomy conclusions because cases of unreliability are piled one onto the other. One should remember, however, that not all traditions are automatically unreliable, even though all have limitations. And one should temper this critical approach with a realization of what oral traditions can contribute.

The genres of oral tradition in oral societies are as diverse as those of documents in a literate one. Their contents range over all aspects of human activity from demographic data of various sorts to data about art.[27] Their range is wider than that of documents in most literate societies and includes the evidence which oral history there unearths. For the near past, there are also great quantities of oral tradition, so great that they seem to be limitless. The number tapers off very quickly beyond a generation before the eldest living members of the community. The time depth may be shallow, but there is great wealth of data for it. Even earlier, going backwards to a century, the amount of data remains substantial, and testifies to human endeavors in most fields. It is only for remote times that the stream of tradition becomes a trickle. Then just a few topics remain themes for oral performances. The quantity and diversity of oral tradition should not be underestimated, nor disdained because most of this traditional wine is young.

One cannot emphasize enough, however, that such sources are irreplaceable, not only because information would otherwise be lost, but because they are sources "from the inside." In oral and part-oral societies, oral tradition gives intimate accounts of populations, or layers of population, that are otherwise apprehended only from outside points of view. Writings by foreigners or by outsiders have their own biases. They select their own topics of interest, which they follow in attributing various activities and qualities to the populations they describe, and their interpretations are shaped through their biases. We have already cited the case of Benin where the overlap between external written and internal oral data is nil and that of the Hadiya where it is small. The Ethiopian texts tell us little about "life among the Hadiya." Only the Hadiya oral sources do. They give us a flavor, a picture of a different kind of past that no written source uncovers, even if it remains itself a limited and biased view.[28]

Without oral traditions we would know very little about the past of large parts of the world, and we would not know them from the inside. We also could never build up interpretations from the inside. The historian interprets from perspectives he knows. Even so, one's interpretation is always steeped in the intellectual life of one's own times and circle. Written historical interpretations too are documents of the present! So, unless there were data to tell us otherwise, we would only attribute past evolutions to factors which make sense to us today, even though the implicit or explicit cultural and social assumptions of our hypotheses are nonsense in that other day and age. Kuba bureaucracy in the eighteenth century was not modern bureaucracy and feudalism in Rwanda is a twentieth-century, European interpretation. By collecting oral traditions and studying them, by internalizing remembered ethnography, which is also tradition,[29] interpretations become more culture-specific, less anachronistic and ethnocentric. Thus R. Packard could come to the insight that rulers in nineteenth-century Bashu states (Zaire) ran into great difficulty whenever droughts occurred because kings were supposed to be rainmakers. Droughts were signs that they failed in their duties, and during droughts their authority withered along with the crops.[30]

One could object and claim that while the argument from the inside holds for historians studying other cultures and societies, it would not be true for those who study the past of their own societies. That view is fallacy, for when in part-literate societies or literate societies that were once (not so long ago) part-literate—such as Europe, India, China, Japan—the historian studies a past beyond the lifetime of living people, he is already an outsider and can only see the oral segments of the society or culture through an outsider's eyes. The argument that as sources from the inside oral traditions are invaluable in contributing evidence and correcting basic biases in foreign historical interpretation holds here as it does elsewhere.

## III. Conclusion

Oral traditions have a part to play in the reconstruction of the past. The importance of this part varies according to place and time. It is a part similar to that played by written sources because both are messages from the past to the present, and messages are key elements in historical reconstruction. But the relationship is not one of the diva and her understudy in the opera: when the star cannot sing the understudy appears: when writing fails, tradition comes on stage. This is wrong. Wherever oral traditions are extant they remain an indispensable source for reconstruction. They correct other perspectives just as much as other perspectives correct them.

Where there is no writing or almost none, oral traditions must bear the brunt of historical reconstruction. They will not do this as if they were written sources. Writing is a technological miracle. It makes utterances permanent while not losing any of their faithfulness, even though the situation of immediate intimate communication is lost. Hence, where writing is widely used, one expects very detailed and very diverse sources of information, which also allow for a very detailed reconstruction of the past.[31] Historians who work with the written sources of the last few centuries in any of the major areas of literacy should not expect that reconstructions using oral materials will yield as full, detailed, and precise a reconstruction, barring only the very recent past. The limitations of oral tradition must be fully appreciated so that it will not come as a disappointment that long periods of research yield a reconstruction that is still not very detailed. What one does reconstruct from oral sources may well be of a lower order of reliability, when there are no independent sources to cross-check, and when structuring or chronological problems complicate the issues. This means that particular research questions remain unsettled for much longer periods of time than when a reconstruction rests on massive and internally independent written evidence. It will take longer to achieve results that are reliable because they are confirmed by other sources. This is no reason to neglect oral traditions, or to denigrate them. The research process may be longer, the researchers may need more patience and more interdisciplinary collaboration, but in the end, reliability of a high order can be achieved. During this process oral traditions occupy the center stage. They tell us which questions to pursue. They set forth basic hypotheses that must be addressed first. Even if in the end we must overcome the limits that are implicit in any set of questions, any *problématique*, nevertheless, oral traditions remain essential as the force that guided further research.

The application of the rules of evidence to oral tradition requires much information that is best gathered in the field, along with the recording of the tradition. Recording traditions as well as collecting the necessary information for their critical appraisal presumes a long stay in the area studied and a true familiarity with the language and culture involved. Local scholars are best equipped to undertake this task, as they are steeped in language and culture, but they also need to be thoroughly conversant with the techniques and critical requirements of history. A case can be made for the special usefulness of foreign researchers, who may well take a very long time to become attuned to their task, but who also may more rapidly discover some fundamental assumptions that underlie that particular culture and society.

The requirement for information along with recorded messages raises further questions. Can a historian who was never there evaluate the work of others? Can one use recorded traditions gathered by others? If not, then oral data are not of much use. The discipline of history evolves as much through reconsideration of older evidence as through the adduction of new evidence, and oral data should be part of this process. This means first that field researchers should make available not only their interpretations, but also their recordings of tradition and, equally important, the necessary data for their evaluation. So far very few have done so.[32] It is possible to reevaluate older recorded traditions when one has access to the linguistic, cultural, and social information required for critical evaluation. Such access has allowed A. Delivré, for instance, to interpret the corpus of information recorded by F. Callet about Madagascar, despite its imperfections.

Oral tradition is so rich that one cannot study all its facets in a single short study. This essay did not attempt to achieve this. It was written to be of use to fieldworkers, and others who study traditions to recover historical evidence, in a concrete way. If others find portions of this work stimulating for their endeavors (sociological, psychological, literary), all the better. Yet this is not all that can be said about the phenomenon of oral tradition; I do not claim it to be complete. I believe that the incredible wealth and versatility of traditions are still not fully realized by social scientists, psychologists, or students of the humanities. May this contribution help to spread more awareness of how intricate, how rich, how revealing these messages from our forebears really are!

NOTES

BIBLIOGRAPHY

INDEX

# NOTES

## Preface

1. *De la tradition orale* (Tervuren, 1961). The *exordium* of my doctoral dissertation (1957) included much of it.

2. I worked among the Kuba (Zaire), in Rwanda, Burundi, and among the Tio (Republic of Congo). Kuba materials have been published in *Geschiedenis van de Kuba* and *Children of Woot*. For Rwanda, see *L'évolution du royaume rwanda des origines à 1900* (Brussels, 1962), and the CRL collection of traditions, *Ibitéekerezo* (Chicago). For Burundi, see *La légende du passé*, and, for the Tio, *The Tio Kingdom*. The Kuba documentation is available in the Memorial Library of the University of Wisconsin–Madison. Further experience was gained during an oral history project in Libya, dealing with the Italo-Libyan war (1911–32), and data are deposited in the archives of the Libyan Studies Centre, Tripoli.

## Chapter One

1. For a recent thorough survey see E. P. Loftus, *Eyewitness Testimony*.

2. G. Greene was present at a revolution in Latvia (Riga, 1938), but did not see it. See *Ways of Escape*, p. 100.

3. J. Campbell, *Grammatical Man: Information, Entropy, Language and Life*, pp. 224–26; E. F. Loftus, *Memory*, pp. 149–69; J. J. Jenkins, "Remember That Old Theory of Memory? Well Forget It"; J. Vansina, "Memory and Oral Tradition," pp. 262–65; A. Lieury, *La mémoire*.

4. In rare cases one can trace accounts back to different rumors. See J. Vansina, *La légende du passé*, pp. 32–54.

5. A. Pagés, *Un royaume hamite au centre de l'Afrique*, pp. 138–40.

6. J. Bird, *The Annals of Natal*, vol. 1, p. 64.

7. M. Wilson and L. Thompson, *The Oxford History of South Africa*, vol. 1, p. 256–59.

8. A. Lieury, *La mémoire;* E. F. Loftus and G. R. Loftus, "On the Permanence of Stored Information in the Human Brain."

9. Of the latter, the most frequent, see for example T. Ore, ed., *Memorias de un viejo luchador campesino: Juan H. Pevez,* or S. Benison, ed., *Tom Rivers.* In general, see L. L. Langness, *The Life History of Anthropological Science.*

10. W. De Craemer, "A Cross-cultural Perspective on Personhood."

11. J. Vansina, "Memory and Oral Tradition"; A. Lieury, *La mémoire.*

12. H. Weinstock, *Rossini: A Biography*, pp. 118–23, for the latest reminiscence. I heard that progression cited on a television program (Fall, 1983). So, *se non è vero, è ben trovato!*

13. F. G. Gamst, *The Qemant,* p. 31 (A place where the hooves of God's horse had imprinted the ground). For Africa, more generally, see H. Baumann, *Schöpfung und Urzeit des Menschen*, pp. 186–87.

14. E. Bernheim, *Lehrbuch der Historischen Methode*, pp. 324, 343.

15. L. Guebels, "Kallina E.," and field notes.

16. J. Vansina, *The Children of Woot*, p. 54. J. Cornet, *Art Royal Kuba*, p. 29, has another story about the appearance of the office of *tataam*, without a folk etymology. In general, see E. Bernheim, *Lehrbuch*, pp. 434, 461.

17. T. Weiskel, "The Precolonial Baule," p. 507.

18. J. Vansina, *La légende du passé*, pp. 174–75.

19. P. Stanislas, "Kleine nota over de Ankutshu." For etiological tales in general, see E. Bernheim, *Lehrbuch*, p. 323 W. Bauer; *Einführung in das Studium der Geschichte*, p. 239; A. Van Gennep, *La formation des légendes*, pp. 69–76.

20. H. Baumann, "Ethnologische Feldforschung und Kulturhistorische Ethnologie," p. 162.

21. J. H. Nketia, *Funeral Dirges of the Akan People.*

22. C. Pellat, *Langue et littérature arabe*, pp. 66–74.

23. R. Firth, *History and Traditions of Tikopia*, p. 12.

24. B. Verhaegen, *Introduction à l'histoire immédiate;* UNESCO, *La Méthodologie de l'histoire de l'Afrique comtemporaine.*

25. P. Thompson, *The Voice of the Past*, pp. 91–164. Concen-

trating on one person are T. Ore, ed., *Memorias,* and S. Benison, ed., *Tom Rivers.*

26. See chapter five, I, 1, c.

27. K. Burridge, *Mambu,* pp. 32, 150–52 (Tangu, New Britain); R. Mayer, *Les transformations de la tradition narrative à l'île Wallis,* p. 73; Ifwanga wa Pindi, "Msaangu: chant d'exaltation chez les Yaka," pp. 203–4. This holds for all the peoples I worked with in Africa (Tio, Kuba, Rwanda, Burundi, Libya). For a less clear-cut case see G. H. Gossen, *Chamulas in the World of the Sun,* pp. 80, 140–42.

28. R. Firth, *History and Traditions,* p. 7; J. Vansina, *Children of Woot,* p. 19.

29. J. Vansina, *La légende du passé,* pp. 55–68.

30. J. Goody, *The Domestication of the Savage Mind,* pp. 118–19, and "Mémoire et apprentissage dans les sociétés avec et sans écriture," p. 32.

31. M. d'Hertefelt and A. Coupez, *La royauté sacrée de l'ancien Rwanda,* pp. 5–7; A. Kagame, "Le code ésotérique de la dynastie du Rwanda."

32. See n. 22. The Arab poet was never the reciter and every poet needed a reciter.

33. R. De Decker, *Les clans Ambuun, Bambunda d'après leur littérature orale,* p. 27.

34. A. Kagame, "Etude critique d'un vieux poème historique du Rwanda," p. 151.

35. J. H. Nketia, *Funeral Dirges,* p. 143.

36. Tamane Bitima, "On Some Oromo Historical Poems," pp. 319–20.

37. A. Kagame, *Introduction au grands genres lyriques de l'ancien Rwanda,* p. 151.

38. See chapter two, II, 1, d, iii.

39. D. W. Cohen, *Womunafu's Bunafu,* p. 14.

40. A. Kronenberg, "The Fountain of the Sun."

41. R. Pernoud, *Les Gaulois,* pp. 9–96 (Bibracte).

42. F. Eggan, "From History to Myth: A Hopi Example."

43. A. Lieury, *La mémoire,* pp. 48–52; J. J. Jenkins, "Remember That Old Theory of Memory?" pp. 790–92; A Tudor example is in E. Leach, *Genesis as Myth and other Essays,* pp. 81–82; R. R. Atkinson, "The Tradition of the Early Kings of Buganda," shows the effects of this process in an extreme way fused with cosmological speculation.

44. J. C. Miller, "Listening for the African Past, pp. 7–8.

45. M. G. Kenny, "The Stranger from the Lake," p. 7 (the story of "the boy and the bead").

46. J. C. Miller, "The Dynamics of Oral Tradition in Africa," p. 86.

47. G. S. Kirk, *Myth*; R. Firth, *History and Traditions*, p. 7 (Malinowski's notion of myth); P. Pender-Cutlip, "Oral Tradition and Anthropological Analysis" (use of the concept by an anthropologist in recent times). Volume 22 of *Paideuma* is devoted to an analysis of myths. Myths there seem to be accounts of origin, believed by the tellers to be true, but held by outsiders to be fiction. C. Lévi-Strauss and other structuralists label any narrative, fictional or not, "myth." I will not use the term in this work.

48. J. Vansina, "Traditions of Genesis"; for an example see chapter three, I, 2. "The Origin of the Chieftaincy of the Ganame."

49. D. Barrere, "Revisions and Adulterations in Polynesian Creation Myths."

50. H. Baumann, *Schöpfung und Urzeit*, passim, and pp. 256–60 for Tower of Babel in Africa.

51. J. Vansina, *La légende du passé*, pp. 55–66. The tale of David playing before Saul is analogous. In the legend about the foundation of the city of Antwerp the young hero Brabo sings for King Druoon Antigoon and slays him, cutting off his hand (folk etymology for the name of the town). This story probably dates from the sixteenth century (humanists!) who knew the Biblical parallel. Did it come to Burundi and Rwanda only after the arrival of the missionaries?

52. J. Vansina, *The Children of Woot*, pp. 34–40.

53. D. Henige, *Oral Historiography*, pp. 88–89.

54. Ibid., p. 100.

55. J. Gates, "Model Emperors of the Golden Age in Chinese Lore"; E. O. Reischauer and J. K. Fairbanks, *East Asia*, vol. 1, pp. 37–38.

56. A. R. Cottrell, *The First Emperor of China*, pp. 136–57.

57. J. C. Miller, "The Dynamics of Oral Tradition," pp. 80–83; G. I. Jones, "Time and Oral Tradition with Special Reference to Eastern Nigeria," pp. 153–57.

58. T. O. Spear, "Oral Tradition: Whose History?" pp. 134–41; J. C. Miller, "Listening for the African Past," table, p. 43; R. G. Willis, *On Historical Reconstruction for Oral Traditional Sources*, table 16.

59. L. Demesse, *Changements techno-économiques et sociaux chez les pygmées babinga*, pp. 135–37. See also, chapter four, II, 2.

60. See chapter six, III, 3.

61. They are found from Ireland to India, in Central Asia, and among the Ainu. In Africa most "epics" are heroic narratives, but some do exist, because they obey special linguistic rules of form. See Kanenari Matsu, *Ainu jojishi Yukarashu* [A collection of Ainu Epic poems] (Tokyo, 1959–65). For Africa, see R. Finnegan, *Oral Literature in Africa*, pp. 108–10; D. Biebuyck, "The Epic as Genre in Congo"; S. Biernaczky, "Folklore in Africa Today"; J. J. Johnson, "Yes, Virginia, There Is an Epic in Africa." For an example, see L. Kesteloot and A. Traore, eds., *Da Monzon de Segou: épopée bambara*,

62. A. Lord, *The Singer of Tales*, pp. 69–77, M. Tamminen, *Finsche Mythen en Legenden*, pp. 14–21; 27–30.

63. A. Ayoub and M. Gallais, *Images de Djazya*.

64. R. P. Pagès, *Un royaume hamite*, pp. 228–335.

65. E. Bernheim, *Lehrbuch*, p. 331; W. Bauer, *Einführung*, p. 237.

66. P. Crépeau, "The Invading Guest"; F. M. Rodegem, *Paroles de sagesse au Burundi*.

67. A. Delivré, *L'histoire des rois d'Imerina*, pp. 203–14.

68. G. Greene, *Journey without Maps*, p. 65.

69. D. Henige, *Oral Historiography*, p. 2.

70. J. C. Miller, "Listening," p. 2: "Oral tradition is a narrative describing or purporting to describe eras before the time of the person who relates it." This comes close to the definition by E. Bernheim or W. Bauer of *Sage*, a subdivision of oral tradition. See E. Bernheim, *Lehrbuch*, p. 318, W. Bauer, *Einführung*, p. 239.

71. This model does not hold for all genres, especially not for historical gossip; See R. Rosaldo, "Doing Oral History," p. 89. For tales, see V. Labrie Bouthillier, "Les expériences sur la transmission orale."

72. T. Bianquis, "La transmission du Hadith en Syrie à l'époque fatimide"; H. A. R. Gibb, *Mohammedanism*, pp. 74–82; J. Robson, *Ḥadīth*; J. Schacht, "A Reevaluation of Islamic Tradition," is considered hypercritical by most later commentators.

73. D. W. Cohen, *Womunafu's Bunafu*, p. 189, and "Reconstructing a Conflict in Bunafu," p. 217–18, fn. 7; R. Rosaldo "Doing Oral History."

74. As against J. C. Miller, "Listening," p. 2, who—in the name of doing away with the documentary analogy—ignores these problems.

75. A. Delivré, *L'histoire des rois*, p. 288 (only problems of succession and of historical progress are retained); Sione Latukefu, "Oral Tradition" (Tonga: mostly battles and succession); P. Irwin, *Liptako Speaks*, pp. 12–21 (Liptako in Upper Volta: male, Fulani, higher status history, mostly about emirs, battles, and holy men).

## Chapter Two

1. H. Scheub, "Performance of Oral Narrative," and "Body and Image in Oral Narrative Performance"; R. Finnegan, *Oral Literature in Africa*, pp. 2–12; D. Ben Amos, "Introduction: Folklore in Africa," pp. 12–16.

2. A. Van Gennep, *La formation des légendes*, pp. 267–71.

3. H. Scheub, *The Xhosa Ntsomi*, pp. 12–16.

4. T. Cope, *Izibongo*, pp. 21–29; H. F. Morris, *The Heroic Recitations of the Bahima of Ankole*, pp. 21–38.

5. J. Vansina and J. Jacobs, "*Nshoong atoot*, het koninklijk epos der Bushong."

6. A. Lord, *The Singer of Tales*, pp. 13–29; M. Tamminen, *Finsche Mythen en Legenden*, pp. 26–27 (*kantele* instrument), pp. 24–25 (swaying).

7. P. Radin, *The Story of the American Indian*, pp. 222–23 (Natchez); S. Latukefu, "Oral Tradition," p. 44 (Tonga); G. Dupré, *Un ordre et sa destruction*, pp. 249–50 (Nzebi); N. Nzewunwa, *The Masquerade in Nigerian History and Culture*.

8. L. Frobenius, *Dichtkunst der Kassaiden*, p. 322.

9. H. Scheub, "The Art of Nongenile Mazithathu Zenani."

10. D. Ben Amos, "Introduction," p. 27; S. Camara, *Gens de la parole*; D. T. Niane *Soundjata ou l'épopée Mandingue*, pp. 1–2.

11. S. Latukefu, "Oral Tradition," pp. 44–48.

12. R. Firth, *History and Traditions*, pp. 15–16.

13. *Notes and Queries in Anthropology*, pp. 195, 204; D. Westermann, *Geschichte Afrikas*, pp. 15–16, 406.

14. S. O. Biobaku, "The Wells of West African History," p. 19.

15. A. Kagame, *La notion de génération*, pp. 9–44; A. D'Arianoff, *Histoire des Bagesera*, pp. 14–15.

16. M. d'Hertefelt and A. Coupez, *La royauté sacrée*, pp. 4–8.

17. A. Kagame, *La poésie dynastique au Rwanda*, p. 39, n. 35.

18. E. Meyerowitz, *Akan Traditions of Origin*, pp. 19–20.

19. P. Pender-Cutlip, "Encyclopedic Informants and Early Interlacustrine History"; G. W. Hartwig, "Oral Traditions Concerning the Early Iron Age in Northwestern Tanzania"; T. Reefe, *The Rainbow and the Kings*, pp. 11–13; P. Irwin, *Liptako Speaks*, pp. 22–26, 32–34 (traditionist). Such informants present their own interpretation of the past and are in that sense "oral historians." M. I. Finley, "Myth, Memory and History," pp. 287–88, 229, discussing why Herodotus can be called a historian while his predecessors cannot, makes evident why encyclopedic performers are not "oral historians": they lack a sense of precise chronology.

20. D. Ben Amos, "Introduction," pp. 27–29.

21. R. Firth, *The Work of the Gods in Tikopia.*

22. D. Ben Amos, "Introduction," p. 27.

23. D. Ben Amos, "Story Telling in Benin."

24. M. Palau Marti, *Les Dogon*, p. 428; G. Dieterlen, "Myth et organisation sociale au Soudan Français," pp. 39–40.

25. E. Loftus, *Eyewitness Testimony*, pp. 24–25.

26. J. Vansina and J. Jacobs, "Nshoong atoot."

27. E. Best, *The Maori*, vol. 1, pp. 65, 73; R. Lowie, *Social Organization*, p. 202.

28. A. Kagame, *La poésie dynastique au Rwanta*, pp. 22–24.

29. A. Kagame, "Etude critique d'un vieux poème historique du Rwanda."

30. A. Lord, *The Singer of Tales*, p. 17.

31. F. Bartlett, *Remembering.*

32. A. Lieury, *La mémoire*, pp. 154–56.

33. H. Scheub, *The Xhosa Ntsomi*, pp. 90–100 and index.

34. D. Sperber, *Rethinking Symbolism.*

35. F. Eggan, "From History to Myth," pp. 50–51.

36. A. Schulze-Thulin, *Intertribaler Wirtschaftsverkehr und Kulturökonomische Entwicklung*, p. 115; R. Underhill, *Red Man's America*, pp. 67–69 (drawing and treaty case).

37. C. H. Perrot, "Les documents d'histoire autres que les récits," pp. 488–89.

38. C. H. Perrot, *Les Anyi-Ndenye et le pouvoir aux 18ᵉ et 19ᵉ siécles*, p. 45.

39. T. Reefe, "Lukasa: A Luba Memory Device."

40. A. Schulze-Thulin, *Intertribaler Wirtschaftsverkehr*, p. 115; R. Lowie, *The Crow Indian*, p. 211, and *Indians of the Plains*, pp. 145–47.

41. G. Niangouran Bouah, "Les poids à peser l'or et les problémes de l'écriture" (summary).

42. W. Brown, personal information.

43. W. Fenton, "Field Work, Museum Studies and Ethnohistorical Research," pp. 78–79, and "Problems in the Authentification of the League of the Iroquois." Calendars needed mnemonic supports, even when quite simple. Thus the Komo (Zaire) hunters and farmers kept track of years by knotting a rope once a year. See W. de Mahieu, "Le temps dans la culture komo," p. 12. The count began after the last moving of the village.

44. C. H. Perrot, *Les Anyi-Ndenye*, p. 23 and *bia* in index.

45. J. Gorju, "Entre le Victoria, l'Albert et l'Edouard," p. 112.

46. P. Chike Dike, "Some Items of Igala Regalia."

47. R. Karsten, *La civilisation de l'empire inca*, pp. 113, 128–37; L. Baudin, *Der Sozialistische Staat der Inka*, pp. 48–50, 103–7.

48. R. Lacey, "On *Tee* Grounds as Historic Places," pp. 282–84.

49. L. Frobenius, *Kulturgeschichte Afrikas*, p. 344.

50. J. Gorju, "Entre le Victoria," pp. 83, 87, 107–9; R. Oliver, "Ancient Capital Sites of Ankole," and "The Royal Tombs of Buganda"; M. Wilson, *Communal Rites of the Nyakyusa*, pp. 42, 70, 85; A. E. Jensen, "Die Staatliche Organisation und die historische Ueberlieferungen der Barotse," p. 94, n. 3; G. Prins, *The Hidden Hippopotamus*, pp. 123–28.

51. S. Latukefu, "Oral Tradition," p. 5, for a Tonga case: historical traditions around the fortress Velata on Lifuka island.

52. I. Cunnison, *History on the Luapula*, pp. 10, 35–38.

53. J. Vansina, *La légende du passé*, pp. 16–17.

54. J. H. Nketia, *Drumming in the Akan Communities of Ghana*.

55. A. De Rop, *De gesproken woordkunst van de Nkundo*, pp. 178–79; T. Reefe, "Lukasa," pp. 10–11.

56. See chapter three, I, n. 5.

57. H. Scheub, *The Xhosa Ntsomi*, pp. 17–43.

58. O. Olajubu, "Iwì Egúngún Chants," p. 159.

59. J. Goody, *The Myth of the Bagre*, pp. 59–60.

60. R. Firth, *History and Traditions of Tikopia*, pp. 15–16.

61. A. Kagame, *La poésie dynastique*, pp. 22–24; H. Lavachery, *Vie des Polynésiens*, p. 37; R. Lowie, *Social Organization*, p. 197; K. Luomala, "Polynesian Literature," pp. 772–89, E. Best, *The Maori*, vol. 1, pp. 57–84; E. S. C. Handy, *Marquesan Legends*, p. 20; J. H. Rowe, "Inca Culture at the Time of the Spanish Conquest," pp. 201–2; L. Baudin, "La formation de l'élite et l'enseignement de l'histoire dans l'empire des Incas," p. 209; H. B. Nicholson, "Native Historical Tradition," p. 609; M. Lunghi, *Oralità et Trasmissione in Africa negra*, pp. 78–79 (Abron, Ivory Coast). The last citation stems from a missionary who was told by a chief about the school, the sanctions for inattention, the schedule of classes, and the curriculum. This information from the 1970s is suspect in that it clearly shows the intent to prove that schools like modern schools existed in precolonial Akan chiefdoms. The case exemplifies problems that may also be present in the other cases cited.

62. E. S. C. Handy, *Marquesan Legends*, p. 20.

63. A. Kagame, "Etude critique," pp. 151–95.

64. A. Lord, *The Singer of Tales*, p. 101.

65. Ibid., pp. 60–61.

66. Ibid., p. 123; D. Biebuyck, *Hero and Chief*.

67. A. Van Gennep, *La formation des légendes*, pp. 267–71.

68. A. Coupez and T. Kamanzi, *Récits historiques rwanda*, pp. 6–11 and passim; J. Vansina, *Ibitéekerezo*, index, *Gakaniisha*.

69. J. Vansina, *La légende*, pp. 32–54, for the case of Macoonco in Burundi. I must refer the reader to this because examples are too long to be detailed here.

70. J. Macpherson, *Fragments of Ancient Poetry*.

71. C. G. Voegelin et al., *Walam Olum or Red Score*; J. B. Griffin, "A Commentary on an Unusual Research Program in American Anthropology," and "Review of *Walum Olum*."

72. D. Henige, *Oral Historiography*, p. 95.

73. D. Ben Amos, "Story Telling in Benin," pp. 22–29.

74. R. Firth, *History and Traditions*, p. 15: he received his first versions in secret from unauthorized persons.

75. See n. 19.

76. A. Kagame, "Etude critique," pp. 153–55.

77. This is known as *probatio pennae*. See, for example, the poem *Laxis fibris* in P. Becker, "Der Planctus auf den Normannenherzog Willem Langschwert."

78. See S. Farrall, "Sung and Written Epics: The Case of the Song of Roland," p. 112 for quote.

79. J. H. Speke, *Journal of the Discovery of the Source of the Nile*, pp. 246–60. He says, "My theory is founded on the traditions of several nations as checked by my own observation of what I saw when passing through them" (p. 246). The famous and erroneous "Hamitic Theory" about the peoples of the great lakes of Africa was first formulated here, as a result of these "traditions" and "observations."

80. I. M. Njoya, *Histoire et coutumes des Bamum*. But see C. Geary, *Les choses du palais*, pp. 38–41.

81. Jiro Tominaga, "Literature," p. 153. The case highlights the difficulties of assigning authorship. Who is the author here? Hieda-no Are? Emperor Mommu? The Chinese scholar?

82. B. Heintze, "Oral Tradition"; O. O. Obuke, *A History of Aviara*, pp. 141 and 141–248; D. Henige, *Oral Historiography*, pp. 119–27. Two text publications are D. Wright, *Oral Traditions of the Gambia*; E. J. Alagoa and K. Williamson, *Ancestral Voices*.

83. H. Scheub, "Translation of African Oral Narrative-Performances"; D. Tedlock, "On the Translation of Style in Oral Narrative." (This is a Zuni case.) Tedlock's proposals for special typographical conventions still are imprecise and in practice unworkable.

84. J. Vansina and J. Jacobs, "*Nshoong atoot.*"

85. L. Haring, "Performing for the Interviewer."

86. P. Thompson, *The Voice of the Past*, pp. 165–85; D. Henige, *Oral Historiography*, pp. 39–54. The literature on interviewing is vast. I cite only E. Loftus, *Eyewitness Testimony*, pp. 88–109, a psychological study which points to the many ways in which interviewers influence informants (passim).

87. D. Henige, *Oral Historiography*, pp. 34–36; E. Loftus, *Eyewitness Testimony*, pp. 94–97.

88. D. Henige, *Oral Historiography*, pp. 51–53; see n. 19, pp. 210–11.

89. M. d'Hertefelt, "Mythes et idéologies dans le Rwanda ancien et contemporain."

90. See n. 68, p. 213.

## Chapter Three

1. V. Goeroeg-Karady, *Littérature orale d'Afrique noire: Bibliographie analytique;* H. Scheub, *African Oral Narratives, Proverbs, Riddles, Poetry and Songs.*

2. M. Jousse, *Le style oral rythmique et mnémotechnique chez les verbomoteurs;* A. De Rop, *De gesproken woordkunst,* pp. 15–16.

3. R. Finnegan, *Oral Literature in Africa,* pp. 55–76; A. Coupez, *Rythmes poétiques africains;* J. W. Johnson, "Yes, Virginia."

4. J. W. Johnson, *Somali Prosodic Systems;* B. Andrzejewski and J. Lewis, *Somali Poetry.*

5. A. Coupez, "Rythmes poétiques africains," pp. 48–49; D. Simmons, "Tonal Rhyme in Efik Poetry"; L. Stappers, "Toonparallellisme als mnemotechnisch middel"; J. Kaemmer, "Tone Riddles from Southern Mozambique."

6. A. Coupez, "Rythmes poetiques africains," p. 55.

7. A. Lord, *The Singer of Tales,* pp. 34–35.

8. V. Propp, *Morphology of the Folktale.*

9. W. Staude, "Die aetiologische Legende von dem Chefsystem in Yoro." The text is first analyzed in terms of formal structure. On the relationship between this and the following discussion in terms of core images see D. Ben Amos, "Introduction," p. 19.

10. H. Scheub, *The Xhosa Ntsomi,* and "Performance of Oral Narrative" developed the concept of 'core image.' In any tale (narrative) an image structure exists. The core image is the "situation of the tale" and undergoes transformations (the action told) leading to a deeper understanding of the core image or linking it to another one or to other core images.

11. H. Scheub, "The Technique of the Expansible Image."

12. V. Propp, *Morphology*, but see reservations of P. Smith, "Le récit populaire au Rwanda," p. 115, and more fundamental objections by B. Nathhorst, *Formal or Structural Studies of Traditional Tales*, pp. 16–29.

13. A. Kagame, "Poésie dynastique," pp. 13–15, and "Etude critique," for an example of *impakanizi*.

14. D. Ben Amos, "Introduction," pp. 3–4.

15. P. Smith, "Le récit populaire," pp. 20–23.

16. F. M. Rodegem, *Anthologie rundi*, pp. 12–16.

17. G. H. Gossen, *Chamulas in the World of the Sun*, pp. 47–55; D. Ben Amos, "Introduction," pp. 4–7 for elements of taxonomies.

18. E. Bernheim, *Lehrbuch*, pp. 255–56; W. Bauer, *Einführung*, p. 162.

19. A. De Rop, *De gesproken woordkunst*, pp. 8–14.

20. R. Finnegan, *Oral Literature in Africa*, passim.

21. A. Jason, "The Genre in Oral Literature," and "A Multidimensional Approach to Oral Literature"; B. Nathhorst, "Genre, Form and Structure."

22. A. Van Gennep, *La formation des légendes*, p. 74.

23. V. Propp, *Morphology*; P. Smith, "Le récit populaire," p. 115; P. Gossiaux, "Comptes rendu," commits precisely this error.

24. E. J. Alagoa and K. Williamson, *Ancestral Voices*.

25. B. Heintze, "Translations as Sources for African History."

26. B. Malinowski, "The Problem of Meaning."

27. R. Thompson and J. Cornet, *The Four Moments of the Sun*, pp. 37–39; K. Laman, *The Kongo III*, pp. 67–172; W. MacGaffey, "Fetishism Revisited."

28. R. van Caeneghem, *Hekserij bij de Baluba van Kasai*.

29. A. Delivré, *L'histoire*, pp. 140–50.

30. J. W. Fernandez, *Bwiti*.

31. A. Coupez, personal communication.

32. P. Ottino, "Un procédé littéraire malayo-polynésien," p. 11. See J. E. Mbot, *Ebughi bifia*, for the practice of creating multiple meanings among the Fang of Gabon.

33. N. Gidada, "Oromo Historical Poems and Songs," p. 329.

34. A. Kagame, *Poésie dynastique*, pp. 14–19.

35. D. Wright, ed., *Beowulf*, p. 22.

36. P. Denolf, *Aan den rand der Dibese*, p. 569.

37. E. Bernheim, *Lehrbuch*, pp. 324–31; W. Bauer, *Einführung*, p. 240; L. Delahaye, *Les légendes hagiographiques*, pp. 30–41; F. Lanzoni, *Genesi e svolgimento*, pp. 74–85.

38. P. Denolf, *Aan den rand der Dibese*, p. 29; I. Cunnison,

*History on the Luapula*, p. 19; M. Plancquaert, *Les Jaga et les Bayaka*, p. 88: J. C. Yoder, "The Historical Study of a Kanyok Genesis Myth," pp. 91–94.

39. On the subject of intentional and unintentional testimony see M. Bloch, *Apologie pour l'histoire*, pp. 23–34, who was a master in their use. The distinction in historical manuals is usually reduced to the opposition between archival and literary sources: archival sources are written for an immediate purpose (e.g., laundry lists); literary sources are written for consultation by posterity. See E. Bernheim, *Lehrbuch*, pp. 230–34, 434–41.

40. M. Herskovits, *Man and His Works*, p. 14. On p. 19 he cites an example from the Pueblo Indians (entry into the house). See also W. Muehlmann, *Methodik der Völkerkunde*, pp. 206–7. Collections of tales soon show how rich this source can be. For Central Africa see, for example, L. Frobenius, *Dichtung der Kassaiden*, gathered in 1904–06, or R. H. Nassau, *Fetichism in West Africa*, pp. 331–86, gathered from 1864 onwards (Ogowe Delta and Gaboon estuary). Many precolonial practices, situations, techniques, social statuses, and roles are preserved there.

41. J. K. Wright, *Map*, pp. 830–31.

## Chapter Four

1. H. Moniot, "Les sources de l'histoire africaine," pp. 134–35.

2. J. D. Y. Peel, "Kings, Titles and Quarters," p. 109; T. O. Beidelman, "Myth, Legend and Oral History"; A. F. Robertson, "Histories and Political Opposition in Ahafo, Ghana"; P. C. Lloyd, "Yoruba Myths."

3. J. M. De Decker, *Les clans Ambuun.*

4. J. Vansina, *The Children of Woot*, pp. 227–34 and index.

5. B. G. Blount, "Agreeing to Agree on Genealogy." The same situation is reported for the Wolof of Senegal. See J. T. Irvine, "When Is Genealogy History?"

6. M. Verdon, *The Abutia Ewe of West Africa*, pp. 257–58. The difference with previous cases is that genealogies were rarely discussed here and were less important for the social present.

7. D. W. Cohen, *Womunafu's Bunafu*, p. 189, and "Reconstructing a Conflict in Bunafu." For a vivid case of actual gossip see P. Irwin, *Liptako Speaks*, pp. 22–23.

8. L. Baudin, "La formation de l'elite"; J. H. Rowe, "Inca Culture," pp. 201–2, and "Absolute Chronology," p. 272; H. B. Nicholson, "Native Historical Tradition," p. 609.

9. E. Meyerowitz, *Akan Traditions*, pp. 21–22.

10. B. Malinowski, *Argonauts of the Western Pacific*, pp. 291–98.

11. R. Lowie, "Primitive Society," pp. 224–32, and *Social Organization*, pp. 131–34.

12. J. Vansina, *Children of Woot*, pp. 123–26 and 49–63. Many other cases can be cited. For instance, see D. Lange, *Chronologie et histoire*, for the Sefawa dynasty of Kanem-Bornu, incorrectly reputed to be the first and only dynasty of that state for a thousand years.

13. E. Meyerowitz, *Akan Traditions*, pp. 21–22.

14. Ibid., pp. 21–22, 84 n. 2, 106 n. 3, 109.

15. R. Lacey, "On *Tee* Grounds as Historical Places."

16. A. Delivré, *L'histoire des rois*, pp. 424–26, for various editions and manuscripts. Delivré's work consists of an interpretation of Callet's materials checked against others, and by work in the field.

17. G. Dupré, *Un ordre et sa destruction*, pp. 249–53.

18. J. Vansina, *Geschiedenis van de Bakuba*, pp. 133–35.

19. W. MacGaffey, *Modern Kongo Prophets*, p. 92.

20. Especially in so-called segmentary lineage systems. See, for example, Lewis, "Historical Aspects of Genealogies in Northern Somali Social Structure."

21. Lord Kinross, *The Ottoman Centuries*, pp. 19, 23, 25.

22. W. M. J. Van Binsbergen, "Interpreting the Myth of Sidi Mhâmmad."

23. D. Henige, *Chronology of Oral Tradition*, pp. 1–120.

24. D. Westermann, *Geschichte Afrikas*, passim.

25. A. Kagame, *Un abrégé de l'ethno-histoire du Rwanda*, pp. 130–31, 133–34.

26. F. Hagenbucher Sacripanti, *Fondements spirituels*, pp. 71–82 (Loango); J. Vansina, *The Tio Kingdom*, pp. 459–63, 470–77.

27. J. A. Barnes, "History in a Changing Society," pp. 1–9; M. Reed, "Traditions and Prestige among the Ngoni."

28. K. I. Blu, *The Lumbee Problem*, pp. 134–68 and passim.

29. A. Kituai, "Historical Narrative of the Bundi People," p. 12.

30. D. Henige, *Oral Historiography*, pp. 83, 87–89, 99.

31. J. Vansina, *Children of Woot*. Compare Shyaam (magician) and Mboong aLeeng (warrior).

32. J. Vansina, *La légende*, p. 208–17 (Mwezi I) to oppose to Ntare I and Ntare II.

33. D. Henige, *Oral Historiography*, p. 88; W. Fenton, "Field Work," pp. 78–80; and "Problems in Authentification."

34. I. Cunnison, *History of the Luapula*, p. 5.

35. C. H. Perrot, "Ano Asema: mythe et histoire," first thought

this person was fictive only to find later he was not. R. Firth, *History and Traditions of the Tikopia*, p. 164, implies that Sako, the culture hero, was a real person who either performed great deeds or created institutions of importance. This may but need not be so. Alexander and Charlemagne became culture heroes. With lesser heroes, such as warriors or law givers, this may be more often the case than with the overall culture hero. Yet even in such cases some figures may have been invented as foils to others (Sancho Panza vs. Don Quixote), as is the case with the Chinese Yao, Shun, and Yü (see J. Gates, "Model Emperors of the Golden Age in Chinese Lore"). For battles see R. M. Dorson, *Folklore and Fakelore*, pp. 413-44. Each party always claimed victory.

36. A. Kagame, *Poésie dynastique*, pp. 158-59.

37. S. Camara, *Gens de la Parole*, pp. 176-96.

38. S. Latukefu, "Oral Traditions," pp. 44-45.

39. P. Denolf, *Aan den rand der Dibese*, pp. 27-29.

40. R. Lacey, "Coming to Know Kepai," especially pp. 76-77.

41. J. Egharevba, *A Short History of Benin*.

42. For a full list of genres see, F. M. Rodegem, *Anthologie rundi*, pp. 12-14; P. Smith, *Le récit populaire*, pp. 20-24 (Rwandan narrative genres); A. Coupez and T. Kamanzi, *Littérature de cour au Rwanda*.

43. J. Helm and B. C. Gillespie, "Dogrib Oral Tradition as History."

44. S. Saberwal, "The Oral Tradition, Periodization and Political Systems," puts their plight well. For some approaches see J. Tosh, *Clan Leaders and Colonial Chiefs in Lango*; J. Lamphear, *The Traditional History of the Jie*; J. B. Webster, *Chronology, Migration and Drought in Interlacustrine Africa*—all for northern Uganda.

45. J. Fernandez, *Bwiti*, pp. 76-87. The longest genealogies were kept in Polynesia. K. P. Emory, "Tuamotan Concepts of Creation," gives one from Fangatau Island running to sixty-two generations, pp. 69-71.

46. J. Vansina, *The Tio Kingdom*, p. 53 n. 33 and p. 445.

47. J.-L. Vellut, "Notes sur le Lunda," pp. 66-69.

48. R. Lowie, "Oral Tradition and History," pp. 164-65.

49. F. M. Rodegem collected well over four thousand proverbs in Burundi alone (see *Paroles de sagesse*), and this is only one of many genres.

50. A. Delivré, *L'histoire des rois*, pp. 16-17, 139-74, 235-83.

51. See chapter six, I.

52. J. Goody and I. Watt, "The Consequences of Literacy."

53. Goody overlooks that written societies are often only partially literate, that manuscripts are not books, that alphabets are not

ideograms, that social pressures tend to push literates to read the same books, and differences between people in oral cultures are greater than he assumes because of specializations and differing interests. There is no specific "oral mentality."

54. K. Burridge, *Mambu*, pp. 158, 250.

55. R. Firth, *History and Traditions*, pp. 176–79.

56. Ibid., pp. 178–79.

57. Ibid., p. 181.

58. J. Vansina, *Children of Woot*, pp. 155–59, and "Traditions of Genesis," p. 320 (palimpsest); R. Sigwalt, "The Study of Historical Process in African Traditions of Genesis."

## Chapter Five

1. B. Berlin and P. Kay, *Basic Color Terms*.

2. J. Goody and I. Watt, "The Consequences of Literacy."

3. The very existence of encyclopedic informants illustrates this point.

4. G. H. Gossen, *Chamulas*, pp. 18–45; Leon Portilla, *Time and Reality in the Thought of the Maya*.

5. W. De Mahieu, "Cosmologie et structuration," pp. 124–26 (Komo); J. Fernandez, *Bwiti*, pp. 103–6 (Fang). J. Vansina, *Children of Woot*, p. 34 (Kuba). W. MacGaffey, "Oral Tradition in Central Africa," links Kongo cosmology and migration accounts. In medieval Europe the Orient was the cardinal direction. Hence "orientation" and *"ex Oriente lux."*

6. E. Ohnuki-Tierney, "Spatial Concepts of the Ainu."

7. E. Ohnuki-Tierney, "Sakhalin Time Reckoning."

8. L. A. Howe, "The Social Determination of Knowledge"; C. Geertz, *The Interpretation of Cultures*, pp. 389–98.

9. T. Spear, "Oral Tradition: Whose History?" p. 140. Opinions shared by R. Willis and J. C. Miller. The concept is too functional, suspiciously elegant, and yet underestimates the complexity of notions of duration and time. The threefold division of periods is not universal. See P. M. Mercer, "Oral Tradition in the Pacific," pp. 140–41.

10. B. Malinowski, *Argonauts*, pp. 300–301; R. Firth, *The Work of the Gods;* M. Eliade, *The Myth of the Eternal Return*. F. Harwood, "Myth, Memory and Oral Tradition" (Trobriand), claims that a succession of places there replaced a sequence of time. The data do not convince. The mythical past there remains timeless, whatever the ordering of places.

11. The complexity of concepts about time is well set out in J. Hoornaert, "Time Perspective." Structuralists had argued that in oral societies duration was interpreted in terms of discontinuities, rather than as a flow of time. As M. Panoff, "The Notion of Time among the Maenge People of New Britain," pp. 456–57, showed, arguing against E. Leach, the Maenge perceive time as a continuum, a homogeneous and irreversible reality appreciated in terms of "long" and "short" and not as sums of discontinuous units. Space, like time, is represented as continuous and infinity in space is "forever" in time. Evidence from many Bantu-speaking peoples in Africa corroborates these points. This dimension of the notion of time is only one of many that we have not taken up in the text, even though it is crucial. Reading Hoornaert makes clear that many other possible and equally relevant dimensions could be explored, but we have not space to do this here.

12. G. H. Gossen, *Chamulas*, p. 81.

13. Ibid., p. 140.

14. G. Van Bulck, "De invloed van de Westersche kultuur," p. 29; B. Malinowski, *Argonauts*, pp. 229–303; P. M. Mercer, "Oral Tradition in the Pacific," p. 143 (Kuma).

15. N. Kouyate, *Recherches sur la tradition orale*, p. 52.

16. J. Vansina, *Children of Woot*, p. 19.

17. L. Lévy-Bruhl, *La mentalité primitive*, pp. 85–93. The title of the first chapter is explicit: "Indifference of primitive mentality to secondary causes." But the reader must keep a distance with regard to the explanation as to why this phenomenon occurs; for example, see pp. 17–85. To me there is no primitive mentality. All people think by the same logic, or use the same processes of analogy. There are no different "modes of thought," but the objects of thought clearly differ from culture to culture. Both substantive and symbolic objects are culture and time specific.

18. J. Goody and I. Watt, "The Consequences of Literacy."

19. A. Delivré, *L'histoire des rois*, pp. 185–92.

20. J. Vansina, *Children of Woot*, pp. 19–20.

21. J. Middleton, "Some Aspects of Lugbara Myth."

22. M. Fortes, *Oedipus and Job* (West African Coast); J. Vansina *La légende*, pp. 30–31 (Burundi). Fate as ultimate cause was a standard notion to Greek *(Moirai)*, Roman *(Parcae)*, and Germanic *(Nornen)* populations.

23. J. Vansina, *The Tio Kingdom*, p. 227.

24. H. Baumann, *Schöpfung und Urzeit*, pp. 361–62.

25. R. F. Ellen and D. Reason, eds., *Classifications in Their Social*

*Context,* for a recent example. But see comments in M. R. Crick, "Anthropology of Knowledge," pp. 293–94.

26. J. Vansina, *Tio Kingdom,* pp. 126, 377. Also A. Kronenberg and W. Kronenberg, *Nubische Märchen,* fn. 57, pp. 294–95.

27. M. R. Crick, "Anthropology of Knowledge," pp. 288–89 for the difficulties involved in using grammatical categories.

28. Stanislas, "Kleine nota," p. 130, shows that the cliché of the bird that could not cross the waters is also found among the Nkutshu (Tetela), northeastern neighbors of the Kuba.

29. See chapter one, II, 2, c. A. O. Wiget, "Truth and the Hopi," shows these conclusions to be true even in accounts relating events of 1680. Apparently, once the reinterpretation had been made such accounts could then acquire great stability.

30. R. Fox, "Child as Plant."

31. Mpase Selenge Mpeti, *L'évolution de la solidarité,* p. 91.

32. J. Fernandez, *Bwiti,* p. 88.

33. See n. 37, p. 216.

34. S. Feierman, *The Shambaa Kingdom,* pp. 43–44; M. G. Kenny, "The Stranger from the Lake," p. 11; L. De Heusch, *Le roi ivre;* J. C. Miller, ed., *The African Past Speaks,* index: cliché, foreign hunter; J. S. Boston, "The Hunter in Igala Legends of Origin"; W. Staude, "Die ätiologische Legende." (See also chapter three, I, 2.)

35. J. C. Miller, "Listening for the African Past," p. 7.

36. R. Firth, *History and Traditions of Tikopia,* p. 164.

37. J. C. Miller, *Kings and Kinsmen,* pp. 169–74.

38. C. McClellan, "Indian Stories about the First Whites in Northwestern America," pp. 116–17.

39. Ibid., pp. 120–24.

40. S. Feierman, *The Shambaa Kingdom,* pp. 40–90. For the cliché see n. 34 above.

41. Ibid., pp. 43–44.

42. Ibid., pp. 82–90. The direction of the route would be questionable only if cosmological representatives favored a southern orientation, especially if Creation was located to the south.

43. Ibid., pp. 56–59.

44. R. G. Willis, "A State in the Making," p. 37: "It is remarkable how readily the mythical concepts and relations translate into key Marxist concepts." Remarkable indeed, but no more so than others who find Weber's or Radcliffe–Brown's concepts hidden in clichés.

45. J. C. Miller, ed., *The African Past Speaks,* pp. 55–88.

46. H. Scheub, "The Technique of the Expansible Image."

## Chapter Six

1. J. J. Jenkins, "Remember That Old Theory of Memory?" p. 793.

2. F. Bartlett, "Remembering," J. J. Jenkins, "Remember," pp. 790–95; E. Loftus, Eyewitness Testimony, pp. 52–87, 108–9. What Jenkins calls fusion, she calls integration (for example, see p. 104).

3. R. Cohen, Womunafu's Bunafu. A good example is in J. Irwin, Liptako, pp. 22–23.

4. V. Labrie-Bouthillier, "Les experiences sur la transmission orale," pp. 14–17. F. Barth, Ritual and Knowledge among the Baktaman of New Guinea, provides a real life proof of the total corpus kept in the minds of 183 Baktaman. See especially pp. 255–67.

5. G. Dupré, Un ordre et sa destruction, pp. 117–22.

6. The main point stressed by R. Mayer, Les transformations.

7. A. Kuper, "Les femmes," p. 42; E. Meyerowitz, "Akan Traditions," pp. 21–22; R. Firth, "History and Traditions," pp. 15–17.

8. J. Vansina, La légende, pp. 32, 55–68.

9. J. C. Miller, "Listening," pp. 35–39; R. Sigwalt, "The Kings Left Lwindi," pp. 143–50. Note origin of contradiction (p. 144) and compromise text (pp. 154–56).

10. J. Vansina, The Tio Kingdom, pp. 440, 457, n. 41; F. Harwood, "Myth, Memory and the Oral Tradition," pp. 787–89, 791–92.

11. S. Thompson, Motif Index of Folk Literature, is the paradigm.

12. P. Denolf, Aan den rand der Dibese, p. 415; J. Vansina, Geschiedenis, p. 318. The slogan is attached to the capital Bulody ("reparation") among the Kuba. The text runs: "The fire burns the villages of people; but his village does not burn." The Lulua text runs "He burns the villages of others but his village, no one burns."

13. J. Vansina, Children of Woot, pp. 30–34.

14. J. C. Miller, ed., African Past, pp. 86, 118; M. Plancquaert, Les Yaka, p. 112; and n. 38, p. 216.

15. H. Baumann, Schöpfung, pp. 256–60. The distribution is even wider in the great lakes area, in Kasai (Zaire), and in West Africa.

16. J. Vansina, Children of Woot, p. 37; D. E. MacGregor, "New Guinea Myths and Scriptural Similarities."

17. J. Vansina, Tio Kingdom, pp. 378 (tyrant), 460 (bell). I have seen both these clichés mentioned in the literature for west central Africa, but their total distribution remains unknown.

18. J. Thornton, "Chronology and Causes of Lunda Expansion," pp. 1–6.

19. U. Braukämper, "The Correlation of Oral Traditions," p. 50. The situation during the Middle Ages in western Europe and in the Arab world until this century confirms this stand.

20. D. Henige, *Oral Historiography*, pp. 80–87.

21. I. Berger, "Deities Dynasties and Oral Tradition"; D. Henige, Royal Tombs and Preternatural Ancestors," pp. 212–15.

22. R. Rosaldo, "Doing Oral History," p. 97.

23. This is the more stringent position as defended by the most positivist historians, C. V. Langlois and C. Seignobos, *Introduction aux études historiques*, vs. E. Bernheim, *Lehrbuch*, pp. 173–74, 444–45, and especially 504–5. Bernheim believes in a criterion of "inner plausibility" which allows for the use of a single source, unlike the Roman adage: "one witness, no witness" *(testis unus, testis nullius)*. The level of plausibility attained by independent confirmation is so much higher than what any single message (written or oral) can attain, that this should be recognized. One uses single sources for lack of anything better —this often occurs with written sources—but one can never claim more than a plausibility in such a case.

24. A. Delivré, *Histoire*, p. 288.

25. J. Vansina, "The Power of Systematic Doubt," where (p. 120) the case for the central role of tradition to initiate hypotheses is made.

26. A. Lieury, *La mémoire*, pp. 35–36, 193–98; M. Halbwachs, *Les cadres sociaux*, is largely vindicated by recent research.

27. C. Lévi-Strauss, *La pensée sauvage.*

28. C. Lévi-Strauss, *Mythologiques.*

29. D. Sperber, *Rethinking Symbolism.*

30. See B. Nathhorst, *Formal or Structural Studies.*

31. The other relationships are similarity, subordination, super-ordination, and co-occurence. See A. Lieury, *La mémoire*, pp. 48–52.

32. J. Vansina, "Is Elegance Proof?" pp. 309–12.

33. F. W. Young, "A Fifth Analysis of the Star Husband," pp. 389–413; E. Swanson, "Orpheus and the Star Husband," pp. 124–26; C. Lévi-Strauss, *L'homme nu.*

34. C. L. Thomas et al., "Asdiwal Crumbles."

35. Structuralism should not be confused with symbolic anthropology. Provided symbolic argument can be verified and replicated by others it is valid. Images and their interrelationships can objectively be shown to be interpreted in a standard way in a culture. Even then readers still will distinguish between the meaning attributed by the majority of members of a culture and interpretations—often on the basis of categories drawn from sociological theories—derived by the scholar who studies the culture.

36. R. R. Atkinson, "The Traditions of the Early Kings of Buganda," pp. 17–57; J. Vansina, *Children of Woot,* pp. 228–33.

37. A. Coupez and T. Kamanzi, *Récits historiques,* gives the repertory of one performer where it is quite evident.

38. A. Kagame, *La poésie dynastique;* M. d'Hertefelt, A. Coupez, *La royauté sacrée.*

39. On this crucial point I strongly agree with J. C. Miller, "Listening," p. 12.

40. E. Leach, *Genesis,* pp. 27, 81–82.

41. A. O. Wiget, "Truth and the Hopi." In the whole literature I found that the above could only be tested with the Hopi case. Others are not necessarily as stable as this one has been. The actual sociopolitical history of a community undoubtedly affects the stability of its traditions directly.

42. R. R. Atkinson, "Traditions of the Early Kings."

43. F. Eggan, "From History to Myth," p. 303.

44. See n. 2, p. 222.

45. A. Lieury, *La mémoire,* pp. 149–53.

46. The most striking experiment showing this is perhaps the one described by J. J. Jenkins, "Remember," pp. 790–93.

47. A. Delivré, *L'histoire des rois,* shows how to achieve this in practice. For my own attempt see *Children of Woot,* pp. 127–71.

48. Even if one takes action because one foresees a chain of events, the foresight antedates the action.

49. For the associated mnemotechnics see chapter two, II, i, d, i; G. D. Gibson, "Himba Epochs."

50. E. Ohnuki-Tierney, "Sakhalin Time Reckoning," p. 288.

51. W. De Mahieu, "Le temps dans la culture komo."

52. J. Vansina, *Tio Kingdom,* p. 501–2, for important events in recent Tio history.

53. Cataclysms are more important in some cultures than in others. Such themes are dominant among the Indians of southern South America; see J. Wilbert and K. Simonean, *Folk Literature of the Toba Indians,* pp. 10–13. A collection of cataclysmic tales of the Toba follows, pp. 68–100. Fire, deluges, long-lasting night, and an ice age all occur.

54. M. Panoff, "The Notion of Time," p. 455, shows how this leads local people to use genealogies as a measurement of time.

55. See chapter four, II, 2.

56. J. C. Miller, "Listening," pp. 13–15.

57. J. Middleton, "Some Social Aspects of Lugbara Myth," p. 194;
B. Malinowski, *Argonauts*, pp. 300–304.

58. J. Vansina, "Is Elegance Proof?" pp. 318–21.

59. J. C. Miller, "Listening," pp. 13–15.

60. J. C. Miller, *Kings and Kinsmen*, pp. 98–103.

61. A. Kagame, *Un abrégé de l'ethno-histoire*, pp. 72, 75, 168–69.

62. J. C. Miller, "Listening," p. 50; A. Delivré, *L'histoire des rois*,
pp. 180–81.

63. F. Eggan, "From History to Myth," p. 301, quoting from A. M.
Stephen.

64. J. Goody, *The Domestication of the Savage Mind*, pp. 74–111.

65. P. Mark, *Economic and Religious Change*, p. 9 (Diola *bukut* in
Senegal); H. A. Fosbrooke, "The Masai Age-group System"; J. Berntsen, "Pastoralism, Raiding and Prophets," p. 60–111.

66. J. C. Miller, "Kings, Lists and History in Kasanje," p. 63.

67. D. Henige, *Oral Historiography*, pp. 98–102. Yet there are exceptions to these generalizations where lists, used as epochs, were quite reliable. See J. Irwin, *Liptako Speaks*, pp. 87–89, and p. 88 for another case, that of the Sereer of Saalum.

68. I. M. Lewis, "Literacy in a Nomadic Society"; W. De Mahieu, "A l'intersection de temps et de l'espace," is the fullest, most elegant analysis of genealogies one can read. In the society (Komo, Zaire) he deals with, every family was autonomous.

69. See n. 5, p. 216.

70. See n. 6, pp. 216–17.

71. D. W. Cohen, "Reconstructing a Conflict in Bunafu," p. 219
fn. 20.

72. L. Delmas, *Au pays du mwami*, is a volume of genealogies of the nobility which allows this to be done.

73. D. Henige, *Oral Historiography*, p. 98.

## Chapter Seven

1. P. Irwin, *Liptako Speaks*, pp. 162–64. I have reservations about the use of "truth" in this context when "occurrence" is meant.

2. Ibid., pp. 65–66, 162.

3. Ibid., pp. 161, 163.

4. F. Van Noten, *The Archaeology of Central Africa*, pp. 75–76
(site of Ryamurari).

5. P. Schmidt, "Cultural Meaning and History in Africa Myth."

6. P. De Maret, "Chronologie de l'âge du fer," pp. 345–65 (Boter-

226 Notes to Pages 188-98

dal Report) on the origin of the Luba and attributions by local people of who the people of Sanga were; A. Samain, *La langue Kisonge*, introduction (origin of the Songye).

7. J. Mack and P. Robertshaw, eds., *Culture History in the Southern Sudan*, pp. 54–55, 63.

8. M. L. Zigmond, "Archaeology and the Patriarchal Age."

9. A. Ryder, *Benin and the Europeans*; R. E. Bradbury, "Chronological Problems in the Study of Benin History."

10. In different genealogies a gap exists between Boyamo, who figures as an early hero, and later generations.

11. U. Braukaemper, "Correlation of Oral Tradition and Historical Records in Southern Ethiopia," pp. 43–44.

12. P. Mai, "The Time of Darkness of Yuu Kuia"; R. J. Blong, "Time of Darkness."

13. D. Henige, *Oral Historiography*, pp. 102–3.

14. J. Vansina, *Children of Woot*, pp. 49, 68, 85.

15. B. G. Day, "Oral Tradition as Complement."

16. P. Irwin, *Liptako Speaks*, pp. 77–81.

17. J. Vansina, "Western Bantu Expansion."

18. M. Mutumba, *Bulozi under the Luyana Kings*, p. 5–6, p. 65.

19. T. O. Beidelman, "Myth, Legend and Oral History," quotation on p. 95.

20. P. Thompson, *The Voice of the Past*, pp. 4–8.

21. P. Irwin, *Liptako Speaks*, pp. 63–64.

22. J. Vansina, *Geschiedenis*.

23. J. Vansina, *Children of Woot*.

24. I. Marrou, *De la connaissance historique*, passim. See p. 232: "History is the knowledge of a human by a human" (repeated p. 296).

25. D. E. L. Haynes, *An Archaeological and Historical Guide*, p. 143.

26. J. Vansina, "The Power of Systematic Doubt in Historical Enquiry," which argues for the crucial, *central* place traditions occupy in an array of disciplines used to study the history of oral societies. Hypotheses must start from tradition. Marshalling evidence is at first shaped by the *problématique* which the traditions propose.

27. L. Ntambwe, "Les Luluwa et le commerce luso-africain," p. 100, on the development of masks and the impact of Cokwe on Luluwa art. This corroborates J. Vansina, *The Children of Woot*, p. 216. On demography see C. H. Perrot, *Les Anyi Ndenye*, pp. 31–34.

28. P. Irwin, *Liptako Speaks*, p. 161, talks about a "style."

29. A. Delivré, *L'histoire des rois*.

30. R. Packard, *Chiefship and Cosmology*.

31. P. Irwin, *Liptako Speaks*, p. 164.

32. D. Henige, *Oral Historiography*, pp. 119–27, ranks this necessity so highly that he concludes his study on this note.

# BIBLIOGRAPHY

*Abbreviations*

APS
: *The African Past Speaks: Essays on Oral Tradition and History.* Edited by J. C. Miller. Folkestone: 1980.

ARSOM
: *Institut Royal Colonial Belge. Section des sciences morales et politiques.* Mémoires in 8°. Later (post-1952), *Académe royale des sciences coloniales. Classe des sciences morales et politiques.* Later (post-1960), *Académie royale des Sciences d'Outre-Mer.*

FFA
: *Forms of Folklore in Africa. Narrative, Poetic, Gnomic, Dramatic.* Edited by B. Lindfors. Austin: 1977.

FO
: *Fonti Orali-Oral Sources-sources orales. Antropologia e Storia-Anthropology and History-Anthropologie et Histoire.* Edited by B. Bernardi, C. Poni, and A. Triulzi. Milan: 1978.

HA
: *History in Africa: A Journal of Method.*

IJAHS
: *International Journal of African Historical Studies*

JAH
: *Journal of African History*

JPH
: *Journal of Pacific History*

MRAC
: *Musée royal de l'Afrique Centrale. Annales. Série in 8°. Sciences humaines.*

MRAC, Archives
: *Musée royal de l'Afrique Centrale. Archives d'Anthropologie.*

OTM
: *Oral Tradition in Melanesia.* Edited by D. Denoon and R. Lacey. Hong Kong: 1981.

Alagoa, E. J., and K. Williamson. *Ancestral Voices: Historical Texts from Nembe, Niger Delta.* Jos Oral History and Literature Texts. Jos: 1983.

Andrzejewski, B., and J. Lewis. *Somali Poetry: An Introduction.* Oxford: 1964.

Atkinson, R. R. "The Traditions of the Early Kings of Buganda: Myth, History and Structural Analysis." *HA* 2 (1975): 17–58.

Ayoub, A., and M. Gallais. *Image de Djazya.* Paris: 1977.

Barnes, J. A. "History in a Changing Society." *Human Problems in British Central Africa* 11 (1952): 1–9.

Barrere, D. "Revisions and Adulterations in Polynesian Creation Myths." In *Polynesian Culture History,* edited by G. Highland, pp. 103–19. Honolulu: 1967.

Barth, F. *Ritual and Knowledge among the Baktaman.* Oslo: 1975.

Bartlett, F. *Remembering.* Cambridge: 1932.

Baudin, L. "La formation de l'élite et l'enseignement de l'histoire dans l'empire des Incas." *Revue des études historiques* 83 (1927): 107–14.

Baudin, L. *Der Sozialistische Staat der Inka.* Translated from the French by J. Niederehe. Hamburg: 1956.

Bauer, W. *Einführung in das Studium der Geschichte.* Tübingen: 1928.

Baumann, H. "Ethnologische Feldforschung und Kulturhistorische Ethnologie." *Studium Generale* 7 (1954): 151–64.

Baumann, H. *Schöpfung und Urzeit des Menschen im Mythus der Afrikanischen Völker.* Berlin: 1936.

Becker, P. "Der Planctus auf den Normannenherzog Willem Langschwert." *Zeitschrift für Französische Sprache und Literatur* 43 (1939): 190–97.

Beidelman, T. O. "Myth, Legend and Oral History: A Kaguru Traditional Text." *Anthropos* 65 (1970): 74–97.

Ben Amos, D. "Introduction: Folklore in Africa." *FFA* (1977): 1–34.

Ben Amos, D. "Story Telling in Benin." *African Arts* 1 (1967): 54–55.

Benison, S., ed. *Tom Rivers: Reflections on a Life in Medicine and Science.* Cambridge, Mass.: 1967.

Berger, I. "Deities, Dynasties and Oral Tradition." *APS* (1980): 61–81.

Berlin, B., and P. Kay. *Basic, Color Terms: Their Universality and Evolution.* Berkeley: 1969.

Bernheim, E. *Lehrbuch der historischen Methode und der Geschichtsphilosophie Mit Nachweis der wichtigsten Quellen und Hilfsmittel zum Studium der Geschichte.* Leipzig: 1903.

Berntsen, J. S. "Pastoralism, Raiding and Prophets: Maasailand in the Nineteenth Century." Ph.D. diss., University of Wisconsin, 1979.

Best, E. *The Maori*. Memoirs of the Polynesian Society. 2 vols. Wellington: 1924.

Bianquis, T. "La transmission du hadith en Syrie à l'époque fatimide." *Bulletin d'études orientales* 25 (1972): 85–95.

Biebuyck, D. "The Epic as Genre in Congo." In *African Folklore*, edited by R. M. Dorson, pp. 257–73. New York: 1972.

Biebuyck, D. *Hero and Chief: Epic Literature from the Banyanga (Zaire Republic)*. Berkeley: 1978.

Biernaczky, S. "Folklore in Africa Today." *Current Anthropology* 25 (1984): 214–16.

Biobaku, S. O. "The Wells of West African History." *West African Review* 29 (1953): 18–19.

Bird, J., ed. *The Annals of Natal, 1495 to 1845*. 2 vols. Pietermaritzburg: 1888.

Bloch, M. *Apologie pour l'histoire ou métier d'historien*. Paris: 1952.

Blong, R. J. "Time of Darkness: Legend and Volcanic Eruptions in Papua." *OTM* (1981): 141–50.

Blount, B. G. "Agreeing to Agree on Genealogy: A Luo Sociology of Language." In *Sociocultural Dimensions of Language*, edited by M. Sanchez and B. G. Blount, pp. 117–36. New York: 1975.

Blu, K. I. *The Lumbee Problem*. New York: 1980.

Boston, J. S. "The Hunter in Igala Legends of Origin." *Africa* 34 (1964): 116–25.

Bradbury, R. E. "Chronological Problems in the Study of Benin History." *Journal of the Historical Society of Nigeria* (1959): 263–87.

Braukaemper, U. "The Correlation of Oral Traditions and Historical Records in Southern Ethiopia: A Case Study of the Hadiya Sidamo Past." *Journal of Ethiopian Studies* 11 (1973): 29–50.

Burridge, K. *Mambu: A Study of Melanesian Cargo Movements and Their Social and Ideological Background*. New York: 1960.

Camara, S. *Gens de la Parole: Essai sur la condition et le rôle des griots dans la société Malinké*. Paris: 1967.

Campbell, J. *Grammatical Man: Information, Entropy, Language and Life*. New York: 1982.

Chike Dike, P. "Some Items of Igala Regalia." *African Arts* 17 (1984): 70–71.

Cohen, D. W. "Reconstructing a Conflict in Bunafu." *APS* (1980): 201–39.

Cohen, D. W. *Womunafu's Bunafu: A Study of Authority in a Nineteenth-Century African Community*. Princeton: 1970.

Cope, T., ed. *Izibongo: Zulu Praise Poems*. Oxford: 1968.

Cornet, J. *Art Royal Kuba.* Milan: 1982.

Cotterell, A. *The First Emperor of China: The Greatest Archaeological Find of our Time.* New York: 1981.

Coupez, A., "Rythmes poétiques africaines." In *Mélanges de culture et de linguistique africaines,* edited by P. de Wolf, pp. 31–59. Berlin: 1983.

Coupez, A., and T. Kamanzi. *Récits historiques rwanda dans la version de C. Gakaniisha. MRAC* 43. Tervuren: 1962.

Crépeau, P. "The Invading Guest: Some Aspects of Oral Transmissions." *Yearbook of Symbolic Anthropology* 1 (1978): 11–29.

Crick, M. R. "Anthropology of Knowledge." *Annual Review of Anthropology* 11 (1982): 287–313.

Cunnison, I. *History on the Luapula: An Essay on the Historical Notions of a Central African Tribe.* Lusaka: 1951.

Daaku, K. Y. "History in the Oral Traditions of the Akan." In *Folklore and Traditional History,* edited by R. M. Dorson, pp. 42–54. The Hague: 1973.

D'Arianoff. *Histoire des Bagesera, souverains du Gisaka. ARSOM* 24. Brussels: 1952.

Day, B. G. "Oral Tradition as Complement." *Ethnohistory* 19 (1972): 99–108.

De Craemer, W. "A Cross-cultural Perspective on Personhood." *Milbank Memorial Fund Quarterly/Health and Society* 61 (1983): 19–34.

De Decker, R. *Les clans Ambuun, Bambunda, d'après leur littérature orale. ARSOM* 20. Brussels: 1954.

De Heusch, L. *Le roi ivre.* Paris: 1972.

Delahaye, H. *Les légendes hagiographiques.* Brussels: 1905.

Delivré, A. *L'histoire des rois d'Imerina.* Paris: 1974.

Delmas, L. *Au pays du mwami Mutara III Charles Rudahigwa: Généalogies de la noblesse (les Batutsi) du Ruanda.* Kabgayi: 1950.

De Mahieu, W. "Cosmologie et structuration de l'espace chez les Komo." *Africa* 45 (1975): 123–38.

De Mahieu, W. "A l'intersection du temps et de l'espace, du mythe et de l'histoire—les généalogies: l'exemple komo." *Cultures et developpement* 11 (1979): 415–37.

De Mahieu, W. "Le temps dans la culture komo." *Africa* 43 (1973): 2–17.

De Maret, P. "Chronologie de l'âge du fer dans la dépression de l'Upemba en République du Zaire." 3 vols. Ph.D. diss., Free University of Brussels, 1978.

Demesse, L. *Changements techno-économiques et sociaux chez les pygmées babinga.* Paris: 1978.

Denolf, P. *Aan den rand der Dibese. ARSOM* 34. Brussels: 1954.

De Rop, A. *De gesproken woordkunst van de Nkundo. MRAC* 13. Tervuren: 1956.

d'Hertefelt, M., "Mythes et idéologies dans le Rwanda ancien et contemporain." In *The Historian in Tropical Africa,* edited by J. Vansina, R. Mauny, and L. Thomas, pp. 219–38. London: 1964.

d'Hertefelt, M., and A. Coupez. *La royauté sacrée de l'ancien Rwanda. MRAC* 52. Tervuren: 1964.

Dieterlen, G. "Mythe et organisation sociale au Soudan Français." *Journal de la société des Africanistes* 25 (1955): 39–76.

Dorson, R. M. *Folklore and Fakelore: Essays towards a Discipline of Folk Studies.* Cambridge, Mass.: 1976.

Dupré, G. *Un ordre et sa destruction.* Paris: 1982.

Eggan, F. "From History to Myth: A Hopi Example." In *Studies in Southwestern Ethnolinguistics,* edited by D. Hymes and W. E. Bittle, pp. 33–53. New York: 1967.

Egharevba, J. *A Short History of Benin.* Lagos: 1934.

Eliade, M. *The Myth of the Eternal Return.* New York: 1954.

Ellen, R. F., and D. Reason, eds. *Classifications in Their Social Context.* London: 1979.

Emory, K. E. "Tuamotan Concepts of Creation." *Journal of the Polynesian Society* 49 (1940): 69–136.

Farrall, S. "Sung and Written Epics: The Case of the Song of Roland." *OTM* (1981): 101–14.

Feierman, S. *The Shambaa Kingdom: A History.* Madison: 1974.

Fenton, W. "Field Work, Museum Studies and Ethnohistorical Research." *Ethnohistory* 13 (1966): 71–85.

Fenton, W. "Problems in the Authentification of the League of the Iroquois." In *Neighbors and Intruders: An Ethnohistorical Exploration of the Indian of Hudson's River,* edited by L. Hauptman and J. Campisi, pp. 262–68. Ottawa: 1978.

Fernandez, J. W. *Bwiti: An Ethnography of the Religious Imagination in Africa.* Princeton: 1982.

Fikry, Atallah. "Wala Oral history and Wa's Social Realities." In *African Folklore,* edited by R. M. Dorson, pp. 237–53. New York: 1972.

Finley, M. I. "Myth, Memory and History." *History and Theory* 4 (1965): 281–302.

Finley, M. I. *The World of Ulysses.* New York: 1954.

Finnegan, R. *Oral Literature in Africa.* Oxford: 1970.

Firth, R. *History and Traditions of Tikopia.* Wellington: 1961.

Firth, R. *The Work of the Gods in Tikopia.* 2 vols. London: 1940.

Fortes, M. *Oedipus and Job in West African Religion.* Cambridge: 1959.

Fosbrooke, H. A. "The Masai Age-group System as a Guide to Tribal Chronology." *African Studies* 15 (1956): 188–206.

Fox, R. "Child as Plant." In *Rethinking Kinship and Marriage,* edited by R. Needham, pp. 219–52. London: 1971.

Frobenius, L. *Dichtkunst der Kassaiden.* Jena: 1928.

Frobenius, L. *Kulturgeschichte Afrikas.* Zürich: 1954.

Gamst, F. C. *The Qemant: A Pagan-Hebraic Peasantry of Ethiopia.* New York: 1979.

Gates, J. "Model Emperors of the Golden Age in Chinese Lore." *Journal of the American Oriental Society* 56 (1936): 51–76.

Geary, C. *Les choses du palais: Catalogue du Musée du palais Bamoum à Foumban (Cameroun).* (English version: *Things of the Palace.*) Wiesbaden: 1984.

Geertz, C. *The Interpretation of Cultures.* New York: 1973.

Gibb, H. A. R. *Mohammedanism.* Oxford: 1962.

Gibson, G. D. "Himba Epochs." *HA* 4 (1977): 67–121.

Gidada, N. "Oromo Historical Poems and Songs." *Paideuma* 29 (1983): 317–40.

Goeroeg-Karady, V. *Littérature orale d'Afrique noire: Bibliographie analytique.* Paris: 1981.

Goody, J., "Oral Tradition and the Reconstruction of the Past in Northern Ghana." *FO* (1978): 285–95.

Goody, J. "Mémoire et apprentissage dans les sociétés avec et sans écriture: la transmission du Bagre." *L'homme* 17 (1977): 29–52.

Goody, J. *The Domestication of the Savage Mind.* Cambridge: 1977.

Goody, J. *The Myth of the Bagre.* Oxford: 1972.

Goody, J., and I. Watt. "The Consequences of Literacy." In *Literacy in Traditional Societies,* edited by J. Goody, pp. 27–68. Cambridge: 1968.

Gorju, J. *Entre le Victoria, l'Albert et l'Edouard.* Rennes: 1920.

Gossen, G. H. *Chamulas in the World of the Sun.* Harvard: 1974.

Gossiaux, P. "Comptes Rendus." *Revue universitaire du Burundi* 1 (1972): 73–77.

Greene, G. *Journey without Maps.* 1936. Reprint, London: 1971.

Greene, G. *Ways of Escape.* London: 1981.

Griffin, J. B. *A Commentary on an Unusual Research Program in American Anthropology.* Bloomington: 1971.

Griffin, J. B. "Review of *Walam Olum.*" *Indiana Magazine of History* 51 (1954): 59–65.

Guebels, L. "Kallina, E." *Biographie Coloniale Belge* 1 (1948): 563.

Hagenbucher Sacripanti, F. *Les fondements spirituels du pouvoir au royaume de Loango.* Mémoire ORSTOM 67. Paris: 1973

Halbwachs, M. *Les cadres sociaux de la mémoire.* Paris: 1925.

Haring, L. "Performing for the Interviewer: A Study of the Structure of Context." *Southern Folklore Quarterly* 36 (1972): 383–98.

Handy, E. S. C. *Marquesan Legends.* Bernice P. Bishop Museum bulletin no. 69. Honolulu: 1930.

Hartwig, G. W. "Oral Traditions Concerning the Early Iron Age in Northwestern Tanzania." *IJAHS* 4 (1971): 93–114.

Harwood, F. "Myth, Memory and the Oral Tradition: Cicero in the Trobriands." *American Anthropologist* 78 (1976): 783–96.

Haynes, D. E. L. *An Archaeological and Historical Guide to the Pre-Islamic Antiquities of Tripolitania.* Tripoli: 1965.

Heintze, B. "Oral Tradition: Primary Source Only for the Collector." *HA* 3 (1976): 47–56.

Heintze, B. "Translations as Sources for African History." *HA* 11 (1984): 131–61.

Helm, J., and B. C. Gillespie. "Dogrib Oral Tradition as History: War and Peace in the 1820's." *Journal of Anthropological Method* 37 (1918): 8–27.

Henige, D. *The Chronology of Oral Tradition: Quest for a Chimera.* Oxford: 1974.

Henige, D. *Oral Historiography.* London: 1982.

Henige, D. "Royal Tombs and Preternatural Ancestors: A Devil's Advocacy." *Paideuma* 23 (1977): 205–19.

Herskovits, M. *Man and His Works.* New York: 1949.

Hoornaert, J. "Time Perspective: Theoretical and Methodological Considerations." *Psychologica Belgica* 13 (1973): 265–94.

Howe, L. A. "The Social Determination of Knowledge: Maurice Bloch and Balinese Time." *Man* 16 (1981): 220–34.

Ifwanga wa Pindi. "Msaangu: chant d'exaltation chez les Yaka. Quelques considérations thématiques et stylistiques." In *Mélanges de culture et de linguistique africaines,* edited by P. de Wolf. Mainzer Afrika Studien, 5. Berlin: 1983.

Irvine, J. T. "When Is Genealogy History? Wolof Genealogies in Comparative Perspective." *American Ethnologist* 5 (1978): 651–75.

Irwin, P. *Liptako Speaks: History from Oral Tradition in Africa.* Princeton: 1981.

Jason, A. "The Genre in Oral Literature: An Attempt at Interpretation." *Temenos* 19 (1973): 156–60.

Jason, A. "A Multidimensional Approach to Oral Literature." *Current Anthropology* 10 (1969): 413–26.

Jenkins, J. J. "Remember That Old Theory of Memory? Well, Forget It." *American Psychologist* 29 (1974): 785–95.

Jensen, A. E. "Die Staatliche Organisation und die historische Ueberlieferungen der Barotse am oberen Zambesi." *Württ. Verein für Handelsgeographie* 50 (1932): 71–115.

Johnson, J. W. "Somali Prosodic Systems." *Horn of Africa* 2 (1979): 46–54.

Johnson, J. W. "Yes, Virginia, There is an Epic in Africa." *Research in African Literature* 2 (1980): 308–26.

Jones, G. I. "Time and Oral Tradition with Special Reference to Eastern Nigeria." *JAH* 6 (1965): 153–60.

Jousse, M. *Le style oral rythmique et mnémotechnique chez les verbomoteurs.* Archives de philosophie 11. Paris: 1924.

Kaemmer, J. E. "Tone Riddles from Southern Mozambique: Titekatekani of the Tshwa." *FFA* (1977): 204–19.

Kagame, A. *Un abrégé de l'ethno-histoire du Rwanda.* Butare: 1972.

Kagame, A. "Etude critique d'un vieux poème historique du Rwanda." In *Symposium Leo Frobenius*, pp. 151–95. Pullach: 1974.

Kagame, A. *Introduction aux grands genres lyriques de l'ancien Rwanda.* Butare: 1969.

Kagame, A. *La notion de génération appliquée à la généalogie dynastique et à l'histoire du Rwanda des X<sup>e</sup>-XI<sup>e</sup> siécles à nos jours.* ARSOM NS. IX, 5. Brussels: 1959.

Kagame, A. "*La poésie dynastique au Rwanda.* ARSOM NS. 9, 5. Brussels: 1951.

Kagame, A. "Le code ésoterique de la dynastie du Rwanda." *Zaire* 1: 363–86.

Karsten, R. *La civilisation de l'empire inca.* Paris: 1949.

Kanenari, Matsu. *Ainu Jojishi Yukarashu.* Tokyo: 1959–65.

Kenny, M. G. "The Stranger from the Lake: A Theme in the History of the Lake Victoria Shorelands." *Azania* 17 (1982): 1–26.

Kesteloot, L., and A. Traore, eds. *Da Monzon de Segou: épopée bambara.* 2 vols. Paris: 1972.

Kinross (Lord). *The Ottoman Centuries: The Rise and Fall of the Turkish Empire.* New York: 1977.

Kirk, G. S. *Myth.* Cambridge: 1970.

Kituai, A. "Historical Narrative of the Bundi People." *Oral History* (Papua, New Guinea) 2 (1974): 8–16.

Kronenberg, A. "The Fountain of the Sun: A Tale Related by Herodotos, Pliny and the Modern Teda." *Man* 55 (1955).

Kronenberg, A., and W. Kronenberg. *Nubische Märchen.* Düsseldorf: 1978.

Kouyate, Namankoumba. "Recherches sur la tradition orale au Mali." DES, Fac. lettres. Alger: 1970.

Kuper, A. "Les femmes contre les Boeufs." *L'Homme* 27 (1983): 33–54.

Labrie-Bouthillier, V. "Les expériences sur la transmission orale: d'un modéle individual à un modéle collectif." *Fabula* 18 (1977): 1–17.

Lacey, R. "Coming to Know Kepai: Conversational Narratives and the Use of Oral Sources in Papua New Guinea." *Social Analysis* 4 (1980): 74–88.

Lacey, R. "On *Tee* Grounds as Historical Places: Holders of the Way. A Study in Precolonial Socio-economic History in Papua New Guinea." *Journal of the Polynesian Society* 88 (1979): 277–325.

Laman, K. *The Kongo 111*. Studia Ethnographica Upsaliensia XII. Lund: 1962.

Lamphear, J. *The Traditional History of the Jie of Uganda*. Oxford: 1976.

Lange, D. *Le Diwān des sultāns du Kānem Bornū: Chronologie et histoire d'un royaume africain (de la fin du X*ᵉ *siécle jusqu'à 1808*. Studien zur Kulturkunde 42. Wiesbaden: 1977.

Langlois, C. V., and C. Seignobos. *Introduction aux études historiques*. Paris: 1897.

Langness, L. L. *The Life History in Anthropological Science*. New York: 1965.

Lanzoni, F. *Genesi e svolgimento e tramonto delle leggende storiche*. Studi e Testi VIII. Rome: 1925.

Latukefu, S. "Oral Traditions: An Appraisal of Their Value in Historical Research in Tonga." *JPH* 3 (1968): 133–43.

Lavachery, H. *Vie des Polynésiens*. Brussels: 1946.

Leach, E. *Genesis as Myth and Other Essays*. London: 1969.

Lévi-Strauss, C. *Mythologiques*. 4 vols. [Vol. 4: *L'homme nu*] Paris: 1964–71.

Lévi-Strauss, C. *La pensée sauvage*. Paris: 1962.

Lévy-Bruhl, L. *La mentalité primitive*. Paris: 1947.

Lewis, I. M. "Historical Aspects of Genealogies in Northern Somali Social Structure." *JAH* 3 (1962): 35–48.

Lewis, I. M. "Literacy in a Nomadic Society: The Somali Case." In *Literacy in Traditional Societies*, edited by J. Goody. Cambridge: 1968.

Lieury, A. *La mémoire: Résultats et théories*. Brussels: 1975.

Lloyd, P. C. "Yoruba Myths: A Sociologist's Interpretation." *Odu* 2 (1955): 20–28.

Loftus, E. *Eyewitness Testimony*. Cambridge, Mass.: 1979.

Loftus, E. F. *Memory*. Menlo Park: 1980.

Loftus, E. F., and G. R. Loftus. "On the Permanence of Stored Information in the Human Brain." *American Psychologist* 35 (1980): 409–20.

Lord, A. *The Singer of Tales*. New York: 1960.

Lowie, R. H. *The Crow Indians*. New York: 1935.

Lowie, R. H. *Indians of the Plains*. New York: 1963.

Lowie, R. H. "Oral Tradition and History." *Journal of American Folklore* 30 (1917): 161–67.

Lowie, R. H. *Primitive Society*. London: 1949.

Lowie, R. H. *Social Organization*. London: 1950.

Lunghi, M. *Oralità e trasmissione in Africa negra*. Milan: 1979.

Luomala, K. "Polynesian Literature." In *Encyclopaedia of Literature*, edited by J. T. Shipley, vol. 2, pp. 771–89.

McClellan, C. "Indian Stories about the First Whites in Northwestern America." In *Ethnohistory in Southwestern Alaska and the Southern Yukon*, edited by M. Lantis, pp. 103–33. Lexington, Ky.: 1970.

MacGaffey, W. "Fetishism Revisited. Kongo *nkisi* in Sociological Perspective." *Africa* 7 (1977): 140–52.

MacGaffey, W. *Modern Kongo Prophets: Religion in a Plural Society*. Bloomington, 1983.

MacGaffey, W. "Oral Tradition in Central Africa." *IJAHS* 7 (1974): 417–26.

McGregor, D. E. "New Guinea Myths and Scriptural Similarities." *Missiology* 2 (1974): 33–46.

Mack, J., and P. Robertshaw, eds. *Culture History in the Southern Sudan*. British Institute in Eastern Africa Memoir no. 8. Nairobi: 1982.

MacPherson, J. *Fragments of Ancient Poetry, Collected in the Highlands and Translated from the Gaelic or Erse Language*. London: 1760.

Mai, P. "The Time of Darkness of Yuu Kuia." *OTM* (1981): 125–40.

Malinowski, B. *Argonauts of the Western Pacific*. London: 1950.

Malinowski, B. "The Problems of Meaning in Primitive Languages." In *Magic, Science and Religion*, pp. 228–76. Glencoe: 1948.

Mark, P. "Economic and Religious Change among the Diola of Boulouf (Casamance), 1890–1940: Trade, Cash Cropping and Islam in Southwestern Senegal." Ph.D. diss., Yale University, 1976.

Marrou, H. I. *De la connaissance historique*. Paris: 1973.

Mayer, R. *Les transformations de la tradition narrative à l'île Wallis*. Ph.D. 3ᵉ cycle. Paris, 1976.

Mbot, J. E. *Ebughi bifia: Démonter les expressions. Enonciations et situations sociales chez les Fang du Gabon.* Mémoires de l'institut d'ethnologie XII. Paris: 1975.

Mercer, P. M. "Oral Tradition in the Pacific: Problems of Interpretation." *JPS* 14 (1979): 130–53.

Meyerowitz, E. *Akan Traditions of Origin.* London: 1952.

Middleton, J. "Some Social Aspects of Lugbara Myth." *Africa* 24 (1954): 189–95.

Miller, J. C., ed. *The African Past Speaks: Essays on Oral Tradition and History.* Folkestone: 1980.

Miller, J. C. "The Dynamics of Oral Tradition in Africa." *FO* (1978): 75–102.

Miller, J. C. "Kings, Lists and History of Kasanje." *HA* 6 (1979): 51–96.

Miller, J. C. *Kings and Kinsmen: Early Mbundu States in Angola.* Oxford: 1976.

Miller, J. C. "Listening for the African Past." *APS* (1980): 1–59.

Moniot, H. "Les sources de l'histoire africaine." In *Histoire de l'Afrique*, edited by H. Deschamps, vol. 1, pp. 123–47.

Morris, H. F. *The Heroic Recitations of the Bahima of Ankole.* Oxford: 1964.

Mpase Nselenge Mpeti. *L'évolution de la solidarité traditionelle en milieu rural et urbain au Zaire.* Kinshasa: 1974.

Muehlmann, W. *Methodik der Völkerkunde.* Stuttgart: 1938.

Mutumba, M. *Bulozi under the Luyana Kings: Political Evolution and State Formation in Pre-Colonial Zambia.* London: 1973.

Nassau, R. H. *Fetichism in West Africa.* New York: 1904.

Nathhorst, B. *Formal or Structural Studies of Traditional Tales.* University of Stockholm Studies in Comparative Religion 9. Bromma: 1969.

Nathhorst, B. "Genre, Form and Structure in Oral Tradition." *Temenos* 3 (1968): 128–35.

Niane, D. T. *Soundjata ou l'Epopée Mandingue.* Paris: 1960.

Niangouran Bouah, G. "Les poids à peser l'or et les problémes de l'écriture." *Symposium Leo Frobenius.* Cologne: 1974.

Nicholson, H. B. "Native Historical Tradition." *American Anthropologist* 57 (1955): 595–613.

Njoya, I. M. *Histoire et coutumes des Bamum, rédigées sous la direction du Sultan Njoya.* Mémoires de l'IFAN, série populations 5. Translated by H. Martin. Paris: 1972.

Nketia, J. H. *Drumming in the Akan Communities of Ghana.* London: 1963.

Nketia, J. H. *Funeral Dirges of the Akan People.* Achimota: 1955

*Notes and Queries in Anthropology.* Committee of the Royal Anthropological Institute of Great Britain and Ireland. London: 1951.

Ntambwe Luadia Luadia. "Les Luluwa et le commerce luso-africain (1870–1895)." *Etudes d'histoire africaine* 6 (1974): 55–104.

Nzewunwa, N. *The Masquerade in Nigerian History and Culture.* Port Harcourt: 1982.

Obuke, O. O. *A History of Aviara: Its Foundation and Government.* Madison: 1975.

Ohnuki-Tierney, E. "Sakhalin Time Reckoning." *Man* 8 (1973): 285–99.

Ohnuki-Tierney, E. "Spatial Concepts of the Ainu of the Northwest Coast of Southern Sakhalin." *American Anthropologist* 74 (1972): 426–57.

Olajubu, O. "Iwì Egúngún Chants: An Introduction." *FFA* (1977): 154–74.

Oliver, R. "Ancient Capital Sites of Ankole." *The Uganda Journal* 23 (1959): 51–63.

Oliver, R. "The Royal Tombs of Buganda." *The Uganda Journal* 23 (1959): 129–33.

Ore, T., ed. *Memorias de un viejo luchador campesino: Juan H. Pevez.* Lima: 1983.

Ottino, P. "Un procédé littéraire malayo-polynésien. De l'ambiguité à la pluri-signification." *l' Homme* 6 (1966): 5–34.

Packard, R. *Chiefship and Cosmology: An Historical Study of Political Competition.* Bloomington: 1981.

*Paideuma.* vol. 22 (1976).

Pagès, A. *Un royaume hamite au centre de l'Afrique.* ARSOM I. Brussels: 1933.

Palau Marti, M. *Les Dogon.* Paris: 1957.

Panoff, M. "The Notion of Time among the Maenge People of New Britain." In *Second Waignai Seminar: The History of Melanesia,* edited K. S. Inglis, pp. 443–62. Canberra/Port Moresby: 1969.

Peel, J. D. Y. "Kings, Titles and Quarters: A Conjectural History of Ilesha. I. The Traditions Reviewed." *HA* 6 (1979): 109–53.

Pellat, C. *Langue et Littérature arabe.* Paris: 1952.

Pender-Cutlip, P. "Encyclopedic Informants and Early Interlacustrine History." *IJAHS* 6 (1973): 198–210.

Pender-Cutlip, P. "Oral Tradition and Anthropological Analysis: Some Contemporary Myths." *Azania* 7 (1972): 6–12

Pernoud, R. *Les Gaulois.* Paris: 1957.

Perrot, C. H. "Ano Asema: mythe et histoire." *JAH* 15 (1974): 199–223.

Perrot, C. H. *Les Anyi-Ndenye et le pouvoir aux 18ᵉ et 19ᵉ siécles.* Paris: 1982.

Perrot, C. H. "Les documents d'histoire autres que les récits dans la société agni." *FO*, pp. 483–96.

Philippi, D. *Kojiki*. Tokyo: 1968.

Plancquaert, M. *Les Jaga et les Bayaka du Kwango*. *ARSOM* 3. Brussels: 1932.

Plancquaert, M. *Les Yaka: Essai d'histoire*. *MRAC* 71. Tervuren: 1971.

Portilla, L. *Time and Reality in the Thought of the Maya*. Boston: 1973.

Propp, V. *Morphology of the Folktale*. International Journal of American Linguistics bulletin no. 24. Bloomington: 1958.

Prins, G. *The Hidden Hippopotamus*. Cambridge: 1980.

Radin, P. *The Story of the American Indian*. New York: 1937.

Read, M. H. "Traditions and Prestige among the Ngoni." *Africa* 9 (1936): 453–84.

Reefe, T. "Lukasa: A Luba Memory Device." *African Arts* 10 (1977): 48–50.

Reefe, T. *The Rainbow and the Kings: A History of the Luba Empire to 1891*. Berkeley: 1981.

Reischauer, E. O., and J. K. Fairbanks. *East Asia: The Great Tradition*. Boston: 1958.

Robertson, A. F. "Histories and Political Opposition in Ahafo, Ghana." *Africa* 43 (1973): 41–58.

Robson, J. "Ḥadīth." *The New Encyclopedia of Islam*, vol. 2. Leiden: 1954.

Rodegem, F. M. *Anthologie rundi*. Paris: 1973.

Rodegem, F. M. *Paroles de sagesse au Burundi*. Leuven: 1983.

Rosaldo, R. "Doing Oral History." *Social Analysis* 4 (1980): 89–99.

Rowe, J. H. "Inca Culture at the Time of the Spanish Conquest." In *Handbook of South American Indians*, edited by J. Steward, pp. 183–330. Washington: 1946.

Ryder, A. *Benin and the Europeans, 1485–1897*. London: 1969.

Saberwal, S. "The Oral Tradition, Periodization and Political Systems." *Canadian Journal of African Studies* 1 (1967): 155–62.

Salisbury, R. E. "Unilineal Descent Groups in the New Guinea Highlands." *Man* 56 (1956): 2–7.

Samain, A. *La langue Kisonge: grammaire, vocabulaire, proverbs*. Brussels: 1923.

Schacht, J. "A Reevaluation of Islamic Traditions." *Journal of the Royal Asiatic Society of Great Britain and Ireland*. (1949): 142–54.

Scheub, H. *African Oral Narratives, Proverbs, Riddles, Poetry and Song*. Boston: 1977.

Scheub, H. "The Art of Nongenile Mazithathu Zenani, a Gcaleka Ntsomi Performer." In *African Folklore*, edited by R. M. Dorson, pp. 115–42. New York: 1972.

Scheub, H. "Body and Image in Oral Narrative Performance." *New Literary History* 8 (1976): 345–67.

Scheub, H. "Performance of Oral Narrative." In *Frontiers of Folklore*, edited by W. Bascom, pp. 54–78. New York: 1977.

Scheub, H. "The Technique of the Expansible Image of Xhosa *Ntsomi* Performances." *Research in African Literatures* 1 (1970): 119–46.

Scheub, H. "Translation of African Oral Narrative-Performances to the Written Word." *Yearbook of Comparative and General Literature* 20 (1971): 28–36.

Scheub, H. *The Xhosa Ntsomi*. Oxford: 1975.

Schmidt, P. "Cultural Meaning and History in African Myth." *International Journal of Oral History* 4 (1983): 167–83.

Schulze-Thulin, A. *Intertribaler Wirtschaftsverkehr und kulturökonomische Entwicklung*. Meisenheim am Glan: 1973

Sigwalt, R. "The Kings Left Lwindi; The Clans Divided at Luhunda: How Bushi's Dynastic Origin Myth Behaves." *APS* 126–56.

Simmons, D. C. "Tonal Rhyme in Efik Poetry." *Anthropological Literatures* 2 (1960): 1–10

Smith, P. *Le récit populaire au Rwanda*. Paris: 1975.

Spear, T. O. "Oral Tradition: Whose History?" *JPS* 16 (1981): 132–48.

Speke, J. H. *Journal of the Discovery of the Source of the Nile*. Edinburgh: 1863.

Sperber, D. *Rethinking Symbolism*. Translated from French by A. L. Morton. Cambridge: 1975.

Stanislas, P. "Kleine nota over de Ankutshu." *Aequatoria* 2 (1939): 124–30.

Stappers, L. "Toonparallelisme als mnemotechnisch middel in spreekwoorden." *Aequatoria* 15 (1953): 99–100.

Staude, W. "Die ätiologische Legende von dem Chefsystem in Yoro." *Paideuma* 16 (1970): 151–58.

Swanson, E. "Orpheus and the Star Husband: Meaning and Structure of Myth." *Ethnology* 15 (1976): 124–26.

Tamene, Bitima. "On Some Oromo Historical Poems." *Paideuma* 29 (1983): 317–40.

Tamminen, M. *Finsche Mythen en Legenden: Het volksepos "Kalevala."* Zutphen: 1928.

Tedlock, D. "On the Translation of Style in Oral Narrative." *Journal of American Folklore* 84 (1971): 114–33.

Thomas, C. L., J. Z. Kronenfeld, and D. B. Kronenfeld. "Asdiwal Crumbles: A Critique of Lévi-Straussian Myth Analysis." *American Ethnologist* 3 (1976): 147–73.

Thompson, P. *The Voice of the Past.* London: 1978.

Thompson, R. F., and J. Cornet. *The Four Moments of the Sun: Kongo Art in Two Worlds.* Washington: 1982.

Thompson, S. *Motif-Index of Folk Literature.* 6 vols. Bloomington: 1955–1958.

Thornton, J. "The Chronology and Causes of Lunda Expansion to the West, c. 1700 to 1852." *Zambia Journal of History* 1, pp. 1–13.

Tominaga, Jiró. "Literature." In *Japan: The Official Guide,* pp. 150–65. Tokyo: 1954.

Tosh, J. *Clan Leaders and Colonial Chiefs in Lango.* Oxford: 1978.

Underhill, R. *Red Man's America: A History of Indians in the United States.* Chicago: 1953.

UNESCO. *La méthodologie de l'histoire de l'Afrique contemporaine.* Etudes et documents. Histoire générale de l'Afrique no. 8. Paris: 1984.

Van Binsbergen, W. M. J. "Interpreting the Myth of Sidi Mhâmmad: Oral History in the Highlands of North-Western Tunisia." *Social Analysis* 4 (1980): 51–73.

Van Bulck, G. "De invloed van de westersche kultuur op de gesproken woordkunst bij de Bakongo." *Kongo-Overzee* 2 (1936–37): vol. 2, pp. 285–93: vol. 3, pp. 26–41.

Van Caeneghem, R. *Hekserij bij de Baluba van Kasai.* ARSOM NS. 3, 1. Brussels: 1954.

Van Gennep, A. *La formation des légendes.* Paris: 1910.

Van Noten, F., ed. *The Archaeology of Central Africa.* Graz: 1982.

Vansina, J. *The Children of Woot: A History of the Kuba Peoples.* Madison: 1978.

Vansina, J. *Geschiedenis van de Kuba van ongeveer 1500 tot 1904.* MRAC 44. Tervuren: 1963.

Vansina, J. *Ibitéekerezo: Historical Narratives from Rwanda.* CRL Microfilm. Chicago: 1973.

Vansina, J. "Is Elegance Proof? *HA* 10 (1983): 307–48.

Vansina, J. "L'influence du mode de compréhension historique d'une civilisation sur ses traditions d'origine: l'exemple kuba." *Bulletin des séances de l'Académie des sciences d'Outre-Mer.* (1973): 220–40.

Vansina, J. *La légende du passé: Traditions orales de Burundi.* MRAC, Archives no. 16. Tervuren: 1972.

Vansina, J. "Memory and Oral Tradition." *APS*, pp. 262–79.

Vansina, J. "The Power of Systematic Doubt in Historical Enquiry." *HA* 1 (1974): 109–28.

Vansina, J. *The Tio Kingdom of the Middle Congo, 1880–1892.* London: 1973.

Vansina, J. "Traditions of Genesis." *JAH* 15 (1974): 317–22.

Vansina, J. "Western Bantu Expansion." *JAH* 25 (1984): 131–49

Vansina, J., and J. Jacobs. "*Nshoong atoot:* Het koninklijk epos der Bushong (Mushenge, Belgisch Kongo)." *Kongo Overzee* 22 (1956): 1–39.

Vellut, J.-L. "Notes sur le Lunda et la frontiére luso-africaine." *Etudes d'histoire africaine* 3 (1972): 61–166.

Verdon, M. *The Abutia Ewe of West Africa.* Berlin: 1983.

Verhaegen, B. *Introduction à l'histoire immédiate.* Gembloux: 1974.

Voegelin, C. F., ed. *Walam Olum or Red Score: The Migration Legend of the Lenni Lenape or Delaware Indians.* Indianapolis: 1954.

Webster, J. B., ed. *Chronology, Migration and Drought in Interlacustrine Africa.* New York: 1979.

Weinstock, H. *Rossini, A Biography.* New York: 1968.

Weiskel, T. "The Precolonial Baule: A Reconstruction." *Cahiers d'études africaines* 72 (1978): 503–60.

Westermann, D. *Geschichte Afrikas. Staatsbildungen Südlich der Sahara.* Cologne: 1952.

Wiget, A. O. "Truth and the Hopi: An Historiographic Study of Documented Oral Tradition Concerning the Coming of the Spanish." *Ethnohistory* 29 (1982): 181–99.

Wilbert, J., and K. Simonean. *Folk Literature of the Toba Indians.* Berkeley: 1982.

Willis, R. G. *On Historical Reconstruction from Oral-Traditional Sources: A Structuralist Approach.* Twelfth Melville J. Herkovits Memorial Lecture. Evanston, Ill.: 1976.

Willis, R. G. *A State in the Making: Myth, History and Social Transformation in pre-colonial Ufipa.* Bloomington: 1981.

Wilson, M. *Communal Rites of the Nyakyusa.* London: 1959.

Wilson, M., and L. Thompson. *The Oxford History of South Africa,* vol. 1. Oxford: 1969.

Wright, D., ed. *Beowulf.* Baltimore: 1957.

Wright, D. R. *Oral Tradition of the Gambia.* 2 vols. Athens, Ohio: 1979.

Wright, D. R. "Uprooting Kunta Kinte: On the Perils of Relying on Encyclopedic Informants." *HA* 7 (1981): 205–17.

Wright, J. K. "Map." *Encyclopaedia Britannica*, vol. 14. Chicago: 1971.

Yoder, J. C. "The Historical Study of a Kanyok Genesis Myth: The Tale of Citend a Mfumu." *APS*, pp. 82–107.

Young, F. W. "A Fifth Analysis of the Star Husband." *Ethnology* 9 (1970): 389–413.

Zigmond, M. L. "Archaeology and the 'Patriarchal Age' of the Old Testament." In *Explorations in Cultural Anthropology*, edited by W. H. Goodenough, pp. 571–98. New York: 1964.

# INDEX